A History of Europe

1648 - 1815

MAURICE ASHLEY

A History of Europe

1648 - 1815

Everything I see is sowing the seeds of
revolution that will inevitably come
about and that I shall not have the
pleasure of witnessing.

VOLTAIRE (1764)

Prentice-Hall, Inc., Englewood Cliffs, New Jersey

Library of Congress Cataloging in Publication Data

ASHLEY, MAURICE PERCY.
   A history of Europe, 1648-1815.

   Bibliography: p.
    1. Europe—History—1648-1789. 2. Europe—
History—1789-1815. I. Title.
D273.A8   940   73-1220
ISBN 0-13-390070-3
ISBN 0-13-390062-2 (pbk)

10 9 8 7 6 5 4 3 2 1

Prentice-Hall International, Inc., London
Prentice-Hall of Australia, Pty. Ltd., Sydney
Prentice-Hall of Canada, Ltd., Toronto
Prentice-Hall of India Private Limited, New Delhi
Prentice-Hall of Japan, Inc., Tokyo

Contents

TEN
Epilogue, 249

Illustrations

A History of Europe

1648 - 1 8 1 5

ONE

Introduction:
A
Revolutionary
Age

"Convinced that Louis is the principal author of all the massacres that have defiled France since the Revolution," declared Citizen Marat in a debate in the National Convention on January 16, 1793, "I vote for death within twenty-four hours." When King Louis XVI of France learned that the Convention had mostly agreed with Marat and voted for immediate execution, he asked his valet to procure for him the volume of David Hume's *History of England* which described the last days of Charles I. For on another January day, 144 years earlier, King Charles of England had likewise been condemned to death as a tyrant, traitor, and murderer, but then the event was described as without a parallel in history. Now the parallel was close and Louis was fully conscious of it. Like Charles I, Louis XVI was a well-meaning if weak-minded monarch, anxious for the good of his people: both came under the ascendancy of their wives; both sought the advice of renegades; both invoked help from outside their kingdoms. But in the light of world history it is hard to look upon either of them as cruel tyrants.

The truth was that both these kings, rulers of two of the richest and most civilized countries in Europe, the first in the middle of the seventeenth century, the second at the end of the eighteenth century, were destroyed by a revolutionary uprising, propelled by a determined minority, aware of long-standing social and political grievances. Each king was accused of planning to make war on his own people, but in fact they were driven to do so to defend their inherited constitutional rights unless they were prepared to abandon them utterly. The revolutionary storms produced twenty years or more of political strife. In England the rule of the revolutionary parliament was succeeded by the Protectorate of Oliver Cromwell; in France the National Convention was to be replaced within four years by the Consulate and then Empire of Napoleon Bonaparte. These revolutionary changes not only transformed the nations in which they took place but overflowed and engulfed their neighbors. The French revolution was but one aspect, though the most important, of a crisis that affected much of Europe from Holland to Switzerland in the years 1763-93, a violent political movement which can also be linked with the American War of Independence in which European colonists shook off the yoke of the Old World. Likewise the execution of Charles I has been seen as part of a revolutionary hurricane that swept across the whole of Europe, from Russia to Portugal in the middle years of the seventeenth century, starting about 1640 and not finally subsiding until the Russian rebellions were suppressed in 1676.

The comparison between the two movements is in many ways striking. In each case the revolution revealed a deep malaise in European social and economic life. The revolutionaries achieved or envisaged political transformations of a startling character. In England John Lilburne and the Levellers thought in terms of a democratic millennium and the overthrow of all restrictions on enterprise. The Church of England was reconstituted and new religious patterns emerged. Yet after King Charles II was restored to power few obvious traces of revolutionary change remained; and when the Bourbons returned to rule in Paris it was said that they had learned nothing and forgotten nothing.

Is it fair to draw so precise a comparison between these two revolutionary outbreaks? If so, why was there a lull between them? It should be noticed that the revolutions which took place during each of these periods were of three different kinds. By a revolution one means an attempt—not necessarily successful—to overthrow the existing government of a country by force. Within this category there were essentially nationalist risings, as, for example, the rebellions of the Dutch and Portuguese against the Spaniards which were victorious about the middle of the seventeenth century; or, to look lower down the scale, the abortive revolts of the Catalans against the Castilians or the Irish against the English, revolts which were repeated more than once. The latter half of the eighteenth century was to witness the rebellions of the Americans against the British monarchy and of the Belgians against the Austro-Hungarian monarchy of the Habsburg Empire. Secondly, class struggles merged into rebellions: the civil war in England consisted at least in part of the rising gentry or a "country party" asserting itself against the irritating remains of feudal monarchy. A similar feeling of class resentment may be detected in the French revolution, while both Russia and Poland had to suffer from desperate risings by downtrodden serfs. Lastly, anger at what was considered to be unfair taxation, usually induced by heavy government debts, was an important and often forgotten factor in rebellion. That factor may be seen, for instance, in the Neapolitan rising of 1647–48, while a battle cry which launched the first French revolution was "Down with the privileged classes!" exempted from such taxation.

What is the explanation for the lull? In the first place, it may be said that it was more apparent than real, that revolutionary currents rarely flowed far below the surface. England experienced another, if bloodless, revolution in 1688; social and political discontent was demonstrated in such events as constant bread riots or revolts against taxation by peasants in France, agitation in the Swedish diet, peasant revolts in Russia and Poland, the Wilkes-and-liberty movement in England. In some countries, however, a period of consolidation was needed after revolutionaries had been victorious, as in Portugal, the United Netherlands, and England. In other countries griev-ances were assuaged for the time being by enlightened governments or at any rate governments that claimed to be enlightened; alternatively repres-sion was effective. But also it has to be recognized that there were elements contributing to the revolutions of the second half of the eighteenth century, such as the growth of the press, which were peculiar to them.

Intellectual and literary movements were significant not so much as the direct causes of revolution, as once used to be thought, but in creating an atmosphere of scepticism which helped to undermine existing institutions. For instance, they helped to destroy the Jesuits who had held Catholic Europe together ever since the Counter-Reformation. A revolutionary atti-tude of mind stemmed from the English philosopher John Locke, whose political theories were used to justify the revolution of 1688, and from Isaac Newton, whose scientific discoveries strengthened belief in a mechanical universe which did not need a Christian God who had to be placated. Two great Frenchmen, Montesquieu and Voltaire, visited England in the first half of the eighteenth century and absorbed these ideas, which were then trans-mitted throughout Europe.

Thus in France, the most intellectually influential kingdom (since French was an international language), traditional beliefs were shaken. The influence of British parliamentary life and relatively tolerant attitude to religious differences were reflected in Voltaire's book entitled *Lettres philo-sophiques,* published in 1728, which has been called "the first bomb thrown at the *ancien régime."* That was succeeded by his play *Brutus,* in which the hero was made to say, "Believe me, liberty, adored by every mortal . . . gives man a courage, inspires grandeur which he would never have found at the bottom of his heart." Brutus was also made to say that the glory of the Roman Senate was to represent the people, an assertion of the democratic ideal never heard before on the French stage.

But between the two revolutionary epochs stability prevailed upon the surface. Basically the Europe that existed during the century between, say, 1660 and 1760 consisted of a family of Christian states, headed by absolute but not arbitrary rulers—kings, princes, grand dukes, doges, and regents—flanked by an aristocracy, whose relations with monarchs were ambivalent, and broad-based on agrarian communities or even landless proletariats, which were dominated by landlords, great and small, possessing many rights and privileges. The nobility would often send their sons to complete their education by going on a Grand Tour of Europe, embracing London, Paris, and Rome; everywhere these fledglings of a ruling class would meet the same kind of people and feel much as if they were at home. Even in times of national wars Grand Tours would continue. But gradually the *ancien régime* was to break down under the impact of new ideas, new inventions and discoveries, new or sharper discontents. It was therefore paradoxically at once an Age of Reason and an Age of Daylight.

Moreover this seemingly accepted dynastic and aristocratic society was, as Napoleon fell, beginning to be split asunder by a rabid nationalism that was to be the curse of Europe for many years to come.

It will be seen, therefore, that between two stirring revolutionary periods of European history, 1640–60 and 1760–1815, while in most countries there was superficial calm and a great deal of political futility, generated largely by dynastic ambitions among rulers, intellectual, social, economic, religious, and antireligious movements were taking place which culminated in political revolutions whose repercussions have been felt throughout the world right on until the present day.

TWO

---

*Europe
after the
Thirty Years' War*

1. The Legacy of the War

Apart from its territorial clauses, the Peace of Westphalia which concluded the Thirty Years' War in 1648 was a milestone in European history. The war had started as a civil war—the revolt of the Czechs of Bohemia against their Austrian King, who was also the Holy Roman Emperor and thus the most powerful ruler in Germany—and had become a general war when first Sweden and then France intervened in German affairs. The peace strengthened France and Sweden but left Germany weakened and divided, licking its wounds. Switzerland and the United Netherlands (modern Holland) ceased even in name to be part of the Holy Roman Empire, though Sweden was now to be represented in the Imperial Diet on account of its territorial gains in northern Germany. The control of two great river mouths, those of the Rhine and the Elbe, was no longer left in German hands.

But more important than the territorial settlement was the religious settlement. The right of Calvinist rulers as well as of Lutheran rulers to reform the Church inside their states was reluctantly accepted by the Emperor. That did not mean that religious toleration was universally established after the fierce contests which had torn Europe apart for nearly a hundred years. It simply meant that every German prince could henceforward choose one of three brands of the Christian religion and impose it upon his subjects. Thus, the Counter-Reformation, launched by the Pope and supported by the Emperor in order to subject the whole of Europe again to Roman Catholicism, had finally been defeated. It was no wonder that the Papal Nuncio in Germany, Fabio Chigi (the future Pope Alexander VII), denounced the Peace of Westphalia as heretical or that the Holy Roman Empire, so divided in religion, gradually lost any sense of political unity and was to become the prey to French aggression. The peace can be said to have marked the end of the Middle Ages in that the ideal of a united Christian Europe which looked to Pope and Emperor for leadership was finally abandoned. Europe became a secular concert of independent nations. Furthermore, once religious differences were accepted, doubt could be thrown on the fundamental tenets of the Christian religion.

The negotiation of the Peace of Westphalia was in itself a remarkable achievement, for it was the product of what may be roughly described as the first modern European congress. The only sovereigns who were not represented there had been the Tsar of Russia, the King of England (who was the prisoner of his own subjects), and the Turkish Sultan. There were actually two congresses, one for the Swedes and German Protestants at Osnabrück, the other for the French and German Catholics at Münster, each with their own mediators. The two towns were twenty-five miles apart, and the coordination of their discussions and of resolutions that were tabled, which went on for three years, owed much to the chief Imperial plenipotentiary riding rapidly between the towns. In the end the Peace of Westphalia became a basic part of the international law of Europe and remained in force until the Holy Roman Empire came to an end in 1806. The Congress of Westphalia set a precedent for other great European congresses, such as those of Utrecht *(1713)* and Vienna *(1815)*.

How did the settlement affect the social and economic life of Europe? It was once thought that it had a devastating effect on Germany—that it so depopulated and despoiled it as to preclude all hope of quick recovery. There is no doubt that a great many people were killed by diseases, plague, and starvation—more than died in the actual warfare. But modern research suggests that the main consequence so far as Germany was concerned was a redistribution of population as a result of large-scale migrations. Many fugitives moved from the west into Kiel, Lübeck, and Hamburg and even into Poland. After the war ended, another migration took place from the agriculturally poorer areas into the mountainous districts of Switzerland and Austria or into different parts of Germany or Alsace in the hopes of finding better land on which to settle. Whereas towns like Göttingen and Magdeburg were temporarily ruined, the populations of Hamburg, Kiel, and Lübeck were swollen. If Magdeburg was razed to the ground and its population slaughtered in 1631, Hamburg became the most prosperous city in Germany. In the countryside the need to feed large armies benefited the peasantry, and after the war earnings rose and prices fell; moreover, the landed gentry required help in restoring their estates. The shacks in which the peasants lived were more easily rebuilt. As to commerce, the negotiators in Westphalia attached considerable importance to trade recovery. Articles 69 and 70 of the Treaty of Münster aimed to allow commerce to flow more freely; the Rhine was to be opened to the trade of all nations. So while understandably voices were raised emphasizing the sufferings of areas which had frequently been fought over, in fact Europe recovered pretty rapidly from the consequences of thirty years of war. Some parts of Europe, such as the United Netherlands and northern Germany, actually profited substantially from the war, while the French and the Spaniards were not too exhausted to go on fighting each other.

It is doubtful if the Thirty Years' War was damaging to the development of culture and science, even in Germany. But the Germans were largely derivative. Baroque art and architecture stemmed from Italy, notably during the papacy of Urban VIII *(r. 1623–44)*. The two greatest patrons of art in Europe were Philip IV of Spain, who, even during the long wars in which his kingdom was engaged, found time and money to spend on Velazquez and Rubens, and Charles I of England, executed just after the Thirty Years' War ended, who acquired a magnificent collection of Italian paintings, which was to be dispersed by the Commonwealth. The Emperor Rudolf II also assembled a superb collection at the outset of the century when he lived and died in Prague, a collection which was to be stolen by the Swedes, while Duke Maximilian I of Bavaria also lost his Dürers and Holbeins to the grasping Swedes. The most successful general of the Emperor Ferdinand II, Wallenstein, a brilliant soldier of fortune, who like Rudolf II, lived in Prague, commissioned the building of magnificent palaces. German novels were published, lyrical poetry was written (for example, by Weckherlin, a Swabian who went to England), plays by Shakespeare were performed, and Dresden became a center of opera and ballet. Heinrich Schütz, a pupil of the Italian Monteverdi, produced an opera there. Epigrams were invented by Friederich von Logau, to be translated into English many years later by Longfellow, and Martin Opitz laid down rules in his *Book of German Poetry*. Two institutions which have survived into our own times, the Frankfort book fair and the Oberammergau passion play, were both established during the Thirty Years' War. Johannes Kepler, another Swabian who won international fame as an astronomer, was in the service of Wallenstein.

It would be wrong, therefore, to say that the Thirty Years' War seriously injured European social and economic life or created cultural desolation. But where it did have evil consequences was in the demobilization of professional armies which had long been employed in fighting and battening upon the civil population. Most of these soldiers were eager to find new masters, for they knew no other trade: they therefore contributed to the perpetuation of European wars. Others became robbers rather than settle down to a peaceful existence. Another result of the war was that its heavy cost fastened burdens on the public finances of governments that they were scarcely able to bear. It was indeed increasing demands for higher taxation which was the principal cause of the revolutions in mid-seventeenth-century Europe.

2. The Mid-Seventeenth-Century Revolutions

The first of these revolutions took place in England when a parliament gathered in Westminster in 1640 for the first time after an interval of eleven years and the leaders of the House of Commons expressed their grievances against the monarchy. These grievances were in fact of three kinds: religious, economic, and political. During the reign of Queen Elizabeth I *(r. 1558–1603)* the House of Commons was often restless. It contained a considerable number of Puritans, that is to say, men who wished to purify the Church of England of all forms of Catholic ritual and services. Strong views were also voiced about foreign policy and about the ways in which the Crown raised money—for example, through the establishment of commercial and industrial monopolies. But Elizabeth ruled with iron hands well covered by velvet gloves. She would not stomach any interference with her royal prerogatives which, she insisted, included the government of the Church and the direction of foreign policy. As the Queen was extremely popular, at any rate since victories at sea had been won against the Spanish Empire, and since she understood how to handle her parliaments, the formation of an organized "country party" in opposition to the Court and courtiers was postponed.

However, when King James I *(r. 1603-1625)* came to the throne, because he was a Scotsman unfamiliar with English affairs the picture changed. The landed gentry, which provided the bulk of the members of the House of Commons, started to demand a larger share of political rights, and the Puritan movement, pretty completely crushed by Queen Elizabeth, began to revive. King James in his dotage and King Charles I *(r. 1625-49)* in his youth got involved in wars with Spain and France and had to try to persuade the House of Commons to pay for them by voting new taxes; for "the power of the purse" was in its hands. When these were refused, Charles collected money by means of dubious legality: he angered the landed gentry and smallholders by the imposition of a new tax, universal in its application, called "ship money" to pay for the fleet and he antagonized the rising merchant class by increasing customs duties; he also revived out-of-date feudal imposts. Furthermore, Charles, unlike his father, had no sympathy whatever for the Puritan movement and backed bishops who aimed to crush it again. So the members of the Commons, though they appealed to ancient but arguable precedents, in fact sought revolutionary changes. Finally they demanded the right to select the King's ministers and control the King's army. Though Charles made many concessions, including putting his signature to the death warrant of one of his principal ministers, he refused to give up all his rights and become a constitutional king. After he had vainly attempted to arrest six leading members of Parliament at the beginning of 1642, he left London for the north of England, and both sides, royalists and parliamentarians, prepared for civil war. The parliamentarians won the first civil war in 1646 when the King was made a prisoner, and in 1648 were victorious in the second civil war after the King had induced a Scottish army to fight in his cause.

Meanwhile the French monarchy was also confronted with civil war and survived with difficulty two rebellious movements, the *Fronde parlementaire* and the *Fronde princière*. In this revolutionary period the French lacked a representative body like the English Parliament to contend with the royal Court. The Parlement of Paris was a supreme constitutional tribunal of the kingdom run by lawyers who had purchased their offices and were known as the nobility *de la robe*. The Parlement had acquired political power because it registered royal decrees. It could and did refuse to register some decrees; but the monarch could always hold a *lit de justice* when he appeared personally before the Parlement and obliged it to accept his decrees. Taking advantage of the weakness of the Regency, the Parlement allied itself with other law courts to promote reforms. On June 30, 1648 these courts met together in the Chambre de St. Louis and drafted a program of reforms. On its advice the Parlement of Paris issued decrees revoking the powers of the intendants, the administrative officers of the Government in the provinces, and reducing the unpopular *taille* or land tax that fell directly mainly on the peasants, by one-fourth. After a victory had been gained over the Spanish army at Lens on August 22, however, the Regency arrested two leading *parlementaires,* though it was compelled to release them a day later. This arrest was therefore as much a fiasco as the attempt which King Charles had made to arrest six members of the English Parliament for treason. The French Regency was obliged to accept the entire program of reform put forward in the Chambre de St. Louis and, because of the pressure of the Paris mob, the royal Court withdrew to the town of Rueil. It was here after three months of war that the first Fronde was brought to an end by treaty.

In August 1649 the Queen Regent and her son Louis XIV returned to Paris and in January 1650 the recalcitrant group of Princes of the Blood, who engineered the second Fronde, were arrested. Rebellions broke out in the provinces; a Spanish army crossed the border; and the Court was obliged to make terms with rebel Bordeaux. In March 1651 assemblies in France were calling for a meeting of the States-General, an institution representing the three Estates of the realm—nobles, clergy, and commons—which had fallen into abeyance. For the time being the Prince de Condé, leader of the princely Fronde, became all-powerful and in the spring of 1652 ruled in Paris where mob violence prevailed and massacres took place. But Condé committed the error of allying himself with the Spaniards, with whom France was at war, and filling Paris with a motley army. Other generals, such as Turenne, rallied against him in the cause of the monarchy and by August 1653 with the capitulation of Bordeaux the second Fronde came to an end.

The English Revolution, which had begun in 1640, ended in 1653 by the summoning of a republican assembly, picked by the Puritan army, which was later to be replaced by the Cromwellian Protectorate. After Charles I's execution there had still been a long period of war when royalist armies in Ireland and Scotland fought against the parliamentarian army. Charles I's eldest son, King Charles II, was finally defeated at the battle of Worcester on September 3, 1651, and escaped to France. France under Mazarin and England under Cromwell became allies and fought against Spain, which was now in the throes of military decline. Thus, after the French rebellions of the Fronde had been defeated, the French Government recognized the English rebels. But following the death of Oliver Cromwell in 1658 England relapsed into a state of anarchy, not dissimilar from that of France during the second Fronde.

If there were notable parallels between the wars of the Fronde and the civil wars in England, the rebellions that beset the Spanish Government had less in common with them. A revolt in Catalonia had begun in the summer of 1640 when the Catalans resented the quartering of a Castilian army upon them. The Catalans had a separate history from the rest of Spain and looked upon Madrid much as the native Irish looked upon London as a remote center of tyranny. In Portugal the rebellion against the Spaniards, beginning in December 1640, was even more nationalist in character and lasted longer. The Portuguese completed a revolution because they eventually overthrew the sovereignty of Spain, but the rebellion in Catalonia was abortive since it was ended when in October 1652 a Castilian army at last succeeded in capturing Barcelona, the Catalan capital. The third rebellion against the Spanish monarchy broke out in Naples, where a republic was proclaimed in October 1647, but by February 1648 the rebellion was crushed.

Yet another revolutionary movement in 1648 occurred in the United Netherlands. The Captain-General and Stadholder, Prince Frederick Henry of Orange, had died in March 1647, and in January 1648 the long rebellion of the Dutch against the Spaniards had concluded with the treaty of Münster, which recognized the independence of the United Netherlands. Nevertheless, the young William II, who succeeded his father as Captain-General, wanted to renew the war in order to expand Dutch rule into the southern Netherlands, and he had quarreled with Holland, the most important state in the Union, over the size of the army. On June 1, 1650 the Estates of Holland ordered the colonels to disband their regiments, but the Dutch States-General, representing the rest of the country, sent under the direction of William II, a "Notable Delegation" to Holland to try to persuade its leading citizens to change their minds about the army. The Notable Delegation was refused admittance to Amsterdam. Thereupon six deputies of Holland were put under arrest and Amsterdam subjected to a siege. Amsterdam yielded on terms, but the death of William II of smallpox at The Hague in November 1650 put an end to the incipient civil war in the United Netherlands. A Great Assembly approved the abolition of the captain-generalship and in February 1651 the able John de Witt became Grand Pensionary of Holland and presided over a republican regime from which the House of Orange was excluded.

Thus the whole of western Europe was aflame around the year 1648. Some rebels became victorious, notably the Dutch and the Portuguese. Other rebels, like the Princes of the Fronde and Oliver Cromwell's army, won temporary victories. The rebellions in Catalonia and Naples were demolished and the ambitions of the House of Orange frustrated. Modern historians have sought to find a common pattern in these various revolutions: they have pointed to the sieges of London, Paris, and Amsterdam; they have drawn attention to the arrests of members of Parliament in England, France, and Holland. They have shown how resentment against arbitrary taxation was a common cause of practically all these rebellions. But on the whole it must be said that the rebellions with which the Court of Madrid had to cope were different in character from the English, French, and Dutch rebellions, though the Neapolitans certainly thought of themselves as the victims of tyranny. The Portuguese and the Dutch managed to tear themselves away from an empire that had grown unwieldy, and the Catalans might have done so too if they had not found the conduct of their allies as distasteful to their ideas of independence as that of the Castilians had been. Yet even if one allows for the difference in character and courses of all these rebellions, they undoubtedly influenced one another and revealed that something was wrong with the social structure of Europe. It was to be twenty-two years before the House of Orange was restored to power, just as the revolution in England spread over a period of twenty years. The revolution in Catalonia endured for twelve years, and it took the Portuguese more than a quarter of a century to establish their independence. Germany too had undergone a civil war which lasted for thirty years, though intensified and perverted by foreign intervention. Isolated rebellions had occurred in Andalusia and a major revolution in the Ukraine. So it is undoubtedly right to regard the mid-seventeenth century as a revolutionary epoch which led to much bloodshed.

It would be wrong, however, to think of this epoch as one of democratic warfare in which the poor were struggling against the rich for new rights. It is true that in Catalonia and Naples and for a time in Paris there was much mob violence. But the principal revolutionaries in France were first middle-class and secondly aristocracy. In England the revolution was on the whole a contest between different sections of the gentry with the bourgeoisie for the most part on the side of Parliament. The average English or French peasant responded only to the orders of his masters. In Holland it was the prosperous bourgeoisie who overthrew the House of Orange. In Portugal the leaders of the rebellion were native aristocrats. Yet there was unquestionably, as Professor Hobsbawm has pointed out, elements of social upheaval at this time, especially in Switzerland and the Ukraine. The years 1647–49 were years of high prices, bad harvests, and agrarian discontent. This may have contributed to bringing about popular revolts or at any rate social unrest, though governments could hardly have been blamed for bad weather. In Moscow a rising took place in 1648 as a protest against the administrative abuses connected with taxation. The Tsar was held in defiance and he was obliged to surrender some of his financial administrators to the mob. Large-scale riots also took place in Novgorod and elsewhere and because of these risings the Tsar in the following year confirmed the establishment of serfdom. Between 1654 and 1682 no Zemsky Sobor (National

Assembly) met and in the years 1667–76 the Government had to contend with the dangerous rising of the Don Cossacks, whose ranks were swollen by migrants from the Ukraine under their leader, Stenka Razin. Razin himself was caught and executed in 1676, but rebellion in Russia was widespread and it has been estimated that one hundred thousand persons were killed during the repression. How far this amounted to a general and concerted European social crisis with common features in the middle of the seventeenth century may be questioned. Similar revolts had taken place in Europe a hundred years before. Insofar as a general crisis existed it may be attributed to the heavy costs of wars everywhere, which did not merely increase taxation but led governments to use new fiscal expedients which, since they fell mainly on the poorer classes, created a resentment that was hard to smother and was to simmer for years to come.

3. The Prospering Countries: The United Netherlands, France, and England

Although the United Netherlands, France, and England were all subject to revolutions in the seventeenth century and had all been involved in war during the first half of the century, each was economically dynamic in different ways. The Dutch had specialized in commerce and had become the middlemen of Europe, having established their economic predominance during the course of the eighty years' war of liberation against Spain, Amsterdam replacing Antwerp as the busiest port and entrepot in Europe. The rich soil of France enabled its farmers to feed a large population, and wine and wheat were valuable exports. England had begun to realize its potentials both in agriculture and in commerce and to some extent in industry. Once internal peace had been established after the victories of Oliver Cromwell *(1649–51)* England began to rival the United Netherlands in shipping and commerce. London, like Amsterdam, became a European entrepot where both luxury goods and necessities were brought from the Middle East and Far East and then reexported to continental Europe and North America. The population of these three prospering countries was equivalent to well over a quarter of that of Europe as a whole, while Amsterdam, Paris, and London were all populous, rich, and architecturally distinguished.

"The Commonwealth of Holland," wrote William Carr in 1692,

> hath worthily been the wonder of all Europe during this last age and perhaps not to be paralleled in the records of former times; for if we consider how many years it was assaulted by the then most potent princes of Europe, who aspired to no less than universal empire, and that how formidable sovereigns they were, yet they not only maintained their pretensions but with uninterrupted prosperity and successfulness advanced their trade, and spread their conquests in all four parts of the world.

The Dutch had some but not many natural advantages. The United Provinces stretched across the estuaries of three great rivers and had many excellent harbors. Thus, they became a nation of seafaring adventurers who did not merely depend upon the resources of their own land. The eighty years' war against Spain presented the United Provinces with a challenge to which they made a lively response, and many of their inhabitants were inspired by Calvinism to believe that they were the Chosen People of God who did their duty to Him by hard work.

Amsterdam, it was said, was built on herring bones. The migration of the herrings to the North Sea in the later Middle Ages provided the Dutch not only with food for themselves but with a product which when salted or smoked became a valuable export. Moreover, the large smacks which were built for fishing could be used to carry exports and imports when not required during the fishing season. By 1680 a thousand fishing smacks were employed in the North Sea. The most important Dutch trade was with the Baltic countries. It is estimated that in the 1660s three-quarters of the capital of Amsterdam was invested in this trade. Dutch ships fetched copper, iron, timber, corn, hemp, and other naval materials from the Scandinavian countries and redistributed them throughout the world. Also with materials thus obtained they developed a busy shipbuilding industry. They not only constructed ships for themselves, including the famous *fluitschip* or flyboat, which was cheap to build, but supplied other countries with ships and crews.

Returning Ships of the East India Company in front of the Harbor of Batavia
Albert Cuyp
Rijksmuseum Amsterdam

Though the foundation of their prosperity was fishing and shipping, the Dutch were not only middlemen. By importing raw materials—such as the timber of Norway, raw wool from Spain, and unfinished cloth from England—they developed large manufacturing industries. Their exports included beer, tiles, glassware, soap, textiles, and ships. They were not unduly concerned, as other nations were, over buying imports with bullion. They obtained gold and silver from the Portuguese and Spanish empires and used it to pay for some of their imports from Scandinavia and in particular for the pepper and spices of the East Indies. They were less dependent than most countries on coin for their business transactions. In 1609 the Bank of Amsterdam had been founded and in 1611 the Amsterdam Stock Exchange. Dutch bills of exchange and stocks and shares were widely valued. Although in many countries a bourgeoisie divorced from the land was expanding in the seventeenth century, alone in western Europe the Dutch Republic was a commonwealth of merchants.

The Dutch Republic was a loose confederation of provinces and towns. Even matters of foreign policy had to be unanimously agreed on in the States-General or referred back to the governments of the individual provinces. Yet this apparently cumbersome system of government worked. In most provinces it was not the nobility that governed but a unique class, or rather caste, known as the Regents. These consisted either of retired merchants who drew their income from houses, lands, and other investments or merchants who only devoted a small part of their time to their own business. Thus, a professional administrative class existed. Although the Regents were unpaid, they often exploited their position to give contracts to their friends or bestow on them public employment. But, on the whole, they were less corrupt than the holders of office in other countries. So the Dutch Republic contained ruthless capitalists and shrewd local administrators as in the United States in the twentieth century. There were also elements of a party system in that at times, as from 1650 to 1672, the Regents ruled and looked to the government of the wealthy province of Holland for leadership, while at other times, as from 1672 to 1702, the country found leadership in the semimonarchical representatives of the House of Orange. But fundamentally the Government was always in the hands of an upper middle class which had the interests of commerce and industry at heart.

It is remarkable that the Dutch were able to maintain an advanced standard of living in a Europe which was so torn by war. But the Dutch besides being successful traders were a warlike people. During the eighty years' war they fought the Spaniards skillfully and actually during the same period carried goods for their enemies at a price. They always kept a large navy, which was essential for the protection of their trade routes. They insisted that neutrals were entitled to carry enemy goods so long as they were not contraband of war. Both their East Indian and West Indian companies fought to establish and sustain markets overseas.

One curious factor was that most Dutch business activity, ranging from insurance and banking to a highly organized commercial network, was concentrated in two of the seven provinces, Holland and Zeeland, situated on the North Sea. Holland contributed about 60 percent of the taxes and shouldered most of the costs of the wars. The other provinces, notably Friesland, depended on horticulture, stock-breeding, and dairy farming. Throughout these provinces (and also in the southern Netherlands) the seventeenth century saw the rise of intensive husbandry. This was necessary because of the smallness of the land available for cultivation and a relatively thick population. New rotations were invented in which the cultivation of clovers for fodder and also turnips played an important part. Frequently, the fallow year, which characterized most European rotations, was eliminated and a fodder crop substituted. Hops proved a profitable crop and Dutch beer was widely exported. So were butter and cheese, for the making of which there was an improvement in tools. But as in industry, it was in Holland and Zeeland that the peasants were best off. "In Guelderland and Overijssel," observes Professor Boxer,

> where the landowners had virtually unfettered control of local justice and administration, the peasantry were less favourably placed than in the two maritime provinces, apart from the fact that the soil was poorer.

An increase of population in Overijssel led to the development of nonagricultural employments like linen making, peat digging, and navigation. During the period succeeding 1648 there was a recession of grain prices, as elsewhere in Europe, and this stimulated the conversion of arable land to pasture for cattle breeding. As in other economic pursuits, the Dutch showed themselves to be enterprising agriculturalists and devoted themselves to reclaiming soil from the sea, to draining the land and developing peat moors. Dutch experts were in much demand in other countries where reclamation of land from the sea and rivers was needed.

The prosperity of the Dutch people must not be exaggerated. A wide gulf existed between the rich and the poor. Frugality was practiced by all classes, but while the mercantile class lived in comfortable houses with solid furniture and artistic decorations, the peasants, even in Friesland, and the lower class of workers in the towns known as the *grauw* or rabble endured a restricted diet, seldom eating meat, while the best butter and cheese were reserved for the export trade. William Carr said that the city of Leiden, a center of the textile industry, had to provide bed and board for 20,000 poor every day and that almshouses were numerous. Methods of dealing with the unemployed and beggars were much the same as elsewhere in Europe: they were pushed from place to place and forced to toil in workhouses. Wages do not appear to have been high. Textile workers are said to have been sweated. The guilds prescribed long hours of labor. And strikes took place from time to time.

Another handicap from which the Dutch workers suffered was a high level of indirect taxation. The Dutch invented the excise and this was imposed on an extremely wide range of goods, including the very necessities of life. Householders had to pay a poll tax on their servants; tolls were levied at bridges and canal crossings for the passage of men and vehicles. William Carr wrote: "Should we in England be obliged to pay the taxes that are here imposed there would be rebellion upon rebellion."

It was sometimes argued, as by the French Minister Colbert, that the Dutch benefited from the wars of the seventeenth century, that trade was the weapon with which they acquired an empire. It is true that the East India and West India companies often set up their trading posts by the use of force. It is also true that the Dutch sold their mercantile shipping services to other countries and were able to charge high freights in war time. On the other hand, the size of their shipping and the extent of their overseas markets made them extremely vulnerable to their enemies in countries more populous than their own. Fishing smacks and "flyboats" were not easy to protect. The aim of the Dutch Regents was invariably to keep out of war. Hence their resistance to the military aims of William II and their reluctance to be brought into wars against France. But war was endemic in the Europe of the seventeenth century. Thus it was vital to maintain a big navy and to possess the means to fight on land. The very proximity of the seven provinces to the Spanish Netherlands and to Germany caused Dutch governments to fear that wars in which they were not directly concerned would spill over into their territories and threaten their independence. Hence their demand from their allies for a barrier of fortresses to preserve their security. The Regent class wanted peace, not war, to uphold the economic leadership of Europe.

Since the beginning of the seventeenth century the government of France had been in the hands of three exceptionally able statesmen: King Henry IV, who was assassinated in 1610; Cardinal Richelieu, who served Henry IV's successor Louis XIII from 1624 until his death in 1643; and Cardinal Mazarin, who in effect governed from 1643 to 1661. The aims of these statesmen were similar: at home to secure stability and abroad to humble the Habsburgs of Austria and Spain. In this they had, on the whole, been successful, although Mazarin had been obliged to face the rebellions of the Fronde. He had allowed the Princes who directed the second Fronde to wear themselves out and he bequeathed to King Louis XIV, who became of age in 1652 but did not assume personal power until after Mazarin's death, a tamed nobility and a humiliated House of Habsburg.

Louis was thus able to rule over the most compact and united population in Europe. When he took over the personal government of his kingdom in 1661 the population of France was some 17 or 18 million compared with 4 or 5 million Englishmen and 2 or 3 million Dutch. The Germans may have had a population of about the same size, but they suffered from the aftermath of the Thirty Years' War and from distractions in the east, and were divided among themselves.

Yet economically the French were not remarkably advanced. Agriculture was predominant, as in most countries, but it was not the subject of technological improvement or even of new ideas. French rural literature, it has been said, confined itself to the study of gardens, hunting fields, and jams. France was, it is true, self-sufficing in foodstuffs and could manage to feed large armies. But until Colbert concentrated his attention on industry and the navy, France had a comparatively small export trade. Its financial mechanisms were primitive. It had no bank and no generally recognized unit of currency. The Dutch at that time owned half the mercantile marine of the world and their ships carried French exports to Amsterdam, where they finished them or adulterated them before they were reexported. The companies of commerce that had been created during the reign of Louis XIII were dying or dead and Colbert had to establish new trading companies, though these did not prove a striking success. The Dutch Stock Exchange was the Wall Street of the seventeenth century and so Dutch finance dominated the French economy just as Dutch shipping for a time almost monopolized foreign trade. French iron tended to be of poor quality; the French armed forces had to purchase their weapons of war or the materials for making weapons from abroad. Steel, copper, and tin were imported and the French metallurgical industries were inadequate.

Under these circumstances, how was France able to support the far-reaching foreign policy of Louis XIV, backed, as it had to be, by the biggest armies hitherto known in Europe? The answer was that the French possessed valuable exports which they were able to exchange for the imports they needed; these included, besides wheat and wines, salt, cloth, and, in particular, linens. French wine was already drunk throughout the whole of Europe, and the vineyards of France were unique. Above all, the French peasantry was hard-working. Many peasants owned their land and some of them were comfortably off. It is true that the fiscal system was anomalous: the bulk of the taxes fell directly on the peasants and the numerous internal customs barriers interfered with the transport of goods from one part of the country to another. Also, for the most part roads were bad, and this explains why there was sometimes starvation in parts of France while prosperity reigned elsewhere. At times bread riots or riots against taxation occurred. Many of the peasants, however, particularly the *métayers*, who had to share the product of their harvests with their landlords, managed to rid themselves of part of their tax burdens; they were often able to conceal the reality of their wealth from the tax collectors. The French peasant frequently combined the functions of a gardener, a wheat farmer, wine producer, weaver or spinner, blacksmith or innkeeper. He was the salt of the French earth. The French economy was thus traditional and powerful. It relied, as Professor Goubert has written, "entirely on the rude, intelligent, unceasing and many-sided labours of a population which, if one takes into account its abundance and great qualities must have been supreme in Europe." Since they were not downtrodden as the serfs of eastern Europe were, they were intelligent enough to recognize the inequities of the social system. Thus they rioted from time to time and in the end backed the Revolution.

England too depended primarily on agriculture. Some 90 percent of the population was employed in it, and whereas the Dutch had to import corn and concentrate on dairy farming and horticulture rather than arable farming, England actually exported corn and extended sheep farming to provide meat and manure as well as wool for domestic consumption. Because of the richness of its soil and the excellence of its water communications both by rivers and along the coasts, every part of the country could be supplied with bread, cheese, and ale; there were no famines or hunger strikes as in contemporary France, and agricultural specialization was on the way, the heavier soils being used as pastureland and the lighter soils as arable. The enclosure of lands, whether to get rid of the medieval strip system or to change from arable to pasturage, was no longer frowned upon in the reign of King Charles II *(r. 1660–85)*, and to keep the price of wheat steady a bounty was paid when prices were low so as to stimulate exports.

To maintain the quality of the soil irrigation or drainage was used and every conceivable kind of fertilizer was employed from animal dung (of which there was never enough) to rags and refuse collected from London and other towns. Although the Royal Society showed an interest in the matter and a number of books were published about agricultural improvement, often derived from the practices of the Dutch, it does not seem that great advances were made in agricultural technology during the seventeenth century. Potatoes were more written about than eaten. Clover seed was imported from the United Netherlands and turnips and carrots constituted new crops, but such figures as we have, as Professor Charles Wilson points out, "emphasize how small was the influence of the new ideas and methods statistically." Farmers were conservative in their outlook and in general the three-course or two-course rotation prevailed. In spite of the bounties, prices for grain stayed fairly low, while prohibitions on the export of raw wool, imposed for the benefit of cloth manufacturers, meant that wool prices were kept down.

Nevertheless, it has been argued that the seventeenth century saw the beginnings of an agricultural revolution. The draining of the fenlands, better irrigation, new forage crops which enabled new stocks of sheep to be fed, conversion of land from arable to pasture and back into arable again (this was known as "up and down husbandry") all demonstrated a spirit of enterprise. Sheep were valued as meat at least as much as for their wool, and enormous meals consumed by the upper classes meant that the fattening of cattle and pigs and the breeding of geese and turkeys were profitable. By and large, agricultural output was on the increase, and every class from the rentier landlords with their businesslike stewards to the agricultural laborer who owned a patch of land behind his cottage benefited. Compensation either in money or land was generally paid for enclosures. Contemporaries, it has been said, were quite clear that they were living through an agricultural revolution.

The English peasants were thus not too badly off and they could see that big landowners were prepared in times of crisis to tax themselves. Thus, although the excise was resented, the English peasants had fewer grievances than the French. They were not revolutionaries. During the civil war they asked only to be left alone to get on with their business. The attempted invasion by the Duke of Monmouth (Charles II's illegitimate son) in King James II's reign *(r. 1685-88)* was the only revolutionary effort to be backed by the lower classes, and these were chiefly mine workers and textile workers. Rioting was to take place in towns and seaports rather than the countryside.

Because of better yields from agriculture the ownership of land was regarded not merely as a means of acquiring social prestige but also as a useful investment. Another form of investment which was open to the speculator was in the joint-stock companies that engaged in distant trade. The English East India Company, like the Dutch one, dated from the beginning of the century. The two companies often came into dispute, and it seems that the English company emerged more successfully from the first Anglo-Dutch war *(1652-54)*, which was largely a trade war. Over a period of six years a United Stock that was created in 1650 distributed a dividend of 205 percent. But monopolies were not popular in Puritan England, and for three years after the war the trade was thrown open to all comers. But in 1657, partly because the company had lent money to the Government (most of which was never repaid) and partly because it threatened to sell the forts, houses, guns, and ports that it owned in India, it was granted a new charter; many of the interloping merchants then joined the reconstituted Company and raised a large stock for seven years; but profits fell and this was again blamed on Dutch competition. Nevertheless, trade with the East continued to grow. The Government favored a Company which employed British shipping and imported such valuable commodities as pepper, spices, and the materials to make gunpowder.

The colonization or conquest of West Indian islands and the building up of an English-speaking community in North America, quite apart from the erection of trading stations in West Africa and southern India, also helped to establish new markets and opened up a reexport trade in such commodities as silks, sugar, and tobacco. The country drew upon the experience of its Dutch competitors, and even before the imposition of protective Navigation Acts *(1651, 1660)* managed to acquire an important place in world shipping. With his much-maligned ship money King Charles I had laid the foundations of a British navy which was able to protect merchantmen

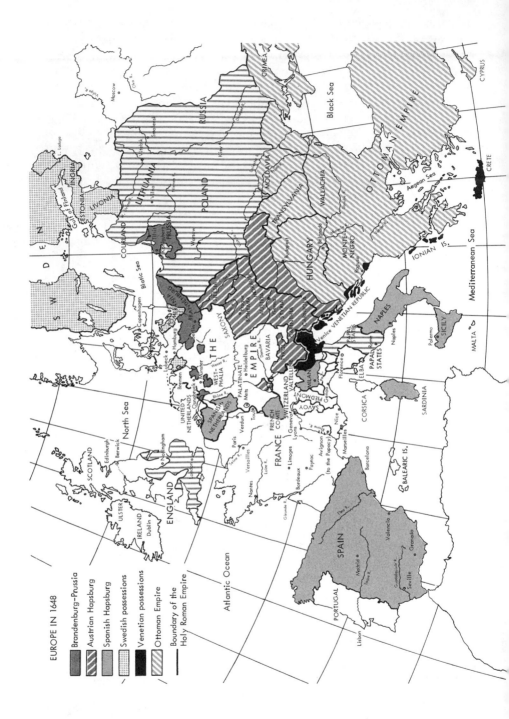

EUROPE IN 1648

Brandenburg–Prussia
Austrian Hapsburg
Spanish Hapsburg
Swedish possessions
Venetian possessions
Ottoman Empire
Boundary of the
Holy Roman Empire

against the depredations of the Dutch and the many pirates and privateers who swarmed the Channel and the Mediterranean. The mere geographical position of the British Isles was conducive to an expanding commerce. Thus, when the group of allies, largely led and financed by Great Britain, finally defeated the French in the War of the Spanish Succession, British traders and shippers were able to obtain substantial economic benefits from the peace treaties. It was this progress in agriculture, in commerce, and later in industry, combined with wiser public finance and bigger opportunities for investment, that made eighteenth-century England into the most prosperous country in Europe, finally outstripping its Dutch rival, and also contributed to political stability in Europe, stilling the dangers of revolutions which were to sweep over mainland Europe.

4. Two Rising Powers: Russia and Prussia

The great rising powers in northeast Europe were Russia and Prussia. In Russia advances took place mainly during the reigns of Peter I and Catherine II, who had much social and economic backwardness to overcome. In 1648 the Tsar of Russia was a minor, Alexis, known as the Gentle, who was to grow into an enlightened monarch and who in later days would have been deemed a suitable constitutional king. He was also to have a considerable statesman in his service in Ordyn-Nashchokin. Mainly because of lack of ports, the country was cut off from international trade and there were few trading towns or manufactures, though Nashchokin established two annual fairs with duty-free goods near Pskov. Mining developed to some extent: metallurgical experts came to Moscow and settled in what was known as the German Quarter.

But conditions in this vast empire were primitive; Sir Bernard Pares wrote of this period that "in different ways the bulk of the Russian people descended into a kind of abyss, of which there is no history." The country was beset by rebellions, and it was with the purpose of upholding order that the Tsar and his ministers strengthened the institution of serfdom, conferring immense powers on the nobility, who could buy and sell serfs with impunity. It has been estimated that at the beginning of this period the population of the country was a mere 10 million, for the serfs lived miserably on the margin of subsistence and were swept away by disease and starvation. Yet the country was by no means poor in resources; if the bulk of the population lived by agriculture, it possessed substantial wealth in its forests and iron foundries; it gradually increased its trade through the Baltic ports selling naval stores throughout Europe. Under Peter I, the son of Alexis, exports exceeded imports. A variety of taxes, including one on beards, raised money to pay for wars that expanded Russian territory both northward and southward and opened up littorals on the Baltic and Black seas. Peter established new industries with the aid of subsidies, loans, and protective tariffs. Besides shipbuilding and gun foundries, he introduced, for example, silk weaving and wine making. A College of Manufacturers was set up to transact business with the lessees of state factories. But of course most of the population was engaged in primitive agriculture carried out by serfs. Peter tried to improve the methods of wheat harvesting by giving orders that scythes and rakes should be used instead of sickles, and sent instructors into villages to teach the peasants how to work with them. But after Peter's death the rights of the nobility were increased and their obligations for service reduced, while the status of the serf was debased. However, Russia's population grew pretty rapidly—it is estimated to have been about 36 million by the end of the eighteenth century, though this was largely due to the acquisition of new territories through war. Throughout the vast Russian Empire there were frequent risings and revolts, owing chiefly to economic causes. Yet when the crux came, national pride overruled the dissatisfactions of the Russian people.

Prussia was less primitive than Russia, though its natural resources were meager. In the Hohenzollerns Prussia had an able generation of rulers. In 1648 the Hohenzollern territories consisted of three scattered portions of northern Europe: in the west Cleves, Mark, and Ravensberg; in the center the Electorate of Brandenburg, which they had governed since 1417; and in the east the duchy of East Prussia, over which, however, the overlordship of Poland was acknowledged. Frederick William, "the Great Elector" *(r. 1640-88),* had acquired eastern Pomerania by the Peace of Westphalia. By 1651 he had cleared the Swedes out of eastern Pomerania, though they remained in possession of western Pomerania, which was the more fertile area. Brandenburg and East Prussia were poor agricultural domains, and the way in which the Hohenzollerns gradually constructed a strong and united kingdom was a fine example of "challenge and response." The wastelands were populated, agriculture and industry were stimulated, and foreign *émigrés* were welcomed—Frisians, French, Swiss, and Jews—who introduced new trades. Yet it was a bleak world which was raised to importance by the ruthless application of military might exercised by a professional army. When King Frederick William I of Prussia *(r. 1713-40)* lay dying they read to him his favorite hymn. At the words "Naked I came into the world and naked I shall leave it" the King broke in: "No, no, I shall still have my uniform."

As in Russia, the position of the nobility or Junkers was strengthened and that of the peasantry debased. The Thirty Years' War had depopulated parts of the country so that the Junkers were obliged to cultivate their lands directly with the help of serf labor instead of letting them for rent. In Brandenburg the peasants had often to work from four to six days a week on their masters' estates. Many peasants were not only tied to the soil but were personally unfree. They were too downtrodden to contemplate rebellion. Though much of the soil was poor and practically no foreign trade existed, it has been estimated that the national revenues were doubled and the national output trebled during the reign of King Frederick William I. Self-sufficiency was the order of the day and on the whole it worked. Under the Hohenzollerns Prussia became a great power which, though first crushed, finally rebelled against Napoleon.

5. Stagnant or Declining Powers

While Russia and Prussia rose to the status of great powers in the eighteenth century, Sweden, Denmark, Poland, and Turkey declined. Because of the strivings of two soldier-kings of genius in the seventeenth century, Gustavus Adolphus and Charles X, Sweden, despite its small population, had been a leading power whose intervention in the Thirty Years' War had been decisive. At the end of the war Sweden had acquired western Pomerania, and then after a war with Denmark wrenched southern Scandinavia, comprising Scania, Halland, and Blekinge, from its neighbor by the Treaty of Copenhagen (1660). Earlier Sweden obtained Estonia in 1561, Ingria and East Karelia in 1617, Livonia in 1629. Thus, it could be said that the Baltic Sea was a Swedish lake, and by its possession of territories on the west coast of Russia as well as the duchy of Finland, Sweden held a stranglehold over Muscovy. But another Swedish soldier-king, Charles XII, who waged war on Denmark, Poland, and Russia, was eventually to be beaten in a war that lasted from 1700 to 1720. After his death the Swedes continued to yearn to regain their losses to Russia but never did so.

Apart from the conquered lands which were to be lost, Sweden-Finland had a population of only about 1½ million and Denmark-Norway about the same. These two kingdoms were traditional enemies, but both had a prosperous agriculture and traded in timber and naval stores with the rest of Europe. Norway also had a thriving fishing industry, but needed to import grain. Sweden exported iron ore and copper as well as timber; Stockholm and Riga were both expanding cities. Denmark was also celebrated for its dairy products. So far as foreign policy was concerned, Denmark devoted itself to acquiring Schleswig and Holstein to the south: after many complicated diplomatic maneuvers and wars this ambition was realized.

Poland-Lithuania was a vast land of wealthy and politically domineering magnates, petty county nobility, German- and Yiddish-speaking burghers, and a feudalized peasantry. It was a country of mixed origins which thrived on the export of grain but whose geography made it highly vulnerable to its neighbors, the Prussians, the Russians, the Austrians, and the Turks. Nevertheless, it could, like Sweden, be counted a major power in the seventeenth century. But as its kings were elective, complicated intrigues took place and anarchy threatened whenever there was a demise of the

Crown. Often the monarchs were little more than puppets in the hands of the higher nobility. But in the second half of the century Poland boasted two capable kings, John Casimir *(r. 1648-68)* and John Sobieski *(r. 1674-96)*. John Casimir was menaced by a revolt of Ukrainians under the leadership of Bohdan Chimielnicki, who in 1654 placed himself under the protection of the Tsar. Charles X of Sweden joined in the war, scenting a prospective partition of Poland. Oliver Cromwell looked with friendly eyes on this enterprise, for he regarded it as part of an anti-Papal crusade. The Great Elector also allied himself with the Swedes. But the Poles fought off all their enemies with some help from the Danes and the Austrians. Chimielnicki died, and peace was concluded with the Swedes at Oliva in 1660; seven years later a treaty concluded at Andrusovo ended the war with Russia. These treaties cost Poland the loss of much territory, including Livonia and Kiev. Yet it survived many dangers and still remained an important European state until internal dissensions opened the way to revolution and conquest.

Just as Poland was menaced by Russia and Prussia, to which it eventually succumbed, the Holy Roman Empire of the German nation, as it was sometimes called or, to speak more realistically, Austria-Hungary, was the subject during the seventeenth century of assaults both from the French in the west and the Turks in the east. It is necessary to remind ourselves of the character of the relationship between the Holy Roman Empire, "Germany," and the Habsburg dominions. Traditionally the head of the Austrian Habsburg family was always chosen Holy Roman Emperor, and he assured the succession in his family by getting his heir created "King of the Romans" in his own lifetime. But this position was more one of honor and responsibility than of concrete advantage. The Emperor was in theory the political leader of eight electors (the Duke of Bavaria became an Elector after the Peace of Westphalia) and hundreds of princes, cities, and Estates. He could invoke their help when they met in the diet of Ratisbon (or Regensburg) and even ask for financial aid. In practice the electors were jealous of the Habsburgs and usually had to be bribed into voting for them or fighting for them. Indeed, alliances had been formed against the Emperor during the Thirty Years' War, and fresh alliances were to be evolved against him in the future. Efforts were made to topple the Habsburgs from their supremacy and to undermine their power.

After 1648 the strength of the Empire was in fact reduced, for the constituent parts had different religions and pursued independent policies. German rulers were allowed to conduct their own foreign affairs (so long as they were not directed against the Emperor); a promise was given that the Estates of the Empire would in future be allowed to vote on important business discussed in the Diet. The Emperor Ferdinand III *(1637-57)* did his best to minimize the consequences of these concessions. Thus, his authority was not in effect materially reduced, and within his own dominions (except for a small part of Silesia) Roman Catholicism remained the exclusive religion. Though Germany was little more than a geographical expression in this age with many centrifugal tendencies and with allegiance to the Emperor its sole tie of unity, external threats from the west and the east helped to hold it together for another 150 years. Moreover, the Court of Vienna was not unskilful in checking rebellions from its discontented subjects, especially in Hungary, and could still make an ideological appeal to Christian allies when confronted with attacks by the Turks.

The Turks were not Europeans, though in earlier times the tentacles of the Ottoman Empire stretched as far west as Sicily. But their fortunes were now on the decline. The last warrior-sultan, Murad IV, who died in 1640, had defeated the Persians; the sultans who succeeded him "generally lived shut up in the seraglio or palace, abandoning themselves to vice." But their grand viziers were able Albanians who looked westward. After a war that lasted twenty years the Turks managed to take Crete from the Venetians, and in 1683 they were to make their second attempt in the seventeenth century to capture Vienna, which could be deemed the frontier town of European civilization.

If Germany—as distinct from the Habsburg empire, which was ultimately to be transformed into Austria-Hungary, and Brandenburg-Prussia, which was to become the heart of a German Empire in the nineteenth century—was in the seventeenth and eighteenth centuries little more than a geographical expression, Italy was even less of a political entity. Until the War of the Spanish Succession in 1701, it was dominated by Spain, which was the mistress of Milan, Naples, Sicily, and Sardinia and in effect controlled Genoa and Tuscany. France had much influence over the House of Savoy, which ruled Piedmont, but had failed in an attempt to create an Italian league against Spain. In the west of the peninsula the power of the Holy See had increased, but its prestige had fallen, while the Venetians became absorbed in their war with the Turks over Crete. As a whole Italy was stagnant economically; it was ravaged by terrible epidemics; for various reasons its commerce and industry were declining; and it was not until toward the end of the seventeenth century that its agriculture revived. But the Italians were always ready to rebel against their masters. Language and culture gave it a potential sense of unity. Thus, nationalist ambitions could be invoked even by foreign conquerors.

6. Spain: A Change of Character

Spain is generally considered to have been a declining power by this time. As the heart of an empire in Europe itself, the authority of Madrid contracted. By the treaty of Münster the independence of the United Netherlands, long obvious, was finally recognized. By the Peace of the Pyrenees with France *(1659),* which ended twenty-four years of war, the border counties of Rosélon (Roussillon) and Cerdaña (Cerdagne), Artois, Gravelines, Landrecies, Philippeville, and Montmédy were surrendered, and in 1668, after nearly twenty years of struggle, the loss of Portugal and Brazil was accepted. But the King of Spain still ruled over much of the southern Netherlands and Italy, while his overseas possessions remained intact. His daughter, Maria Teresa, was married to the King of France, and he might hope at last for peace along the Pyrenees. What happened in fact was, as Professor Juan Reglá has written, that "Spain abdicated her position as a great power [in Europe] and withdrew within herself."

The tremendous effort made by the Spanish Minister Olivares, a man of considerable talents and wide-ranging ambitions, to strengthen and centralize the Spanish Empire during the reign of Philip IV *(r. 1621–65)* failed, largely through lack of financial and economic resources and the defiant independence of many of its subjects. It was not so much that the silver

The Duke of Olivares
DIEGO VELAZQUEZ
Prado, Madrid

Da de Comer al Pobre el proueche. El Pobre Come & Diego Satisfecho.   Mira en el Pobre à Dios y desupecho,   I aun tiempo Exercitando vida activa
Rezive Diego de que el Pobre Coma, El dar las Gracias por Su quenta toma.   Caridad todos à Dios le ofrece alguna,   El Santo Seza la Corona dichosa.

St. Diego of Alcalà Feeding the Poor
BARTOLOMÉ E. MURILLO
Mansell Collection

imports from America had begun to dry up in the 1630s as that the Castilian
peasants were unable any longer to sustain the heavy taxes imposed upon
them. Spain itself was a pretty barren kingdom which had to import wheat
to feed its population and had only wool and salt to export. Nor was it
industrially advanced. The principal industries—woollen textiles, silk manufacture, and metallurgy—entered upon a decline, though protected industries such as ceramics and glass were able to supply the home market with
its needs. Ninety-five percent of the population were in fact peasants and 95
percent of the land was owned by the Crown, the nobility, and the Church.
Population fell, the currency was debased, and twice, in 1647 and 1653, the
Government had to admit to bankruptcy.

Nevertheless, the Spanish Habsburg monarchy managed to weather the
storms of the mid-century. The kingdom did not break up into its constituent parts as it might have been expected to do. The rebellion in Catalonia

was finally put down when Barcelona surrendered to the army of Don Juan of Austria in 1652, while neither Aragon nor Valencia had shown any inclination to help the Catalans or to rebel themselves. Afterward Catalan trade revived and Barcelona replaced Seville (which lost half its population in a plague in 1649) as the most thriving port in Spain. At the end of Philip IV's reign and during the reign of his son Carlos II, there was a considerable immigration of foreign artisans and merchants into Spain, including not only Frenchmen and Portuguese but even a number of Protestants who contributed to the replacement of the half-million hard-working Moriscoes who had been expelled by Philip III. The policy of centralization pursued by Olivares was abandoned; this stimulated in particular the progress of trade and industry in Catalonia, and by 1680 economic recovery had set in. Moreover, the Spanish Government never completely lost control in its overseas empire, which remained loyal to the motherland. Though the population of Spain itself was only about 6 million in the middle of the century, that of Spanish America rose to more than 10 million.

Thus, after Spain lost its former hegemony in Europe, there were considerable compensations. The population began to rise, earnings improved, and trade expanded. If Cervantes and Velazquez were dead (Velazquez died in 1660), Spanish literature was by no means negligible, the theater flourished under Pedro Calderon de la Barca, and Spanish art could boast the names of Murillo, Ribera, and Zurbaran. While the grandees who helped to rule Spain were often incompetent and sometimes impoverished (Professor Elliott has spoken of the nobility's "moral and intellectual bankruptcy"), a deep-rooted spirit of Spanish nationalism was to reveal itself during the eighteenth century, first in alliance with the France of Louis XIV and later in the course of the contest against Napoleon. Thus just as in the Austrian Habsburg Empire there were nationalist stirrings as well as rebellious outbreaks in Hungary, so in Habsburg Spain nationalism began to emerge as a genuinely patriotic feeling, even though there were always centrifugal trends in Catalonia and in the Basque country.

7. The Power Vacuum

The power vacuum left by the changed character of Spain had a profound effect upon the political history of Europe. When Philip IV died in 1665 he was succeeded by his four-year-old son, Carlos II, who was physically and mentally retarded because of years of inbreeding in his family. His tongue was too large for his mouth and his legs too frail for his body. It was therefore widely assumed that he was not going to live long or to have children; moreover, during the regency of Philip IV's widow, Queen Mariana, which was principally directed by a Jesuit from the Tyrol named Father Nithard, there was a constant threat of civil war, as Don Juan, the half-brother of the new King, headed a group of nobles who were discontented with the new regime. Both King Louis XIV of France and the Emperor Leopold I, who ascended the throne in Vienna in 1657, were sons of Spanish princesses and married to Spanish princesses; therefore, they could hope to profit from the imminent break-up of Spain. In fact, the second half of the seventeenth century was to witness French dominance over Europe, replacing that of Philip II's magnificent Spanish Empire. Habsburg Spain, more modest in its pretensions, had survived four revolutions and was to survive the dangers of an internal civil war, while the last period of French Bourbon greatness was so to strain the French people that it was to pave the way to revolutions more far-reaching than the two Frondes.

But before the evolution of French greatness is considered, the social, intellectual, and artistic structure of seventeenth-century Europe must be examined.

THREE

The Social, Economic, and Intellectual Structure of Europe, 1648–1715

1. Social Structure

There are two outstanding facts about the history of Europe in the second half of the seventeenth century: the first is that the total population declined; the second is that the price of grain tended to fall. It has been estimated that the size of the population was reduced from 118 million in 1648 to 102 million in 1713. This reduction was not evenly distributed: it certainly was most marked in Spain and Italy (owing mainly to economic causes) and in some parts of Germany (because of devastation and disease); on the other hand, population rose, or at any rate did not fall, in the more prosperous countries—England, France, and the United Netherlands.

The reason for the decline in population has been variously assessed. It is generally accepted that warfare, which was usually in progress in most parts of Europe, was not directly an important factor. Armies suffered more from medical casualties than from actual losses in battles. Epidemics were still common; the Great Plague of 1665 cost the London area alone one hundred thousand dead, and about the same number may have died in Naples in 1656 from the same kind of plague. Secondly, it has been contended that the average age of marriage among ordinary people rose: it has been discovered that in England women did not usually marry until they were twenty-four and men until they were twenty-eight or more; also, girls began to menstruate later. Thus a fall in the birth rate contributed to a smaller European population. Though members of the ruling classes married earlier, intermarriages between royal families were rarely conducive to fertility: Carlos II of Spain had no children by two wives; Charles II of England had no legitimate children; William III of Orange was childless; only one of Louis XIV's children survived infancy.

What was the social structure of this population of a hundred million or so Europeans? Two generalizations which are often made require qualification. One is that it can be divided between the "privileged" and "unprivileged"; the other is that it consisted of a stepped pyramid with the monarchs, princes, and higher nobility constituting the upper layers and the huge mass, vaguely called the peasantry, providing the broad base. Professor Andrew Lossky has lately argued forcibly that each class in society in fact had its own privileges handed down by custom and long possession and sometimes embodied in charters. Even the obligations of serfs in eastern Europe were generally minutely defined so that they could be said to have a legal personality; the privilege of a slave was that he was exempt from taxation. But in practice the rights of peasants, especially in eastern Europe, were eroded, and it can hardly be argued that in western Europe cottagers and landless men, who struggled to survive on a bare subsistence level, enjoyed anything that can be realistically thought of as effective privileges. As to the stepped pyramid, Professor Lawrence Stone has suggested that for preindustrial society a better model is that of "San Gimignano"—a series of vertical towers upon a hill. The hill represents the unprivileged, or at any rate the poor, and the towers land, church, law, commerce, and government office.

One thing at least is certain about society in the mid-seventeenth century, and that is that it was fundamentally based on agriculture. Bad weather which ruined harvests would shake the whole of European society, and the pressure of population on the means of subsistence was real enough. In many parts of Europe, including France but not England, peasants at times literally starved to death; malnutrition was common because many peasants could not grow or buy enough food to sustain the health of their families. Servants who sat at their lords' or masters' tables were usually better fed than poor cottagers.

The peasantry—perhaps countrymen is a better word—represented an enormous class which ranged from the poverty-stricken, the cripples, the chronically sick, the unemployables, who were dependent on charity or parish relief, to the wealthy farmers, either freeholders or renting their land on long leases, who could aspire to live like the gentry. In Beauvais in France, for example, although the peasantry actually owned about two-fifths of the land, most of it was of poor quality, and four-fifths of the peasantry possessed only tiny plots, a few acres in extent, including fields which would yield a little grain, gardens which grew vegetables and apples, two or three hens which lived on scraps, and perhaps a skinny cow: they had no horses or pigs. Out of these resources they tried not only to maintain their families, but to buy seed and hire a plough. The principal way in which they could do this was by selling their services to large farms, which were glad of cheap labor during the summer and at harvest time. These French countrymen lived on soup and rye bread or maslin (a mixture of wheat and rye), gruel, and a little milk; but only the strong could survive a bad winter: the old—and men were reckoned old at forty—and the very young would die off. In England Gregory King reckoned that there were 1.3 million cottagers and paupers out of a total population of 5.5 million, and that their average yearly income was £6 10s ($15.60).

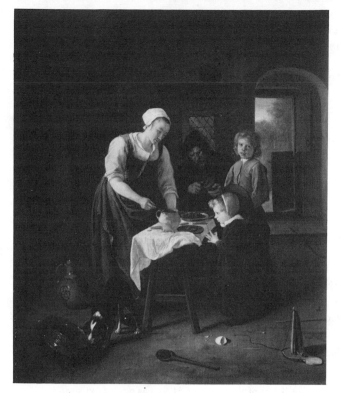

A Peasant Family at Mealtime
Jan Steen
National Gallery, London

Whether one should place above this class of cottagers (sometimes called cotters or smallholders or, in France, *manoeuvriers*) the landless laborers and out-servants who worked for wages is questionable. Gregory King considered that they were financially twice as well off in England as the cottagers. They could count more or less on regular employment, they could eat at their master's table, they were furnished with sleeping accommodation, if it was only in a shed, and they paid no taxes. Dr. Kerridge believes that both outdoor servants and indoor servants lived well in England on cheese, beef, beer, and rye bread. In Spain the agricultural laborers were extremely numerous as compared with the "peasants" proper, that is to say, smallholders. They too were reasonably well off in busy seasons, but when a slump occurred and they could find no work they often starved. In some eastern countries—Russia, for example—the number of landless laborers was fewer because the big landlords preferred to call upon the labor services of tenants, to which they were entitled by law for next to nothing, than to have to pay a wages bill. Even then a laborer was lucky if he earned more than a few cents a week.

The top class of peasantry—the *laboureurs* in France, the yeomen in England—were often reasonably well-to-do. They farmed upwards of 30 or 40 acres of land; they possessed cows, pigs, sheep, and always horses and a plough. They were not ashamed to be seen at church: they saved enough money to buy decent furniture and could even manage to lend it to smaller peasants; and they left property to their heirs. But this class of peasant was a fairly rare specimen. Even if one adds together those whom Gregory King classes as "freeholders of the better sort" and "freeholders of the lesser sort" in England, they totaled only a fraction compared with the mass of small tenant farmers, cottagers, and agricultural laborers which everywhere constituted the bulk of the countryfolk.

Everywhere in Europe peasants had to find taxes for the state, at any rate in time of war, which was almost perpetual, and tithe for the Church; moreover, the vast majority had to pay rent to their landlords and often provide services in labor and in kind as well as seignurial dues. They had to take their corn to be ground at the landlord's mill, to bake their bread at the landlord's oven, to make their wine at the landlord's presses, to pay tolls when they moved their produce, to work on the roads if they were required to do so, and to stomach hunting over their land. Historians of every country dilate upon the hardships of the peasantry. In Spain (especially in Castile, which harbored the major part of the population) the tillers of the soil were sacrificed to the big wool interests and the peasants were called upon to pay new kinds of taxes; in Italy

> the most regular condition of the peasant's life was one of extreme poverty punctuated by periods of real starvation. In 1648 free pardons were offered to bandits who ravaged the *campagna* if only they would bring corn into Rome.

In Brandenburg the privileges of the Junkers in relation to the peasants were strengthened by law; if peasants complained of their treatment, they could be evicted from their holdings or sent to prison. In Sweden, which prospered through the demand from other countries for its copper, iron ore, and tar, the peasants were reluctant to move into the towns and preferred to cultivate their lands by antiquated methods on an out-of-date strip system. In the forest areas Finns cleared the land by burning it over and sowed in the ashes (as is still done in backward parts of Europe today). In Russia a long process of enserfment was completed; the bulk of the rural population, many of whom had once been free tenant farmers, became bound to the person of their landlord and completely subjected to his will. The serfs, observed Klyuchensky, divided their labor between the state treasury and the landowners' estate offices. In France, says Professor Mousnier, most people were badly fed, of poor health, and lived a short life: the population always tended to outgrow the means of subsistence, and famine was endemic. In almost every country there was chronic underemployment in agriculture. Yet the peasants were supposed to pay most of the taxes. A French historian, writing of the seventeenth century, has said: "The peasant was the beast of burden in this society."

Before returning to the lot of the peasants, let us consider the other classes which made up the society of the time. Much has been written about the rise of the bourgeoisie or middle classes in the seventeenth century, but they are by no means easy to define. What seems undoubtedly true is that the professional classes expanded, particularly doctors and lawyers. The term *bourgeois* should perhaps be confined to burghers who lived in towns and earned their livings by other means than agriculture. Capital cities grew in size during the century, including Paris, London, Stockholm, Naples, and Copenhagen. Amsterdam was the leading commercial and financial center in Europe, and Antwerp, Danzig, Hamburg, and other north German towns still flourished. While merchants themselves were not noble, apprentices who rose to be prosperous merchants came, in some countries at least, from the gentry class, and sons of wealthy merchants might buy their way into the nobility. An administrative class had also become well established. To increase their revenues governments in most countries sold offices on a huge scale: the only important exception was in the United Netherlands. These officials have been described as a meritocracy, and they were certainly recruited from educated men. But again it is difficult to assign them definitely to a middle class: court officials consisted of nobility; in England the gentry jumped at the opportunity of buying their way into offices; exceptionally a merchant, like Lionel Cranfield, Earl of Middlesex, rose from being an apprentice to the highest offices in the state.

One point that has recently been emphasized by specialist historians is that there were often two classes of officials: there were those who bought their way into administrative positions and were able to sell or bequeath their offices (in France this was subject to a down payment known as the *paulette*), but at the same time governments made use of commissioners whose job it was to supervise or control the privileged officeholders both at the center and in the localities. In England the assize judges had wide supervisory powers. In France the King made use not only of intendants in the provinces but also of army intendants, judicial intendants, and intendants of police to act as overseers and report back to the Council of State. Tax commissioners may also be assigned to this class, although they were not always easily distinguishable from tax farmers, who bought their offices by advancing money to the Crown. But not all countries possessed an expanding middle class. The Spaniards relied chiefly on foreigners and Jews to run their financial and commercial affairs. "Our republic," wrote Gonzales de Cellorigo at the beginning of the century,

> has come to be an extreme contrast of rich and poor, and there is no means of adjusting them to one another. . . . We lack people of the middle sort, whom neither wealth nor poverty prevents from pursuing the rightful kind of business enjoined by natural law.

It is strange that this should have happened in Spain, because it might have been assumed that a large mercantile class would have been built up centered on Seville in response to the growing trade with the Americas. In fact, however, by the middle of the seventeenth century the Spanish bourgeoisie had been converted into a rentier class who preferred living on incomes derived from investment in government securities to risking their capital in commercial or industrial enterprises. So the Spanish monarchy grew weaker and the aristocracy stronger, and men who might have formed the nucleus of a middle class bought their way into the nobility to avoid paying taxes.

The nobility everywhere was divided into different categories: at the peak were the wealthy aristocrats, who enjoyed rents derived from their huge estates, spent most of their time at Court, and profited from offices conferred on them by the Crown which were mainly sinecures. Next came the provincial or country nobilities, who lived chiefly on their own estates, dwelling in imposing houses and supervising the administration of their domains. Finally there was a country nobility, who, although like the rest of the nobility were exempt from taxation, often found it hard to make both ends meet, their expenditure necessary to maintain status generally exceeding their income. In France such noblemen were known as *hoberaux,* in Spain as *hidalgos,* in Poland as *szlachta,* and in England as lesser gentry. As a whole the nobility lived on their rents and paid no taxes (though exceptions to this may be found in Prussia, Russia, and to some extent in England): the only occupations that they were permitted to fill, apart from service at Court, were in the army or navy or in the Church. A gentleman never worked with his hands. The higher clergy were nearly always recruited from the nobility and may be equated with it; the lower clergy might sometimes be equated with the lower gentry, but in the majority of cases were hard to differentiate from the peasants.

At the apex of society were of course the monarchs and the princes of the blood, who constituted a more or less closed circle: the only exceptions were in the few republics like the United Netherlands or Venice, which were ruled by oligarchies. The relations between the monarchies and their nobilities varied. On the one hand, a feeling of social solidarity existed between them. Louis XIV addressed all dukes as his cousins. But monarchs who aspired to be absolute often found it necessary to keep their aristocracy in check. Both in the English and French civil wars members of the nobility fought against the Crown, and at no time were they exempt from imprisonment or even execution. Moreover, they had duties as well as privileges. They were expected to lead armies and risk their lives in war; to furnish troops and give or lend money to the Government; in peace they might be required to supervise local government as lords lieutenant in the English counties and the viceroys in the Spanish Empire. On the whole, the later part of the seventeenth century was a golden age for the aristocracy. In most countries an "inflation of honours" took place as kings found the creation of new titles a useful way of raising money. Philip III began this in Spain, as

James I did in England. There were 41 grandees in 1627 and 113 in 1707, and the lower nobility expanded correspondingly. In Sweden Charles XI *(r. 1672–97)* created many noblemen who acquired money and land. In Prussia the privileges of the nobility were confirmed and extended by the Recess of 1653 in return for a substantial monetary grant. There the nobility, writes Professor F. L. Carsten, "remained free from taxation, its social position and economic privileges were reinforced and it remained the absolute ruler over its peasants and the burghers in small towns." In Russia before the end of the century the only rights left to the peasants were those their lords allowed them. Even in France, where it is often said that Louis XIV deprived the old nobility of its political functions, in fact he created a new nobility; the families of his leading ministers like Colbert and Louvois were all ennobled. In 1696 Louis XIV sold over two thousand patents of nobility. Moreover, the lawyers who formed the *noblesse de la robe* were as powerful and influential as the hereditary aristocracy, the *noblesse de l'épee.*

In one important respect a difference of interest existed between the monarchy and the aristocracy. This was particularly noticeable in France. The nobles were dependent for their income (apart from officeholding) upon the peasantry, who furnished them with rents in money and in kind and with labor services. Since most of the peasants lived on or below the margin of subsistence, it was difficult or impossible for them both to pay their dues to their landlord and their share of taxes owed to the Government. Thus, especially when harvests were poor, French peasants were incited to riot against the royal tax collectors and were actively encouraged in doing so by their landlords. For the peasantry the King and his Council dwelt far away and appeared to ignore the advice of the privincial nobility and to attack local liberties. Thus, lord and peasant had a common interest in conflict with the King and his taxation system. The provincial nobility might be persuaded to relax their requirements from their peasants in hard times; consequently, it was rarely wise for the peasants to antagonize their immediate masters, who alone could protect them from royal pillage. As Professor Mousnier has shown, popular uprisings were fomented by the upper classes in France, who thus sowed the seeds of revolution to which they themselves were to succumb.

The idea, therefore, that there existed a balanced European society consisting of a hierarchy by degree, each class possessing well-defined privileges and duties, cut off from one another by ancient usages, each wearing its own robes, dresses, or uniforms, is vitiated by hard economic facts. Moreover, a far larger amount of social mobility both horizontal and vertical prevailed than once used to be thought. In his detailed examination of the peasants in Beauvais, Professor Goubert has shown how difficult it was for them to live on the produce of their own land. Because the peasant had to pay *taille* to the Crown, tithe to the Church, and *champart* (tributes in kind) to his *seigneur* in order to survive and feed his family, he had to grow twice as much as he required for the last purpose alone. To do this he would have needed a farm of 30 acres in years of plenty and of twice that size in years of scarcity. But most *manoeuvriers* had only 25 acres under cultivation. Then how could he live? The answer is that some peasants starved, especially in bad years. For when shortages forced up prices, it was to the interest of the landlords to sell their grain promptly; for example, grain was exported from Languedoc in the middle of the seventeenth century while the poor died of starvation in the streets of Narbonne.

But of course they did not all die. How then did the peasants manage? What they did was to supplement their earnings by finding other kinds of work: they spun wool, they made lace, they carved wood, they undertook transport, they obtained temporary jobs on the larger estates, they poached, and they begged. Furthermore, the evidence suggests that the peasants did not necessarily stay put. In some English villages a third to a half of the population changed in ten years. Evidently the younger people left home and sought work in neighboring towns or on big farms. If they were successful, they might return one day to their birthplaces. Unskilled or semiskilled laborers found their way into lowly paid jobs, becoming servants, peddlers, or petty dealers. In England complaints were heard of laborers "running and shifting from town to town and county to county." The authorities did not much care for this kind of social mobility, and the Statute of Artificers, the Statute of Apprentices, and the Act of Settlement all aimed at keeping the poor where they were and imposing on them regular hours of work and conditions of employment.

From Prussia many peasants fled abroad in bad times. But Russia provided the most striking examples of peasant mobility. By the middle of the seventeenth century there were in Russia some 7 million serfs who could say: "Our body belongs to our sovereign, our soul to God and our back to the master." Under the impact of this growing servitude the only recourse that the peasantry had against the exactions of their masters and their governments was flight or violence. They ran away to Siberia or to the White Sea; they joined the Cossacks; they sought employment with more generous masters who were not above poaching serfs from their neighbors to work on their domains. Vainly the Tsarist Government tried to stop the free movement of the peasantry by introducing exit fees and permitting migration only at specific times of the year. Throughout the seventeenth century the hand of the law tightened on the Russian peasants. In the end they were forbidden to move at all, and any time limit previously imposed on landlords after which they could not recover fugitive serfs was abolished. Nevertheless, peasants continued to flee or even to be kidnapped. The authorities had good reason to be afraid of peasant unrest. For Stenka Razin, a Don Cossack leader, formed an army out of runaway peasants and controlled much of the Volga area before he was caught and executed in 1671. This was an example of the revolutionary stirrings which always threatened European society.

If a good deal of mobility existed among the peasantry, so too it did in other classes of the community. In Germany, as has already been noted, there was a huge shift of population after the Thirty Years' War. The Jews were always on the move, and found the friendliest welcomes in England, Holland, and Brandenburg. Protestants from Roman Catholic states frequently emigrated to Protestant countries, a movement that culminated in the dispersal of the Huguenots after 1685. Some countries felt the need for skilled immigrants: for example, a considerable Dutch population settled in Sweden in order to develop commerce and industry there. Mercenary soldiers were hired by France, the United Netherlands, and finally by Russia, and many of them afterward settled in the lands of their paymasters. Scientists and artists knew no nationality. The philosopher Descartes spent much of his life in Holland and died in Sweden. Sir Peter Lely came from Westphalia to make his name as a portrait painter in England, and he was followed by Sir Godfrey Kneller from Lübeck. Finally, emigration took place out of Europe mainly to the Americas and the West Indies. Thus, both economic and religious factors contributed to social mobility: the vertical movement was stimulated by the expansion of professional classes and by the growth of commerce and industry; the horizontal movement was brought about by the unceasing urge upon hard-pressed and exploited agriculturalists to find other jobs, discover richer soil to cultivate, or achieve a higher standard of living in the towns.

2.   Commerce and Finance: The Beginnings of "Mercantilism"

The fact that in Europe as a whole the second half of the seventeenth century was a time of stagnant or falling populations and stagnant or falling prices meant that there was little to stimulate economic progress. Outside the United Netherlands and England agricultural methods remained more or less unchanged, and although this was reckoned a scientific age, technological advances were small. Nor was industry highly developed. On the other hand, owing to overseas expansion, which had begun in the sixteenth century, something like a commercial revolution was taking place.

Though most countries engaged in commerce and had merchant communities, a shift in emphasis occurred by the middle of the seventeenth century. The opening of the Atlantic had brought an end to the supremacy of the Mediterranean, so that Spain and Italy entered upon a period of decline. Baltic trade continued to be important: Scandinavian timber and naval stores were much in demand, but the commerce was chiefly in the hands of the Dutch. In the Atlantic the once-flourishing commerce between Spain and the Americas was much reduced with the decline in the output of the silver mines, while Portuguese commerce was interrupted by wars first with the Dutch and then with the Spaniards, and was also much damaged by shipwrecks and piratical attacks as well as by the rivalry of the Dutch and the English. In fact it was mainly these last two nations which, often by unscrupulous means, stimulated European commerce eastward as well as westward.

The Dutch set the pace in commercial advance. In 1656–57 the Dutch East India Company conquered Ceylon from the Portuguese, and the surrender of Nagapatam in July 1658 enabled the company to link Ceylon with India, where later it also took Cochin on the Malabar coast. In 1666 an expedition from Batavia, its chief port in Java, subdued Macassar in the Celebes. Ceylon was valuable for cinnamon and Malabar for pepper. By the end of the seventeenth century the Company had become an impressive power in India, Ceylon, Malacca, and the Malay archipelago, though the dream of permanent Dutch settlements in the east was not realized. The Dutch West India Company was somewhat less successful. For a time it laid its hands on Brazil, which had been part of the Portuguese Empire, but by 1654 it had lost its main trading station at Recife. Equally important, though the New Netherlands in North America had been established as a Dutch colony by the middle of the century, it was surrendered to the English, who surrounded it in September 1664. The Dutch also had strong posts in the Gold Coast and elsewhere in West Africa, where the English, Swedes, and Danes traded as well. Gold, ivory, rubber, and ostrich feathers were exchanged for tools, arms, and textiles. The Dutch Admiral De Ruyter was hired to counter the depredations of the English in West Africa; he recaptured Goree and took Cormantin. Thus, despite certain setbacks, such as the loss of the New Netherlands and Formosa, during the second half of the century Dutch trade and shipping stretched around the world.

The principal commercial rivals of the Dutch were the English, with a population about double that of the United Netherlands, a growing mercantile marine, and a powerful navy. English shipping, protected by the Navigation Acts, steadily increased in size, and if English merchants could not compete successfully with the Dutch in the Baltic or East Indies, new markets were opened in the West Indies and North America. Not only were textiles exported (they were still easily the most valuable exports during this period), but coal, tin, and grain were sold abroad and reexports of sugar, tobacco, cotton wool, and dyes were added to native products. While London was still the chief port and entrepot, other ports, such as Bristol and Liverpool, benefited from the growing transatlantic trade. It has been estimated that the value of exports increased by at least 50 percent between 1660 and 1700, and that a deficit in the balance of trade was transformed into a surplus.

Besides the English East India Company, whose charter was renewed in 1657, another joint-stock company that prospered was the Royal Africa Company, which was founded in 1672 and had the advantage both of active royal patronage and of the support of the Royal Navy. Though it had to compete with the Dutch West India Company and other European companies, it did a busy trade exchanging textiles and arms for gold, ivory, hides, and other commodities. It also bought slaves, which it sold to the West Indian islands and to Virginia. A third smaller company, the Hudson's Bay Company, was also successful, and laid the foundations for British imperialism in Canada.

The justification for the monopolies conferred upon these companies was that they needed fixed capital in the form of port facilities and fortresses and because they even had to hire warships to protect their markets. In European trade much less fixed capital was needed. English merchants were able to raise the resources they needed from commercial banks that were coming into existence; these bankers were originally goldsmiths who furnished safety deposits for cash and discounted bills. In 1694 the Bank of England was founded by act of Parliament; it advanced the whole of its capital to the Government and began to issue notes. A Bank of Scotland was founded at the same time. Although the goldsmith bankers were at first suspicious of it, the Bank of England overcame many difficulties, including the issue of a new silver coinage, and eventually it became the bankers' bank.

Thus banks facilitated the operations of public finance, for it was no longer necessary to borrow money from Italians, Jews, or tax farmers. But in nearly every other country except England and the United Netherlands there was deficit financing. Governments borrowed money wherever they could and often failed to pay it back. But in the absence of sophisticated banking systems, methods of public borrowing were crude, and governments from Spain to Russia debased their currencies in order to keep afloat. Indeed, so great was the shortage of sound money that tradesmen were obliged to resort to credit transactions, and barter was widespread. It was largely because Great Britain and the United Netherlands acquired viable systems of public finance and banking, while the French relied on antiquated methods of raising money, that the latter lost two great wars against the Maritime Powers.

In his famous book *An Inquiry into the Nature and Causes of the Wealth of Nations,* which the Scottish philosopher Adam Smith published in 1776, he argued that the economic policy which prevailed in Great Britain roughly between the middle of the seventeenth and the middle of the eighteenth centuries was governed by what was called the "mercantile system." The self-interest of merchants and manufacturers, he thought, had shaped government policies not only in Great Britain but in other European countries. "The encouragement of exportation and the discouragement of importation" were "the two great engines by which the mercantile system proposed to enrich every country," and "its ultimate object was always the same—to enrich the country by an advantageous balance of trade." This policy, Smith believed, is full of fallacies. In particular, the conferring of bounties and subsidies on producers and the protection of their industries by tariff walls is to approach economic policy from the wrong end; for

> consumption is the sole purpose of all production; and the interest of the producer ought to be attended to only so far as it may be necessary for the promoting of the consumer.

Adam Smith's interpretation was subsequently adopted and refined by historians, notably by the German Gustav Schmoller, and the word *Mercantilismus* was applied particularly to the policies of the English and French Governments in the late seventeenth century. But the aims of the system were never exactly and generally defined. Did it aim at plenty or did it aim at power? Did it accept the belief that wealth consists of money and that there is only a limited amount of money to go round? Or did it believe, in Professor Charles Wilson's words, that "the economic welfare of the State can only be secured by government regulation of a nationalist character"? One thing that seems certain is that the idea that wealth consists of money—usually described as bullionism—was never generally accepted. For it was proved by the experience of the various East India companies and also by the dealings of the Dutch in the Baltic that the export of bullion could stimulate trade and bring valuable goods into the homeland at low cost.

As to the question of whether there is also a limited amount of wealth in the world and whether one country's gain is another country's loss, this was certainly not a difficult doctrine to maintain when population was static and world prices were steady or falling. Undoubtedly, under pressure from merchants and manufacturers governments did attempt to increase the wealth of their countries by artificial means. If new industries were to be established, they had to be encouraged with subsidies and protected by tariffs. It was a persuasive argument to put forward, and, unless conflicting interests were involved, not a difficult policy to carry out. But the question which has perplexed historians writing in the twentieth century is whether such ideas and policies can really be assigned to any particular period of modern history. They were of course lit up by the coming of the commercial revolution. But today hardly a government is not concerned with the welfare of highly articulate producers and is not guided by consideration for its balance of payments. Modern mercantilism may be more sophisticated than it was in the seventeenth and eighteenth centuries, but basically economic policies remain much the same. The erection of tariff walls, the fostering of new industries, the subsidizing of agriculture by bounties are as common now as they were then.

Professor Eli Heckscher has contended that in the seventeenth and eighteenth centuries statesmen pursued this mercantile policy not so much to maximize the welfare of their peoples as to increase their political power and unity. Even Adam Smith commended the English Navigation Acts because, he wrote, "defence is of much more importance than opulence." It does not seem, however, that—except in the case of shipbuilding—English statesmen in those days were primarily guided in their economic policies by considerations of national power. But one man certainly was: that was the French Minister Colbert. Not only did he attempt to make his country richer by employing the direct authority of the Government to increase industry and commerce, but he neglected agriculture, to which France was best suited. He honestly believed that the amount of wealth in the world was limited, and that a larger share of it could be gained by France if its Government adopted a deliberate policy of attacking its rivals by every means at its disposal. He aimed at self-sufficiency at home and the creation of a colonial empire abroad in order to enhance the greatness of his King. Unless the word is used in a loose sense that may be applied to all countries at all times, Colbert was, as Professor Coleman has written, the only true "mercantilist" who has ever lived. But Colbert's policies failed. Hence France did not participate in the commercial revolution as much as he hoped. His King was little interested in matters of commerce and finance—even less than Cardinal Richelieu had been. Thus, once again France dragged behind the two Maritime Powers, whose wealth helped to destroy French political supremacy by enabling them to build navies and hire soldiers to fight for them in wars that lasted intermittently for over twenty-five years.

3.   War and Society

What impact had war on the structure of society? It tended to strengthen monarchies, which were able to exact services and taxes from their subjects that were unobtainable in peacetime. Though it was to the interest of some trading companies to promote wars against their rivals, most merchants preferred peace. That was why Amsterdam, as the wealthiest city in Europe, after some little experience, became stubbornly opposed to war. Adam Smith was to write that

> it is to the interest of the general not to rob the peasants, because
> it would be difficult to march an army carrying all its provisions
> through the country of an enemy.

Marshal Villars once had thirty soldiers shot for disobeying his orders not to set cottages on fire and force the peasants to flee, since, as he wrote to the French Secretary of State for War, afterward "the peasants who were fleeing ten leagues around brought their chickens and butter to my camp." But probably it was not so much the smallholders who were enriched by the rising demand for farm produce and livestock created by war. The average peasant had only a small surplus to sell, and villages were easily overrun and burnt down by armies which were brought to a halt by the fortified walls of large towns. The principal areas of European fighting, such as the southern Netherlands and northern Italy, were frequently the scenes of agricultural ruin and intensified poverty.

But whatever the sufferings of individuals may have been, the wars which were fought throughout Europe in the second half of the seventeenth century stimulated economic demand and output just as the total wars of the twentieth century have done. The Scandinavian countries in particular profited from the sale of metals, such as brass, from which cannon were manufactured, and of timber, from which warships were built. Sir George Clark has written that

> During the reign of Louis XIV the expansion of government activities, especially in war and warlike preparations, created new employment at every level from that of the ruling few to the manual workers, and as the numbers of men employed increased, their tasks inevitably became more specialized.

Thus, wars stimulated the division of labor which characterized the industrial advance of Europe. But at the same time it must not be forgotten that wars also brought in their train epidemics, dysentery, and cattle plagues, and that therefore the damage they did to the social life of the people as a whole may well have offset the economic advantages. By injuring agriculture, as distinct from commerce and industry, war engendered discontent.

4.   The Revolution in the Arts

By the middle of the seventeenth century what art historians call high baroque was nearing the end of its popularity in western Europe. It is true that three of its masters—Sacchi, Borromini, and Cortona—were still living, and that Bernini, the most famous of them all, was not to die until 1680 at the age of eighty-two, but the painters who had shed such luster on the first half of the century had (except for Rembrandt, whose old age was sad) all passed away: architecture, painting, and sculpture were now carried out by a third generation of baroque artists who, writes Professor Wittkower, "were respectable, versatile and talented, but lacked the universality and fullness of vision of their elders."

Of course, contemporaries did not speak of the work of these artists as baroque, though the word is to be found in late-eighteenth-century dictionaries and usually deprecatory. It was thought to have derived from the Portuguese word *barroco,* meaning an imperfectly rounded pearl. Writing of music in the French *Encyclopédie,* Jean-Jacques Rousseau, that self-made genius, said "baroque music is that in which harmony is confused, full of modulations and dissonance." In 1797 the celebrated German writer on esthetics, Winckelmann, observed: "Baroque is the ultimate in the bizarre; it is the ridiculous carried to extremes."

The French were less attracted by baroque than other nations and mostly preferred classicism in imitation of Greece and Rome. But there had been a Roman Catholic reaction against the classicism of the Renaissance, notably at the Council of Trent, where it was thought to have exhibited pagan characteristics. Thus the Italian artists of the late sixteenth century had practised an anticlassical style of "mannerism" which verged on the fantastic. Baroque artists were less extreme. Nevertheless, baroque was exuberant, uninhibited, exciting, and very colorful, and can be seen at its most typical in the large and dramatic paintings of Rubens. In architecture it made much use of entablature, set-in columns, and domes, in music of emotionally expressed melody. High baroque also welded together the arts of architecture, sculpture, and painting as they had never been before.

The heart of the baroque movement was Rome, where Carlo Fontana *(1634–1714)* exerted great influence; and it was between 1656 and 1667 that Bernini created his finest masterpiece, the piazza of Saint Peter's Cathedral in Rome. Here the open colonnades help to give an impression of grandeur and spaciousness which remained an inspiration to urban designers for almost two hundred years. But after the Peace of Westphalia had been signed the patronage of the Popes declined, and Italian artists found other patrons in northern and southern Italy, particularly in Genoa, Venice, and Turin. Indeed, Guarino Guarini *(1624–83)* with his daringly designed churches turned Turin into one of the outstanding baroque cities of Europe.

From Italy the baroque style penetrated into Spain, where Toledo Cathedral was a supreme achievement, but it came rather more slowly to Austria-Hungary. Its pomp and majesty had appealed to Wallenstein, but it was not really until after the Turks had been repulsed from Vienna in 1683 that the great period of high baroque or authentic baroque began there. Between 1685 and 1720 there was in Austria an epoch of distinguished architects, painters, and sculptors, of whom the most celebrated were Fischer von Erlach, Johann Lukas von Hildebrandt (an admirer of Guarini), and Jakob Prandtauer. Fischer von Erlach built the Schönbrunn Palace, an Austrian Versailles, for the Emperor Leopold I, while Hildebrandt designed the Upper Belvedere for Leopold's victorious general, Prince Eugene. Prandtauer, who was a sculptor as well as a mason, was responsible for the Benedictine monastery of Melk, which dominates the Danube and although mostly enclosed by high walls opens up the west front by a low arched screen through which the twin towers and façade of the church are visible. Italian architects were also welcomed in Austria: Andrea Pozzo, who had designed a unique ceiling for the church of Saint Ignatius in Rome, was invited to transform the interior of the University of Vienna. Southern German baroque was, if anything, more elaborate and fantastic than that of

Italy and Spain: in particular, the German architects embodied gothic towers in their designs. By such means Prague was transformed. And because baroque came much later to southern Germany than to Italy, it dissolved more easily into the even more elaborate style of rococo.

The baroque style was not confined to southern Europe. It spread to northern Germany, Poland, Russia, and the Ukraine. In Munich Saint John of Nepomunk was an extreme example of baroque church architecture, while the Zwinger at Dresden and Sans Souci at Potsdam were typically splendid baroque palaces. Guarini was invited to Paris to design the church of Saint Anne la Royale, and in England Sir Christopher Wren borrowed freely from Borromini.

It is sometimes said that the baroque style sprang initially from decisions taken at the Council of Trent; that its aim in church architecture and religious painting was to inspire overwhelming spiritual emotions and for that reason particularly invoked the devotion of the peasants. The fact that many examples of baroque are to be found in Brandenburg-Prussia, in Russia, and in England, which were not Roman Catholic countries, does not necessarily vitiate this line of argument; nor does the fact that high baroque never took the same hold on Roman Catholic France as it did on Italy and to a lesser extent on Spain. Unquestionably baroque architecture, sculpture, painting, and music were all deliberately used to heighten the emotional and majestic appeal of Roman Catholic churches. It may in fact be contended that while the Counter-Reformation had suffered from a violent setback in the Thirty Years' War, baroque artists proved better missionaries than the Emperor's mercenaries. The appeal of baroque differed fundamentally from the almost austere grandeur of the gothic cathedrals. They were symbols of an age of faith which united the Christians of Europe and inspired men's minds to soar toward heaven. Baroque art was more uninhibited, striving, as it were, by its very vitality and colorfulness, to distract the mind from a malaise which had inflicted mid-seventeenth-century Europe.

It is perhaps symbolic that in France, which had emerged as a conqueror in the middle of the century after having first defeated the Austrian Habsburgs and then the Spanish Habsburgs, baroque never took the same hold as it did in southern and eastern Europe. Yet the fame of that style, stemming from Rome, was not at first without its influence. Rubens had celebrated the life of Henry IV's Queen with supreme examples of the baroque style in painting, and in the 1660s a French academy was established in Rome so that French artists might sit at the feet of the Roman masters. But an event which took place at this time marked the parting of the ways. Bernini was invited to Paris to draw up a plan for a new Louvre. The rejection of his plans constituted a turning point against the baroque in France. Bernini's original scheme was for an immense oval pavilion flanked by two concave wings joining two rectangular pavilions of the same height. The central pavilion was surmounted by a gallery with round windows in the form of a crown.

Although Bernini was treated with the greatest possible consideration and generosity when at the age of sixty-seven he arrived in Paris, the opposition to his far-reaching designs was headed by Louis XIV's leading Minister, Colbert, who was not only the Protector of the French Academy of Arts but also the Finance Minister, who had to find the money for the project. Colbert insisted that in all of the three plans that he submitted Bernini had sacrificed function to decoration. Bernini thought that the buildings in Paris were too regular, and argued that a palace should be compared with a man's body: the principal building in the center of the Louvre should produce the effect of a head dominating the rest, as a head dominates a body. Thus, in his final plan the central pavilion was to be of a colossal size capped by an imposing cornice with a balustrade and a row of statues. The French King hesitated to reject the designs of this world-famous artist, and before Bernini left Paris in October 1665 the first stones were actually laid. But later the King was persuaded that Bernini's plans were too grandiose and expensive, and the task of enlarging the Louvre was handed over to French architects.

It is impossible to say what might have happened if Bernini's plans had been followed. Conceivably Louis XIV would have remained in Paris and his withdrawal to the palace which he was to build at Versailles with its profound consequences for the history of France and of Europe would never have taken place. As it was, though Bernini's designs had an influence outside France, the French went on to evolve their own style, which became known as *le style Louis XIV*.

Colbert held sway henceforward over the French arts and indeed dragooned the artists, employing as his agent the versatile Charles Le Brun; the factory of the Gobelins was created not only for the manufacture of tapestries but of furniture and all sorts of artistic decorations, and promising young artists were sent there as pupils to master the French academic style. Just as Boileau, who dominated French literature at this moment, detested the "baroque literature" of Italy, so Le Brun turned away from baroque and back to the ideals of classical art. It was not that Le Brun rejected grandeur in his designs, for that was necessary to glorify his King. He was no lover of simplicity but thought that magnificence and a sense of movement created the kind of glory for which his master sought. So he did not accord to color the first place in his designs, nor did he look for the dazzlement of light or the prestige conjured up by architectural illusions. The authoritative state, Sir Kenneth Clark has remarked, "gives French classical architecture a certain inhumanity. It was the work not of craftsmen, but of wonderfully gifted civil servants." The heavy classicism of Versailles owes virtually nothing to baroque influences. "Versailles," writes Sir Anthony Blunt,

> offers little in either painting, sculpture or architecture which is of the first quality in itself. Louis XIV aimed first and foremost at a striking whole, and to produce it his artists (Le Vaux and J. H. Mansart) sacrificed the parts.

Two French artists who preceded the period of Colbert and Le Brun's domination, and in fact spent most of their lives in Rome, contributed to the creation of a distinctive French style. Between 1643 and 1653 Nicolas Poussin executed a series of paintings which were intended to appeal to the mind rather than to the eyes. He concentrated on biblical and stoic figures who, like the principal actors in Corneille's tragedies, manifested the triumph of the will over the passions. These paintings—calm, contemplative, cool, and philosophical—have been described as the purest embodiments of French classicism. Poussin's last works were also designed to convey "general truths." The other great painter who lived in Rome, Claude Lorrain, specialized in landscape painting that recalled the countryside of Virgil's days. Both Poussin's and Lorrain's paintings were eagerly bought in Paris. Their mainly small canvases contrasted with the baroque exuberance of a Rubens or Velazquez.

After the death of Colbert in 1683, the influence of Le Brun and the strictly classical style declined somewhat. Louvois, Louis XIV's War Minister, took Colbert's place as patron of the arts and preferred the rather indifferent Pierre Mignard as his guide. The result was that some painters and sculptors showed tendencies toward the baroque style which had until then been frowned upon. But the French artists never combined architecture, painting, and sculpture in the manner of the high baroque; and the Louis XIV style has generally been described as dramatic but cool and even cold. It had nothing of the emotional appeal of baroque at its best.

Thus in the latter half of the seventeenth century and the outset of the eighteenth century there were three distinct artistic styles which, to a considerable extent, reflected the character of the countries concerned. In the Netherlands and in England art tended to be realistic. By realistic is meant photographic and devoid of any elaborate ornamentation. The portraits by Lely or the seascapes of the Dutch somehow reflect the kind of commercial world in which the Dutch and English merchants moved; the palaces designed by Sir John Vanbrugh, such as Blenheim, used baroque elements to pay tribute to the British aristocracy, who were the real rulers of the kingdom. In France *le style Louis XIV*, based on classical principles, appealed to the servants of an absolute monarchy, but hardly to the French peasants who supported the lopsided social and political system. In Germany and Russia, both rising powers, baroque came later; its elaborations there glorified aspiring monarchs. The Roman Catholics of Italy, Spain, and southern Germany were offered the emotional appeal of the high baroque, while the Protestants of northern Germany, Denmark, and Sweden were mostly influenced by the French style, less emotional, better balanced. It is interesting that when Nicodemus Tessin, the Swedish architect who had studied in Rome and was known as the Bernini of the north, submitted plans to his martial King, Charles XII, then in exile in Turkey, the King rejected Tessin's ideas of sculpture and ornamentation and pronounced in favor of the classical style. The rulers of the eighteenth century regarded themselves as Caesars and not as apostles of the Church.

5. Intellectual and Scientific Progress

If the outstanding painters of the seventeenth century were dead or had passed their prime by 1648, philosophy and science—generally called "natural philosophy"—had already made strides forward. William Gilbert published his book on magnetism in 1600; William Harvey had discovered the circulation of the blood; Kepler's three laws of planetary motion, which gave substance to Copernicus's speculations about the movement of the earth around the sun, had also been known; Kepler showed that the planets travel on an elliptical course; Galileo Galilei, a descriptive astronomer and physicist of genius, died in 1642. The scientists were aided by the invention of the telescope, the barometer, the air pump, and the pendulum clock. In 1648 English scientists were meeting in London to form the nucleus of a club which was to become famous as the Royal Society, where experiments in technology were given and discussed. René Descartes, a Frenchman born in 1596, who many claim to have been the first modern philosopher and who was also a considerable mathematician, published his *Principia Philosophae* in 1644 and was to die in 1650; Thomas Hobbes, a political philosopher who based his arguments on elementary psychology, published his *De Cive* in

Newton's Second Reflector
Royal Society, London

1641 and was to finish *The Leviathan,* his masterpiece, in 1651. Francis Bacon, who had earlier written persuasively about the virtues of induction—that is to say, inferences based on an accumulation of observed facts—though he died in 1626, was to become the inspiration of the Royal Society.

Science and philosophy, like arts, were cosmopolitan: most treatises were written in Latin or French, international languages among learned men. But, unlike with art, there were no recognized centers of philosophy, and scientific experiments were undertaken from Italy to Sweden. The most startling discoveries were in astronomy and dynamics. These undermined the hitherto accepted classical teaching. Moreover, the fact that the earth had been proved a minor planet of the sun was enough to make men wonder whether the world was, after all, the focus of the universe. Descartes believed that all things are either bodies or minds, bodies being spatial and minds conscious, each working according to the laws of physics, which leaves little room for an active diety. God, whose existence as an infinite being Descartes did not doubt—and indeed claimed to have proved—thus becomes a clockmaker who sets minds and bodies at work, though Descartes never resolved the problem of their relationship or their "dualism." The Abbé Malebranche got around this difficulty by arguing that God is "the place of minds" or spirits, just as space is the place of bodies. Geulincx, a Dutch follower of Descartes, solved the problem by assuming that God treats the body and mind like two clocks that keep perfect time. When the body is thirsty and the mind feels sorrow, one clock indicates thirst and the other indicates sorrow, the two chiming together. This theory left little room for free will, for mind and body are equals and both are operated by the unchanging laws of physics.

To Descartes God was therefore an infinite being who had created a mechanical and dualistic world. Baruch de Spinoza, a Portuguese Jew who spent all his life in Holland "accepted from Descartes and his contemporaries a materialistic and deterministic physics and sought within this framework, to find room for reverence and a life devoted to the Good." Descartes had taught that there are three "substances," a body which is spatial, a mind which is conscious, and a deity which is infinite. Spinoza admitted the existence of only one "substance": an infinite God. Thus, the courses of men's lives are determined for them and God enters into everything they do (this was called pantheism). Therefore, Spinoza urged that whatever occurs as a physical event also occurs as a mental event. So the problem of the relationship between mind and body was solved. God is not the clockmaker who created the world; he *is* the world. But Spinoza thought that if men realize that their life is determined for them, then they will replace an evil passion such as hatred by a good passion such as love. True knowledge consists of the intellectual love of God.

Thomas Hobbes claimed that philosophy can only treat of bodies, and must leave everything spiritual to revelation. For him ideas and wants were held at bottom to be activities of the body. Sensations are caused by the pressure of objects on bodies. Thoughts are not arbitrary but governed by laws of association. The idea of free will, he thought, is absurd. Men are naturally equal and aggressive, eager to dominate each other. Therefore, if they are to live in peace, they have to create by means of a contract or convention agreed among themselves a mortal god, a Leviathan, who determines for them what is justice and what is religion.

Hobbes *(1588-1679)* and Spinoza *(1634-1677)* were in agreement that in order to meet the secular needs of men, who require peace, order, and the security of their property, the State must be supreme and the Church must be subordinate to the State. Hobbes was conscious of the dangers of anarchy and therefore thought that any government, however bad, must be obeyed. Spinoza agreed that there is no right of rebellion, although, unlike Hobbes, who believed that subjects only retain the right of self-defense, Spinoza maintained that they retain other rights, such as freedom of opinion. Spinoza, like Hobbes, had lived through an age of revolution and sought to prevent the disruption of society by accepting the absolutism of the State. The Dutchman Grotius and the German Puffendorf also felt that the unfettered supremacy of government is essential to the preservation of peace, order, and property, and that rebellion endangers the very structure of civilized society. All these philosophers, therefore, were influenced by the dangers of revolution or rebellion, which they regarded as evils to be avoided at all costs. Thus, they justified absolute sovereignty not by an appeal to its divine origins but by commonsense arguments. Though these arguments might be applied to any established government, Hobbes thought that monarchy is best; other seventeenth-century writers also maintained that monarchy is the most natural form of government. "Mixed governments" (that is to say, parliamentary governments) were regarded as a contradiction in terms. Thus, the absolutism that prevailed in most European countries until the French Revolution was given an intellectual justification.

Gottfried Wilhelm Leibniz *(1646-1716)*, like most of the other philosophers of the time, was a man of many interests: he was a courtier and a historian, and invented the infinitesimal calculus at about the same moment as Newton. (There was some sort of quarrel about this, and that was why Leibniz did not accompany his master, King George I, to England, but died in Hanover.) Leibniz aimed to reconcile the mechanical and spiritual views of the world. He accepted the mechanical interpretation of the world, but believed it had an efficient cause. He therefore invented a force-substance, which is basic to everything, and he called it a "monad." The monad is a nonphysical force; every monad is independent and can neither experience nor exercise influence. On the other hand, each monad mirrors the universe, though with different degrees of distinctness. The lowest monads are in matter; the central monad is God. The monads harmonize with each other throughout creation; they are like an infinite number of clocks that all strike at the same time. A human body is entirely composed of monads, including one dominant monad which is in the mind. The monads realize the ends of the creative universal spirit, that is to say, God.

Leibniz produced four reasons for the existence of God. He insisted that God exists as an absolute necessity, on which everything else depends. Leibniz also invented a "principle of sufficient reason" why a thing should be as it is determined by God. But as Leibniz wished to leave room in his theory for freedom of will, he added that the principle of sufficient reason "incline[s] without necessitating." The whole doctrine has been called vitalism; it provides variety within unity; it offers a mechanical explanation of the universe while leaving men with the control of reason over their sense and passions. Sin can therefore exist. But God created the best of all possible worlds.

Just as England, lying on the western edge of Europe, had never accepted baroque art in the same way as it had been accepted in Roman Catholic countries, so it was far less receptive to the metaphysical theories of Continental philosophers. Bacon, Hobbes, Locke, and Newton were all empiricists—that is to say, they based their theories on observations and experiments, not on simple assumptions. Locke and Newton thought that the various theories about "substances" were medieval nonsense. On the other hand, they accepted from Descartes the mechanical explanation of nature. Isaac Newton took it for granted, and by proving mathematically the theory of universal gravitation he showed how the whole universe can be reduced to one fundamental system of scientific law. But at the same time Newton thought that the wonderful uniformity of gravitation throughout space made the existence of God logically necessary; and indeed, the mechanical explanations of a clockwork universe strengthened the hands of religious groups, like the Calvinists and Jansenists, who held that, since God is all-powerful, His is the choice of which men shall be saved and which shall be doomed.

Among the things that Newton disproved in his *Principia (1687)* was Descartes's theory that the planets are held in their place by a series of vortices or whirlpools. But Newton was a typical absent-minded professor who dressed in a slovenly way, lectured to empty classrooms, had few friends, did little entertaining, was neglectful of his meals, and managed with only four hours sleep at night. He was extremely touchy over the thought that his ideas might be appropriated by others, and so when he came to write his masterpiece he deliberately made it as abstruse as possible in order that only fellow mathematicians would be able to understand it. Moreover, he refused to offer an explanation of the origin of gravitation, sometimes seeming "privately to favour the view that the cause was in the ether, . . . gravity representing the tendency of all bodies to move to the place where the ether was rarer." At another time

> he seemed to think that this gravitation of his represented an effect that had to be produced by God throughout the whole of space—something that made the existence of God logically necessary and rescued the universe from the over-mechanization that Descartes had achieved.

The result of Newton's making his work so abstruse and keeping his speculations to himself was that many scientists, including Leibniz and the eminent Dutchman Christian Huygens, were critical of his system, and it was fifty years before it became generally accepted in Europe.

Nearly all these scientists were believers in God. Descartes was proud of his proof of God's existence and Leibniz of his four proofs. Newton once wrote to a friend: "When I wrote my treatise about our system, I had an eye upon such principles as might work with considering men for the belief of a Deity." Newton's friend John Locke, in addition to writing his *Essay concerning Human Understanding* and his two treatises on government, produced a book called *The Reasonableness of Christianity.* Robert Boyle, often called the father of chemistry, left £50 a year to establish a lectureship defending the Christian religion against infidels. But although these philosophers and scientists assumed the existence of God and often called themselves Protestants, that did not mean that they assented to all the tenets of orthodox Christianity. Leibniz tried to reconcile the Protestant and Roman Catholic religions. Neither Newton nor Locke believed in the doctrine of the Trinity—that is to say, the belief that Father, Son, and Holy Ghost are one godhead, three in one and one in three. One of Newton's biographers states that he did not believe that Jesus Christ was divine at all, but merely a man and therefore not an object of prayer. Locke in his *Reasonableness of Christianity* showed his disbelief in the doctrine of the Trinity; he also did not believe that all men were born sinful, and he thought that Christ was a messiah who came to preach immortality. Professional Christians fought a losing battle against these scientists with their varied views about God. Clergy found it hard to accustom themselves to the idea that the earth is not the center of the universe, that the planets do not move in a circular but in an elliptical motion, and that men are machines wound up like clocks. Although some Jesuits accepted Cartesianism, Descartes's works were placed posthumously on the Index (or under Papal ban) as not being suitable reading for good Catholics. But the new ideas stimulated theologians in England to harmonize science and religion, and they also led the way to deism (the belief that there is an unfathomable God), which was to be so popular among the French *philosophes* of the eighteenth century.

Scientific discoveries were not confined to astronomy and physics. Robert Boyle rejected Aristotle's view that substances can be resolved into four elements—earth, water, air, and fire—and aimed to "beget a good understanding between the chemists and the mechanical philosophers who have hitherto been too little acquainted with one another's learning." Progress was also achieved in biology and zoology. Antoni Van Leeuwenhock, a self-trained biologist who made four hundred microscopes for his own use, discovered spermatazoa in 1677 and was the founder of protozoology, the study of the simplest types of animals. Finally, this period saw the invention of modern statistics, its joint founders being two Englishmen, John Graunt and William Petty, while Gregory King's estimates of population are still used by historians today. Most demography, however, was guesswork. In 1696 the English Government inaugurated the first statistical office successfully conducted by a western European state, that of Inspector-General of Imports and Exports. William Petty in Ireland and Marshal Sébastien Vauban in France excelled in the science of surveying and mapmaking. The collection of facts and the practicing of experiments revealed the insatiable curiosity of educated seventeenth-century minds. But although scientists—especially in the English Royal Society—were conscious of the importance of practical problems, such as improvements in agriculture, it was not really until the eighteenth century that applied science came into its own.

6.   The Impact of New Ideas

Such was the economic, cultural, and intellectual situation at the end of the seventeenth century. The first half of the eighteenth century is often looked upon as a period of stability and placidity for most Europeans, only interfered with by the outbreak of futile dynastic wars. But if one takes into account the nonpolitical aspects of life, one detects a slow but potentially explosive development of ideas. Baroque art was emotional and dynamic, and ultimately undermined the classical approach, upholding things as they are or were. It was not a mere coincidence that the classical style was preferred by absolute monarchs like Louis XIV and Charles XII and also later by the Emperor Napoleon. Similarly, the discoveries of science undermined established ideas. The triumph of the mechanistic philosophy altered the nature of scientific explanation. As Professor A. R. Hall has noted, "it was no longer sufficient to ascribe the pattern of events to divine purpose or the necessary conditions for human existence." Both scientists themselves and the popularizers of their discoveries aimed to reach a wider audience. Galileo, Descartes, and Locke preferred to write books in the vernacular instead of Latin, the academic language. In England members of the Royal Society and in France men as different as Vauban, the Abbé Saint-Pierre (author of a project of perpetual peace), and Archbishop Fénelon (tutor of Louis XIV's grandson, the Duke of Burgundy) were moved by a questioning spirit which reacted against political orthodoxy. Vauban criticized economic privileges, Fénelon attacked the bases of autocracy, Saint-Pierre wanted government to be improved by scientific methods. Toward the end of the seventeenth century, John Locke's defense of the right of rebellion, which he propounded in his treatises on government, gave a new impulse to political thought, but it took a long time to penetrate. Even the great and influential author, the Baron de Montesquieu *(1689–1755)*, sometimes called the first sociologist, who, like Voltaire, visited England in search of political guidance and also toured the republics of the United Netherlands, Venice, and Genoa, was distressed by the tyranny and corruption he discovered, and realized that the transformation of European autocratic and aristocratic societies lay a long way off. So for nearly a century the arguments for enlightened absolutism, tempered by a privileged aristocracy, were held to be good. Nevertheless, fear of rebellions similar to those that had taken place around the year 1648 continued to agitate the minds of the educated and propertied classes. If drastic reforms were pressed, might not revolution follow?

FOUR

*Europe
in the Age
of Louis XIV*

1. Louis Assumes Personal Power

Louis XIV, who was born in 1638 and had spent much of his boyhood witnessing the wars of the Fronde, was carefully prepared for the profession of kingship. Cardinal Mazarin, who had ruled France since the death of Richelieu, believed that in him Louis "had the stuff for several great kings and one good man." When Louis was a teenager the Cardinal occupied several hours a day with him analyzing matters of politics. And Louis wrote that even when Mazarin was dying he "gave the last moments of his life on earth to the love that he had always had for the good of my state and my *gloire*." It would be wrong to say that Louis was never young, but the Frondes gave him a realization of the seriousness of political life. However, he was not without youthful pleasures: he acquired a love of food and a love of women that remained with him all his days. Also, he enjoyed playing at soldiers and became a crack shot. In the garden of the Palais Royal a miniature fortress was built for his benefit. He played war games with his younger brother, in which he usually came out on top.

When Louis announced that he would be his own First Minister after Mazarin's death, he had at his disposal a relatively stable administration and an army which gave him opportunities for enterprise abroad. During the '60s he wrote a number of memoirs for the benefit of his son in which he embodied the gems of political wisdom he had acquired from Mazarin. Professor Goubert points out that four words frequently fell from his pen: *"ma dignité, ma gloire, ma grandeur, ma réputation."* Louis recognized that kingship was a unique institution blessed by God which demanded hard work and careful thinking. Some historians have expressed the opinion that the French word *gloire* is not exactly equivalent to the English word *glory* and that it would be wrong to suggest that the driving force in Louis's life was self-glorification. In the contexts in which he generally used it the word *gloire* is equated with honor, and there can be little doubt that what the King most thought about was the honor of the monarchy and the honor of his kingdom. Glory was a delicate plant that needed prudent attention: "Love of glory," he wrote in his memoirs, "requires the same delicacy of touch and approach as love of a woman."

From the beginning the King took his own decisions and rapidly built up a system of personal rule, excluding from his councils members of his own family and princes of the blood, relying on some nine hundred secretaries. But he also had able ministers and generals and experienced diplomatists. After a few years he resolved to employ his diplomatic service and newly created army to fulfil his *gloire*.

Far-reaching policies had been advocated by Louis XIV's predecessors. Sully urged that France should seize all those French-speaking parts of Europe that had once belonged to it. Richelieu favored reviving the boundaries of ancient Gaul, the Rhine, the Alps, and the Pyrenees. Detailed modern historical research, however, has brought out clearly that Louis did not base his foreign policy on any particular shibboleth such as "the natural frontiers" formula. "If he pursued any constant aim," writes Professor Andrew Lossky, "it was to increase the grandeur of his state and of the House of Bourbon; as for the means, he tended to be opportunist." This certainly applies to the first actions of his reign, when he went out of his way to uphold French "honor" abroad.

Apart from this, three other incidents occurred during the early years of Louis XIV's personal rule. He bought the towns of Dunkirk and Mardyck from England, which Oliver Cromwell had acquired in 1658 when he had allied himself with Mazarin. The sale was not popular in England, but it is probable that Cromwell's idea of acquiring bridgeheads on the European mainland was impracticable, as they would have been difficult to defend even with support from the sea. Louis also tried to buy Lorraine from its duke. The Duke, who was hard up, was willing to cede his estates to the French Crown in return for a large annual income and the promise that the princes of Lorraine should enjoy immediate precedence over the French princes of the blood. But over this question of precedence negotiations broke down, and it was not until 1766 that Lorraine became part of France. Lastly, the Most Christian King chose at that time to demonstrate his power against the Turks. He sent a contingent to fight alongside the Austrians, and the French soldiers distinguished themselves at the battle of Saint Gothard *(1664)*; this victory enabled a truce to be concluded between the Austrians and the Turks for twenty years (this was known as the Treaty of Vasvar). An amphibious expedition against the pirates of Algeria turned out less well and had to be withdrawn.

2. The Emperor Leopold I and his Problems

The Emperor Leopold I, like Louis XIV, ruled over a large area of Europe, was destined to enjoy a reign of nearly fifty years, and also announced (in 1665) that he intended to be his own First Minister. He was only sixteen when he took over the Habsburg possessions which stretched from Bohemia and Silesia in the northwest to Transylvania in the east and Dalmatia in the south. Leopold had come to the throne unexpectedly in April 1657 owing to the premature death of his elder brother; he had been called to the throne when studying theology in Spain. He was a sincere Christian and devoted Roman Catholic with impeccable morals. He was also a cultivated man, a lover of music, and a collector of books and paintings. After fifteen months he was, like his father and brother before him, elected Holy Roman Emperor and thus the political leader of Germany.

The major problem that he had to face during the whole of his reign was a dual threat to his possessions from the east and the west. The eastern threat from the Turks was temporarily warded off by the Treaty of Vasvar. But from the west he had to contend with the ambitions of Louis XIV. On the other hand, he, like Louis, was conscious of the possibility from 1665 onward of the break-up of the territories belonging to the Spanish Habsburgs, as, for example, those in Italy and the southern Netherlands.

3. Louis XIV's Diplomacy and Wars

At the beginning of his personal reign Louis XIV had been able to wave the French flag victoriously over a peaceable Europe. But in 1667 he met with a difficulty. His cousin, Charles II of England, who had been restored to power in 1660, was involved by his Parliament in what became known as the Second Anglo-Dutch War. In the First Anglo-Dutch War, fought while Charles was still in exile, the English had been victorious. Louis had concluded a defensive alliance with the Dutch in 1662. Therefore, when the English fleet attacked the Dutch in 1665, he was reluctantly obliged to honor the treaty.

The war lasted two-and-a-half years. As in the First Anglo-Dutch War, the English tried to capture the wide-flung Dutch mercantile marine, and the Dutch admirals attempted to destroy the English fleets. The two sides were evenly matched. In the first big battle at Southwold bay the English won a victory and killed the Dutch admiral, but allowed most of his fleet to escape. On the other hand, an attempt by the English to capture a Dutch merchant fleet at Bergen in Denmark was a failure, and brought the Danes into the war on the Dutch side. Although in 1666 the English held their own at sea, a bubonic plague struck England in the spring of 1665 and caused much loss of life in London; this was followed in September 1666 by a great fire in the English capital. These two events damaged British commerce and credit and contributed to a decision to seek peace. Meanwhile in 1667 the larger ships of the English navy were laid up, and it was resolved, partly owing to shortage of money, to limit the war effort to commerce destroying, while British merchant ships were forbidden to put to sea. The Dutch took advantage of this policy to send across a naval expedition which sailed up the Medway and attacked English warships at anchor off Chatham. "By God," wrote the diarist Samuel Pepys, "I think the Devil shits Dutchmen." This operation, so humiliating to the English, hurried up the peace negotiations, and a treaty was signed at Breda in July 1667. The Dutch retained the island of Pula Run in the East Indies, obtained a modification of the Navigation Acts, which had injured Dutch trade, and strengthened their hold on West Africa. The English were allowed to retain the New Netherlands; the town of New Amsterdam was renamed New York after the title of Charles II's brother and proved a valuable addition to the British settlements in North America. This war has been called the first war over trade in European history; but the English gained little from it.

One reason for the Dutch willingness in the flood tide of victory to conclude peace with England was the behavior of their ally, France. It is true that in January 1666 King Louis XIV had declared war on England and sent a small force to deal with England's only ally, the Bishop of Münster, but French support at sea—and this was essentially a naval war—had been negligible. Louis XIV did not care for battles fought solely at sea; he thought that to begin his reign with one would be a shabby start. At sea it was, he thought, impossible to distinguish the really brave from the rest, and a king ought not to expose himself to the caprice of the oceans. Thus, though he had declared war on England, he hastened to assure Charles II that this was only because he could not break his word to the Dutch; he found it extremely embarrassing; also he had wider ambitions.

When in September 1665 King Philip IV of Spain died, the elaborate French diplomatic machine was set intensely to work. It secured alliances wherever it could, notably among the German princes, and at the beginning of 1667, to sooth the Emperor Leopold, it was suggested that he should agree with France to a partition of the Spanish Empire in the event of the death of the little Spanish King. When the Emperor refused, the French were not unduly distressed. Their King was ready and anxious to show the paces of his land forces immediately. After concluding a treaty with Portugal which, it was hoped, would keep the Spanish armies occupied in the peninsula, a French army of seventy-two thousand men was launched in the spring of 1667 upon the Spanish Netherlands. Such an act of aggression threatened the security of the Dutch, who quickly ended their war with England. The Spanish Governor of the Netherlands had only a small and scattered army at his disposal (although a subscription list was opened on his behalf in Madrid), and the advance of the French under the experienced generalship of Turenne was like a triumphal march. Before the next campaigning season began, the Emperor changed his mind about the proposed partition. The French had laid claims to large parts of Flanders on the ground that according to local laws a daughter by the first marriage had the preference in inheritance over a son by a second wife. Thus, this was known as the War of the

Queen's Rights. But Leopold was staggered by the swiftness of the French advance. Supposing King Carlos II of Spain should die, might not the French gobble up the whole of the Spanish Empire? One of the Imperial ambassadors, L'Isola, had just published a pamphlet warning Europe that the French King was aiming at "a universal monarchy." To prevent this Leopold, on January 19, 1668, signed what became known as the first partition treaty: the lion's skin was to be divided before he was dead.

Meanwhile, the Dutch had not been inactive. In the same month the Dutch and English concluded a treaty by which they undertook to mediate between France and Spain or, if France refused to accept their proposals, to wage war against it. King Charles II was not happy about this treaty, but the defeat in the Anglo-Dutch War and the crises at home had undermined his personal position, and he had been obliged to dismiss his chief Minister, Clarendon, making him a scapegoat for political failure. Later Sweden, tempted by the promise of subsidies, joined in the treaty, which became known as the Triple Alliance. The French King was ignorant of these negotiations, and the war went on. In February the Prince de Condé occupied the area known as Franche-Comté, which lay south of Lorraine. When Louis XIV learned of the offer of mediation by the Triple Alliance, he was at first very angry but then decided to acquiesce. The choice was given him between retaining his conquests in Flanders or permanently occupying Franche-Comté. He chose the former alternative because he thought the northern fortresses would make a good starting point for another offensive later on. Therefore, by the Treaty of Aix-la-Chapelle in May 1668, Franche-Comté was restored to Spain.

Historians are not in harmony about why Louis agreed to the Treaty of Aix-la-Chapelle after two such victorious and almost unopposed campaigns. Some say that he was influenced by the signature of the partition treaty; for why go on fighting if by agreement with the Austrian Habsburgs much more Spanish territory would soon fall into his hands? On the one side it is said that the Triple Alliance had nothing to do with it. On the other attention is drawn to the secret article in which England and the United Netherlands agreed to make war on France unless reasonable terms were accepted. The fact was that both these powers were extremely sensitive over the strategic importance of Flanders. The nation that commanded the Channel and North Sea ports could hold Holland in fee and menace the security of the British Isles. Although Charles II personally was pro-French, he twice, in 1668 and 1678, was ready, if necessary, to wage war on France rather than allow the whole of this coastline to fall into French hands. The political history of western Europe for the next fifty years was to be largely of a struggle between France and the two Maritime Powers for the control of the northern European plain on which so many wars were to be fought.

During the following four years Louis devoted his energies to destroying the Triple Alliance. He bought off the Swedes and brought them over to his side; he concluded a secret treaty with Charles II for an offensive alliance against the Dutch; he arranged alliances with a number of German princes; and he prepared an army of a hundred thousand men to punish the Dutchmen for "their ingratitude, bad faith and insupportable vanity."

The Dutch had only a small army, and most of it was scattered on garrison duties. In 1672 the French armies moved forward with little resistance. The Rhine was crossed on June 12, and William, Prince of Orange, who at this time of peril for his country had been given his father's old office of Captain-General, was forced to abandon the line of the Yssel. He had only twelve thousand men under him, and the return of some of them was being demanded by the threatened Dutch provinces. Overyssel was ravaged by German troops allied to the French. Arnhem was taken by Turenne. On June 20 Utrecht surrendered. The Hollanders cut their dikes, and by allowing the sea to flow into the polders made an island out of Amsterdam. But they could not count on the inundations providing a permanent defense, especially as the English navy had joined their enemies. The Dutch States-General therefore sought peace on abject terms, which were refused. But the waters round Amsterdam did not subside or turn to ice, and the French were baffled. Louis XIV returned to Paris, leaving the war to his generals.

After one campaign Louis XIV's *Blitzkrieg* had ground to a halt, and by 1675 half of Europe was in arms against him. Moreover, the French people themselves showed resentment at new taxes that were imposed to pay for the war; in 1674 there had been trouble in Bordeaux and Guienne: the King retorted by billeting troops for their winter quarters in the disaffected areas. "After having hanged thousands of his subjects," writes Professor Goubert, "the King was able to send his troops back to fight the allies." In the next two years the land war resolved itself into a series of sieges in which the French on the whole were more successful than their enemies.

Throughout the long war, peace negotiations continued. A conference was opened in Nymegen in 1676 in which the English, having withdrawn from the war earlier, offered their mediation. In 1677 William of Orange, who was the nephew of Charles II of England, married his cousin Mary, Charles's niece, and William was soon trying to bring the English over to the side of the allies. How far this threat worried Louis XIV is not clear, but the French capture of Ghent in 1678 speeded up peace negotiations. By the terms of the Treaty of Nymegen the French gained Franche-Comté from Spain and a line of fortresses running between Dunkirk and the Meuse. The Dutch lost nothing and in fact obtained better trading terms from France.

The Peace of Nymegen has generally been considered to represent the height of the French King's success in war. At the expense of Spain he had strengthened the fortifications to the northeast of his kingdom and given added protection to Paris. He had also shown that his armies and navy were capable of fighting much of the rest of Europe on equal terms. On the other hand, he had aroused the Germans against him and made them more susceptible to the leadership of Leopold I. Also, Louis had antagonized many of his own subjects and had severely damaged the efforts that his Controller-General of Finance, the Marquis of Colbert, was making to build up the industry and commerce of the kingdom. Let us consider what Colbert had been attempting to do.

4. The Policy of Colbert

Colbert has been described as "a practical opportunistic agent" whose principal aim was to provide the money necessary for his master's wars. Taxes, notably the *taille* or land tax, fell mainly on the French peasants, and both the nobility and clergy were largely exempt. Colbert tried all sorts of expedients. He reformed the administration of the *taille* and aimed to reduce the number of people exempt from it; he also improved the system of collecting profits from the *gabelle* or State salt monopoly; he cut the rate of interest paid on government loans or *rentes*. He attempted to eliminate waste and reduce the profits of tax farmers and tax collectors (a fiscal chamber of justice had been established by Colbert's predecessors), but in 1674 he was forced to depreciate the currency. Apart from technical reforms in Government finance, he tried to build up French industry and commerce so that the country and consequently the monarchy should grow richer. As he once explained to Louis XIV,

> the universal rule of finances should always be to watch and use every care and all the authority of Your Majesty to attract money into the kingdom, to spread it out into all the provinces so as to pay their taxes.

To Colbert the progress of the economy was sought as if it were itself an act of war. Subsidies were given to native industries, and skilled workers were imported from abroad to introduce new ones. Although, on the whole, he disapproved of industrial monopolies, he issued detailed instructions on how manufactures should be run. To facilitate the internal economy he abolished some of the numerous tolls and attempted to improve roads and canals. But particularism in the French provinces was hard to overcome.

So far as external trade was concerned Colbert used all the devices of protectionism. In 1667 he imposed heavy import duties on Dutch goods, and a tariff war was waged until the outbreak of real war in 1672. Colbert was effectively to subsidize merchant shipping and succeeded in enlarging the French navy. He dreamed of a vast French colonial and commercial empire. To this end he created companies as armies to fight the war of trade. An East Indian Company was founded in 1663, chiefly financed from royal funds. The idea was to use Madagascar as a trading station, but this was a failure.

Of twelve ships that sailed to the East Indies in 1670–75 only seven returned. A French West India Company followed in 1664, but the Dutch had a stranglehold on trade in the French West Indian islands. Large numbers of colonists were sent to Canada and elsewhere in an effort to rival British settlements. An effort was also made to open up French trade with northern Europe. But none of these chartered companies survived for long. The reason was that whereas the Dutch and English companies sprang from a union of merchants who had spontaneously gone into the trade and then sought government support, the French companies were largely constituted from above. Moreover, Colbert was unfortunate in that he started his companies at a time when prices were stationary or declining and had to operate during the war against the Dutch, who were already established merchants and had an experienced navy to protect their shipping.

Colbert paid less attention to agriculture than he did to industry and commerce. Jean Meuvret points out that French agricultural literature was poor and that most of the books published dealt with gardening. Amateurs and gourmets cultivated cherries and plums; ordinary peasants specialized in luxury goods for the rich when they could, such as nosing out truffles in Périgord or hunting ortalans. Agricultural laborers engaged in other work outside harvesting time, such as lace making taught to them by Venetians. Just as low prices discouraged commerce, so the French peasants in the second half of the century obtained poor prices for their grains and wine. But at least they were better off than in times of famine, such as occurred in 1693. Thus, in spite of the richness of the French soil and the diversified character of French agriculture, people who lived in the towns prospered more than countrymen because they could buy cheap food and drink and were exempt from most taxes. On the whole, Colbert was a failure as a financier. He created no bank from which money could be borrowed by the State (as Napoleon was to do), and it was not until the end of Louis XIV's reign that a serious effort was made to extend taxation (by *capitation*—a graduated poll tax—and *dixièmes* or *vingtièmes*—a tax on incomes) to all the King's subjects. The fiscal system was so bad and so deeply rooted that it could only be destroyed by a revolution. Moreover, Colbert labored without much assistance from his master. In the end he came to realize that

> the greatest of kings who ever mounted the throne . . . preferred war to anything else and had reckoned the administration of his finances . . . as a tiresome detail which was not the natural or ordinary concern of kings.

5. Louis XIV's Domestic Affairs

The decade that succeeded the Peace of Nymegen was the only long period of relative peace during Louis XIV's reign. It was also a period of economic recovery when huge sums of money were spent on building which, after the waging of war, was the King's greatest passion. In 1679 the construction of the palace and gardens of Versailles moved forward rapidly. Work on converting his father's shooting lodge into the centerpiece of his Court and Government had begun in 1669, and it was not to be completed until 1709. But the Court moved from Paris to Versailles in 1682. There were housed the King and Queen, the princes and leading members of the nobility, hundreds of officials, and over ten thousand servants. The premises must have been overcrowded and, as Professor Wolf has remarked, it was neither as roomy nor as palatial as the government offices of modern Washington. But here the King could keep his nobility under his control, for he was always mindful of the threat to the monarchy of the princely Fronde. Louis preferred to give his nobles accommodation and ceremonial duties, and even on occasion to pay their gambling debts, but he allowed them no real power: they were domesticated.

In July 1684 Louis's Spanish Queen, to whom he had been consistently unfaithful, died, and within six months he married his current mistress, the pious Madame de Maintenon as his morganatic wife. In the same year Colbert died. Colbert had not approved of the move to Versailles, which he thought unduly costly and unnecessary, and would have preferred Louis to stay in Paris at the Louvre. But Versailles symbolized the King's supremacy and absolutism. Yet France was not as centralized as has sometimes been thought. It was still a "mosaic of provinces more than a unified kingdom"; local rights and privileges were recognized and accepted; even the inten-

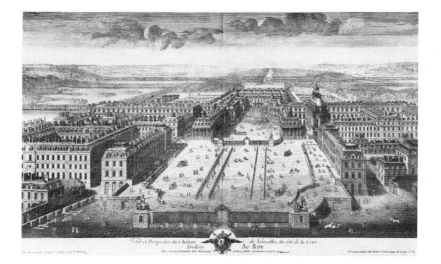

The Palace of Versailles
Menant
New York Public Library

dants, the King's representatives in the provinces, enjoyed some degree of independence if only because it took so long for royal instructions to reach them.

It was to some extent under the influence of his new wife that Louis began to think seriously about the conversion of heretics—that is to say, the non-Catholics in his kingdom—even though he refused to admit the claims of the Pope to discipline himself as the Most Christian King. The King's relations with the Papacy were therefore ambivalent. There was a prolonged quarrel over the right of the *régale,* the royal prerogative to exercise the temporal and spiritual rights belonging to the diocese of a bishop from the time the incumbent died until his successor was instituted. The right dated from the reign of Francis I, but it had been extended and was resented by Innocent XI when he became Pope in 1676. The Gallican Church rallied behind the King, and in 1681 propounded four articles maintaining that the Pope had no right to overrule the King on temporal matters. The quarrel lasted a considerable time; at one point thirty-five dioceses had no consecrated bishops. However, there was a certain amount of playacting about the affair, because the King needed the support of the Papacy in keeping the Gallican Church united. First the Jansenists presented a problem. They were named after a Flemish bishop, and had affinities with the Calvinists in that they believed in the virtues of an austere life and accepted the doctrine of predestination. The Jansenists would not admit that they were heretics, and although Papal bulls were issued against them, it was not until the eighteenth century that they were more or less brought under control. Their disruptive ideas may have contributed to the Revolution.

More important to Louis than the Jansenists were the Huguenots, a million French Protestants who had been given special privileges by Henry IV in the Edict of Nantes of 1598. At first the King had acquiesced in the policy of the Edict of Nantes, but now, under the influence of Madame de Maintenon and Louvois, his Minister of War, he sponsored a campaign to convert them all to Roman Catholicism so that they should cease to form a state within a state. Modern research seems to suggest that the King was not fully aware of the drastic methods adopted by Louvois to achieve this end. Originally money or special exemptions from taxation were offered to Huguenots to procure their conversion. But later dragoons were billeted in the homes of rich and influential Protestant households, Huguenot schools were attacked and their churches shut down. Much brutality was employed. The King was persuaded that the conversion campaign had been so startlingly successful that the Edict of Nantes had become superfluous; it was therefore replaced in 1685 by the Edict of Fontainebleau, which provided, among other things, for the exile of Huguenot ministers who refused to abjure their faith and severe punishment for any Huguenots who tried to leave the kingdom. In fact two hundred thousand persecuted Frenchmen escaped abroad and found a welcome in Protestant countries, while many of the new converts who remained continued to practice their religion in secret and to nurse their political grievances.

6.   Louis XIV and the Arts

How far is it true to say, as Voltaire averred and Lytton Strachey repeated, that the flowering of the French arts in the age of Louis XIV— particularly in poetry, prose, and the theater—was deeply indebted to the encouragement of the King and his Government? In the early years of the seventeenth century French poetry tended to be "precious" (it was ridiculed as such later by Molière), but at least three geniuses of very different characters reached their prime before Louis began his period of personal rule and well before Versailles became the home of the Court: these were Pierre Corneille, whose passionate dramas were built upon classical poetry; René Descartes, who wrote his philosophic theories in translucent prose; and Blaise Pascal, who died before his masterpiece in defense of Christianity was completed.

In fact, Cardinal Richelieu set the example of stimulating the arts by founding the French Academy (though admittedly three great Frenchmen— Descartes, Diderot, and Flaubert—never became members); Richelieu even wrote a play himself and cared for the purity of the language. The legend that he was jealous of Corneille and therefore hindered his progress has recently been refuted. Under Louis XIV Lully was given an overlordship of music, Charles Le Brun of painting, and Colbert of building. It was actually during the ten years or so before the French King got himself involved in European wars (before the Dutch started to thrust back the French armies in the autumn of 1673) that royal patronage was most effective. Colbert reconstructed the Royal Academy of Painting and Sculpture, founded in 1648, and also persuaded his master to establish one in Rome. Louis lent his aid to the two great dramatists whose plays were performed at his Court, Racine and Molière; Boileau, more successful as a critic than an original author, influenced French prose and poetry in the direction of compactness and clarity; Molière created French comedy and Lully (an Italian by birth) French opera. "All these great men," remarks Voltaire, "were known and protected by Louis XIV with the exception of La Fontaine." Nevertheless, La Fontaine's novel poetic fables became popular enough, but the simplicity of his life made him out of place at Versailles.

The adjective that applies to much of the French (and English) literature of this period is "worldly." La Rochefoucauld's epigrams or "maxims" were based on the belief that self-love is the mainspring of every action. Molière mocked the middle classes, from which he himself came, and also by implication the practice of Christianity. La Fontaine was an Epicurean, that is to say, a follower of the philosopher who taught that pleasure is the highest good. The letters of Madame de Sévigné, the memoirs of Madame de Motteville, and the novels of Madame de Lafayette were all essentially worldly in their outlook and corresponded with the summer of the French King's life when he was bewitched by beautiful women.

But later a change came about, as the monarch turned to the enforcement of a united religion and was faithful to the widowed governess, Madame de Maintenon, of whom Voltaire wrote that she was "filled at once with ambition and piety, neither striving for the mastery." Then Racine, a Jansenist, lost favor and died after ten years of silence in 1699; money became tighter for the arts as it was poured into the making of wars; French Calvinists fled the country to practice their literary arts and other crafts elsewhere. Bishop Bossuet *(1627-1704)* became the acceptable figure in this latter age, his funeral orations being reckoned masterpieces of rhetorical prose. Bossuet was the veritable trumpeter of absolutism who never wavered in his beliefs in a Christian God and a Most Christian King. On the other hand, Archbishop Fénelon—whose greatest work, part novel, part poetry *Télémaque,* fraught with moral ideals and open-minded attitudes, was published toward the end of the reign—pointed to the more liberal times that were to come under the Regency, during the reign of Louis XV and possibly to the Revolution.

Even Lytton Strachey, who attributed much of the magnificence of this age in French arts to the autocracy of the King and the glitter of Versailles, observes that it faded away during the later years of the reign. La Bruyère, whose book *Les Caractères* was completed in 1694, was scornful of the vanity, emptiness, and worldliness of the Court. By then the political ambitions of the Sun King were shattered, his bigotry exemplified, and poverty and discontent were stalking the land.

7.   The Threat to Germany

It has been suggested that the French King was unaware of the cruelties used against the Huguenots because he was absorbed in foreign affairs. After the Treaty of Nymegen he kept a large army in being, while his late enemies disarmed or were distracted by events elsewhere. Louis was advised that the French frontiers could be greatly extended and improved if full advantage were taken of some of the vague clauses in the treaties of Westphalia and Nymegen. French historians have sometimes argued that this policy of "reunions," as it was called, was perfectly justified by the correct legal interpretation of ancient feudal tenures. Others have called the whole method blackmail by a threat of force. In any case, substantial territorial gains were acquired in Franche-Comté, Alsace, Lorraine, and the three bishoprics of Metz, Toul, and Verdun. By the summer of 1680 the free Protestant city of Strasbourg was the only town in Alsace not in French hands.

After witnessing the success of the reunion policy, Louis decided in September 1681 to occupy Strasbourg on the ground that it had by implication been assigned to France in the Peace of Westphalia. On the same day that Strasbourg fell French troops took over the strategically valuable town of Casale on the Franco-Italian frontier, and in November another force laid siege to Luxembourg. France's neighbors were understandably frightened by the swift progress of the French armies at a time of nominal peace. Even the English Parliament expressed concern.

But many of the German princes were Louis XIV's clients, and indeed the French King seems to have hoped that he might be elected the next Holy Roman Emperor. The existing Emperor, Leopold I, was paralyzed by menaces from the east, where the Grand Vizier Kara Mustafa was preparing an army of a hundred thousand or more men to march up the valley of the Danube to besiege Vienna. When in 1681 Leopold appealed to the Imperial Diet at Ratisbon to raise an army to protect central Europe against the Ottoman Turks, he was promised only forty thousand men. It was therefore impossible for him to defend his eastern frontiers as well as to impose restraint on Louis XIV. To sooth anxieties Louis temporarily lifted the siege of Luxembourg. Is it possible that he believed that should Vienna fall, he himself would be acclaimed Emperor and acquire the glory of defending the rest of Europe from Turkish infidels? Whatever his ultimate motives were, after Vienna had been saved and the Emperor was concentrating on driving the Turks out of Hungary, Louis XIV offered a truce in the west. But before he did so he resumed the siege of Luxembourg and captured the town. Only Spain, now enfeebled beyond belief, dared to declare war upon him. The Germans accepted a twenty-year truce at Ratisbon in 1684. Even the Dutch, in spite of protests by William of Orange, acquiesced in the truce. For once, a *Blitzkrieg* appeared to have paid off, and it looked as if Louis XIV had reached the summit of his power in Europe.

But Louis XIV did not trust the Emperor Leopold to honor the truce, and he hoped that further acts of terror might induce the whole of Europe to accept his conquests by treaty. He ordered the bombardment of Genoa because the Republic had supplied ships to the Spaniards. He sent a fleet to Cadiz. He forced the Duke of Savoy to massacre his own Protestant subjects, the Vaudois, because they had aided the Huguenot refugees. He picked another quarrel with the Pope and seized the Papal territory of Avignon, just as earlier he had occupied Orange, the enclave in France from which William III took his title. In Germany, when the Elector Palatine died Louis put forward claims to the inheritance on behalf of his sister-in-law, Elizabeth Charlotte, who was the sister of the dead Elector: these claims he modestly referred to the Pope. He also tried to persuade the Pope to make his creature Fürstenberg, Bishop of Strasbourg, into the Coadjutor Archbishop of Cologne so that when the Archbishop himself, who was ailing, died, Fürstenberg could take his place. Innocent XI refused these requests, and the German princes began to draw together in self-defense. In July 1686 the

Emperor and certain other members of the German Diet signed the Treaty of Augsburg, agreeing to defend each other if breaches were made in the existing treaties or the Truce of Ratisbon. The French King then decided on yet another *Blitz,* hoping to force the Emperor's hand before he had completed his war against the Turks and the dissident Hungarians.

On September 24, 1688, France declared war on the Emperor. Leopold was blamed for refusing to convert the Truce of Ratisbon into a treaty, for joining the League of Augsburg, and for opposing Louis's wishes over the Palatinate and the Electorate of Cologne. Louis sent a large army through Liège to attack Philippsburg and another smaller force to occupy part of the Electorate of Cologne. But although at one stage he offered King James II of England warships to protect him in case of invasion from Holland by his son-in-law, William of Orange, he had neither men nor ships to spare when the crisis came. James, whose arbitrary conduct aimed at giving civic equality to his fellow Roman Catholics and other nonconformists had aroused resistance against him, was left alone to face his son-in-law, who insisted that he was invading England on behalf of the liberties of its people and the rights of his wife. William had organized three armies: one to invade England, one to protect the United Netherlands, and a third to guard the Electorate of Cologne. The invasion of England in November 1688 was bloodless. The army and navy deserted to William. By Christmas William III and his wife Mary were proclaimed King and Queen of England. The first thing that William did was to declare war on the French who had been assisting James II in Ireland. On May 12 the Emperor and the Dutch signed an offensive and defensive treaty to which England, Spain, and the Duke of Savoy acceded, thus creating what was known as the Grand Alliance. So Louis's second *Blitzkrieg* had failed, and he was engaged in a war against half of Europe.

8. The Decline and Death of Louis XIV

The war between the Grand Alliance and France lasted for nine years and was fought on five fronts. The principal front was in the Netherlands: here William of Orange came over from England at the beginning of each campaigning season to shake himself free from distasteful party politics in England and to engage in maneuvers against the various French generals amid the rivers and fortresses of Europe's northern plain. The war was waged too in Germany both in the Rhineland and on the Danube; also in northern Italy after Victor Amadeus, Duke of Savoy, had thrown in his lot with the Grand Alliance. While Victor Amadeus threatened France from the south, the French invaded Catalonia once again. The Spanish Empire was unable to contribute much to the alliance, and was more of a debit than an asset to the coalition. Sea power played an important part in the war. Because

Colbert had succeeded in building up a large French navy, the French were able to land the exiled James II in Ireland, where he tried to regain his throne with the assistance of an Irish Roman Catholic army and French military advisers. On June 30, 1690, an English fleet was defeated off Beachy Head; in May 1692, however, the French were decisively beaten at the battle of Barfleur. Henceforward the Anglo-Dutch command of the sea brought pressure to bear on French land operations, particularly on the shores of the Mediterranean. But an English attempt to disembark a force in France in 1694 failed, nor could the English Mediterranean fleet prevent the fall of Barcelona. There was in Europe a third force which might have had repercussions on the war. This consisted chiefly of the Baltic states, which were the source of naval supplies to both sides. They did not care for interference with their commerce, and Sweden offered to mediate; in the end Swedish mediation was accepted.

The war degenerated into a battle of the lines in Flanders. In 1692 France itself was invaded by Victor Amadeus, and in 1693-94 there was actual starvation throughout almost the whole of France, the price paid for shouldering a world war and for an inability to prevent the blockade of French ports. By 1694 stalemate supervened in the Netherlands as well as in Germany. Louis was obliged to think of concluding peace on the best terms he could get. Peace negotiations were initiated by the Dutch under Swedish mediation. A basic diplomatic fact was that it had been reported that Carlos II of Spain was dying childless. A secret clause in the treaty of the Grand Alliance had provided that the two Maritime Powers would support the claims of the Austrian Habsburgs to the inheritance of the entire Spanish Empire. Thus, if the war in France was still being fought when Carlos II died, the Emperor would be in a strong position to assert his claims. Louis XIV for his part was eager to bring the Nine Years' War to a close so that his armies and fleets could recuperate sufficiently to enforce the Bourbon claim to the Spanish inheritance. The French would certainly have been unable to do this if actually fighting the Spaniards when their King died.

So the French King put forward large offers in the negotiations of 1696-97. London and Amsterdam, which had borne much of the financial burden of the war, were eager to conclude peace; William III, whose health was never good, was tired of the political squabbles in England and the selfishness of the Habsburg Emperor. Moreover, he was as conscious as Louis XIV and the Emperor of the looming question of the Spanish succession. So the Treaty of Ryswick was signed in 1697 providing for the abandonment of the French gains since 1678, apart from Strasbourg, and the renunciation of the ambitions with which Louis started the war. Furthermore, Louis agreed to recognize William as King of England and to cease from giving support to James II. England rejoiced at the peace, and its Parliament hastened to demobilize the army. The politicians, who were resentful over William's Dutch interests, turned to framing an Act of Settlement which arranged not only for the succession of the Crown in the House of Hanover (the direct descendants of James I), but restricted the rights of the monarchy more severely than ever before. After the revolutions and many years of foreign war the English people looked for peace and stability. But in fact the Spanish succession question ensured that the Treaty of Ryswick would no more provide for European peace than the Truce of Ratisbon had done, and stability was not to come to England for another twenty years.

The problem of the Spanish succession was incredibly complicated. It had two aspects—legal and political—and the political aspect was the more important. Carlos II of Spain was impotent, and the two chief claimants to the whole of his empire were Louis XIV and the Emperor Leopold I. On paper Louis XIV's claims were better, since he was the son of an elder Spanish Infanta and the husband of an elder Spanish Infanta. The Emperor Leopold had been the son and husband of younger sisters. But if either of these rulers succeeded to the Spanish inheritance, the entire balance of power in Europe would be upset and the great trading nations of the United Netherlands and England placed at a disadvantage. Moreover, it was unlikely that either Louis or Leopold would passively agree to the other scooping the pool. The Emperor, after he had signed the Treaty of Ryswick, played a waiting game. He was absorbed in ending a long war against the Ottoman Turks, and was unwilling to consider any compromise about the future.

Louis XIV, on the other hand, was in favor of a compromise plan. He had just emerged somewhat battered from a nine years' war, and at the age of sixty, with a set of pacific advisers surrounding him since the death of Louvois, was not eager to start such a war again. However, unlike the Maritime Powers, he kept his army in being, and since his hereditary claims to the succession were so good he was in a strong bargaining position. During the war his respect for William III as a diplomatist and soldier had risen, and it seems that the first approach to a compromise solution came from the side of France. William proved willing to meet his old enemy halfway; so two partition treaties were signed, the first in 1698 and the second in 1700, but as neither the Emperor Leopold nor the King of Spain was a party to them they meant little. Finally, in 1701 Carlos II himself made a will bequeathing the throne to Prince Philip of Anjou, who was Louis XIV's grandson but not in the direct line of succession to the French throne. If Louis refused this gift, it was to be offered to Philip's younger brother, the Duke of Berri, and if he did not want it, then the whole Empire was to go to Archduke Charles, the second son of the Emperor.

A month after the will was signed Carlos expired. Louis XIV was therefore set the problem of whether he should accept the huge inheritance for his grandson (on the understanding that the kingships of France and Spain should always be kept separate), or whether he should abide by the partition treaty of 1700. It was a delicate question. Ultimately, on November 1, 1700, Louis in the presence of his Cabinet and the Spanish ambassador announced that he accepted the legacy on his grandson's behalf; the Spanish ambassador tactlessly observed that "the Pyrenees are no more." This saying was afterward attributed to the King himself and did him immense harm.

At first only the Emperor expressed public indignation at Louis's acceptance of the will; he set about seeking allies in Germany and sent his best general, Prince Eugene, to confront the French in Italy. But the rest of Europe was less excited. Torci, the French Foreign Minister, a descendant of Colbert, sent a memorandum round the capitals pointing out the pacific intentions of his master. He had deliberately refused the direct gains to France provided for in the second partition treaty, and he undertook that the crowns of Spain and France should never be united. Neither London nor Amsterdam was prepared for or wanted another war. But a series of events induced the Maritime Powers to change their minds. In the first place, the Regency of Spain, established since the new King Philip V was still a boy, handed over the administration of the country to Louis XIV. Secondly, as a military precaution French soldiers laid hold of fortifications in the Spanish Netherlands and expelled Dutch garrisons which had been there with Spanish permission since the signature of the Treaty of Ryswick. Thirdly, letters patent were issued declaring that Philip retained his divine right to succeed to the French throne, which was (wrongly) taken to mean that one day the French and Spanish crowns would be united. Moreover, the merchants of both maritime countries began to wonder what would happen to their Mediterranean trade if the Bourbons controlled the ports of Italy. This fear was underlined when French troops were dispatched to the Milanese. Louis XIV himself once said that this was a war for trade.

Thus, within a year of the death of Carlos II the governments of the Maritime Powers, which had at first reluctantly recognized Philip V as his successor, altered their attitudes. On September 7, 1701, they signed a Grand Alliance treaty with the Emperor which committed them to presenting an ultimatum to Louis XIV. They demanded that the Spanish Netherlands and the Spanish possessions in Italy should be given to the Habsburgs; that French trade should be excluded from the Spanish colonies; and that the separation of the Spanish and French crowns should be solemnly reaffirmed. The Elector of Brandenburg, who had been recognized as King in Prussia by the Emperor, also acceded to the treaty. Louis XIV did his cause no good when in defiance of the Treaty of Ryswick he recognized the elder son of James II (who died in September 1701) as King James III of England. The English Whigs, who had never been fond of William III, were not going to have their Glorious Revolution upset. William's sister-in-law, Anne, peacefully succeeded to the throne on March 8, 1702, and on May 15 the English, Dutch, and Austrians began war on France.

As before, the war was fought on different fronts, in Spain, Italy, Flanders, and northern and southern Germany. In the first years of the war there was fighting in Italy in which Eugene, Prince of Savoy, more than held his own, and off Spain an allied fleet captured a Spanish treasure fleet in Vigo Bay. These events were the consequences of the allies persuading both the Duke of Savoy and the King of Portugal, who were originally French supporters, to change sides in 1703. Portugal gave the allies access to Spain, while the French were forced onto the defensive in northern Italy. The British general, the first Duke of Marlborough, captured Bonn in the Electorate of Cologne, which was knocked out of the war, and Louis XIV was reduced to two allies, Spain and Bavaria. In the summer of 1704 Marlborough and Eugene joined forces in Bavaria and imposed a crushing defeat on the Franco-Bavarian army at the battle of Blenheim. Bavaria was afterward devastated, and the Elector became of little use to the French as an ally. In the same month an English fleet captured the Rock of Gibraltar, and the French Marshal Berwick, who had invaded Portugal from Spain, was forced to retire. In 1706 Marlborough won another victory at Ramillies, and the whole of the Spanish Netherlands was overrun by the allied armies. Though in 1707 the French were victorious in Spain itself, by the end of 1708 France was threatened with invasion after the Battle of Oudenarde and the fall of the fortress of Lille.

His Grace The Duke of Marlborough
Detail from tapestry at Blenheim Palace, England

So Louis XIV was obliged to think in terms of an honorable peace. Louis warned his grandson that he might have to give up Italy and the Netherlands, both of which were in enemy hands. But he was satisfied that Philip was strongly entrenched in Spain itself. The defeats of 1708 were followed by a terrible winter in France. A severe frost succeeded by a sudden thaw ruined the spring crops. Famine menaced the whole country. Even the King's wife had to eat bread made from oats. The King decided to sent Torci to The Hague to beg for terms of peace. The Dutch refused to negotiate without consulting their allies. A humiliating ultimatum, euphemistically called the Preliminaries of The Hague, was presented to Louis. Philip of Anjou was to renounce all his claims; French conquests during the last fifty years were to be restored, an elaborate fortress barrier was to be provided for the Dutch, including some towns in France itself. In return for all this the allies merely offered a truce to last two months during which the French King himself was to secure his grandson's expulsion from Spain.

These harsh terms were not acceptable, Louis being particularly indignant at the idea that he should fight his own grandson. Stupendous efforts were made to rally the French people behind their King; it was even proposed to summon the French States-General. Troops consisting largely of young soldiers were concentrated under Villars to prevent the invasion of France. Villars fought the Battle of Malplaquet in an attempt to save Mons. The losses on both sides were heavy, but Mons fell. In 1710 French victories in Spain and the unwillingness of the allies to risk another battle on the French frontier after the "murdering" Battle of Malplaquet contributed to a change of feeling about peace negotiations. In England the Whigs, who were reckoned the war party, were defeated in a general election. In April 1711 the Emperor Joseph I, the elder son of Leopold I, who had succeeded to the throne in 1705, died and was replaced by the claimant to the Spanish Empire, the Archduke Charles, who became the Emperor Charles VI. It was obvious that if he held the whole of both empires, the balance of power in Europe would be destroyed. Moreover, the Austrian army had to be withdrawn to Germany to protect the new Emperor's election, while at the end of 1711 for party reasons Marlborough was relieved of his command. When Prince Eugene, the Austrian commander-in-chief, returned from Germany, he suffered defeat by Villars in 1712, the British having received secret orders not to fight. All this aided the French.

9. Consequences of the War of the Spanish Succession

Treaties were signed at Utrecht in April 1713 between France, on the one hand, and Great Britain, the United Netherlands, Portugal, Savoy, and Prussia on the other. By their terms Philip V was to remain sovereign of Spain and its overseas empire, but most of the Italian possessions were to go to the Holy Roman Emperor Charles VI and the Dutch were to control the Spanish Netherlands until they settled their barrier with the Emperor, as they did in 1715. Great Britain gained Gibraltar and Minorca together with trading privileges in the Spanish Empire, and from France received Newfoundland, Hudson's Bay, Acadia, and Saint Kitts in the West Indies. Anne was recognized as Queen of England and Frederick I as King in Prussia; the Duke of Savoy was to become the King of Sicily. The other parties received back all they had lost during the fighting. The Emperor Charles VI was reluctant to assent to these terms, but defeats in the field compelled him to acquiesce in the Treaty of Rastatt in March 1714: by this France retained Strasbourg but returned other towns captured in the war to the Empire.

Curiously enough, Spain, which was the victim of this long European war, appears according to recent research, to have been far less injured by it than might be assumed. It was not war but climate that caused Spain itself to be faced with the specter of starvation in the second decade of the eighteenth century. The size of the civil population was not reduced by the war, nor were the civilians much involved in it, for the fighting was done by others. It is true that bandits and pirates interfered with normal Spanish life, yet, on the whole, the war years were a time of economic revival except in Catalonia. The war actually stimulated Spanish industry, hitherto in a state of decline, and, as Henry Kamen has written, "may well have shaken the Spaniards out of their stupor." Thus, when Louis XIV's grandson succeeded to the Spanish throne as a result of the Peace of Utrecht, he found the Spaniards ready for the regeneration of their country, which at the outset of the war had appeared decadent and feeble beyond all hopes of recovery. Moreover, during the war a Spanish national spirit had come into being which was to be demonstrated a hundred years later in the revolution against Napoleon.

The treaties of Utrecht and Rastatt marked the end of an era in European history. The long conflict between the Bourbons and the Habsburgs, initiated by Henry IV of France, had resulted in the placing of a Bourbon on the throne of Spain and a consolidation of the frontiers of France, so that it was no longer possible for the Habsburgs to exert a stranglehold on all sides. In fact, before the eighteenth century was over Bourbon France and Habsburg Austria were to become allies, and later Napoleon I was to aim at a European settlement by marrying a Habsburg princess. The Austrian Emperor was to extend his rule to Italy and modern Belgium as well as Hungary and Transylvania; but the Holy Roman Empire and its Diet at Ratisbon had become no more than the shadowy leaders of Germany. The German princes ceased to follow the Emperor. Belgium was always a burden, especially as the Maritime Powers were not going to allow the Emperor to exploit its economic advantages, and the possession of Italy was to lead to losing wars in the nineteenth century. Great Britain and, to a lesser extent, the United Netherlands were to benefit substantially from the economic and

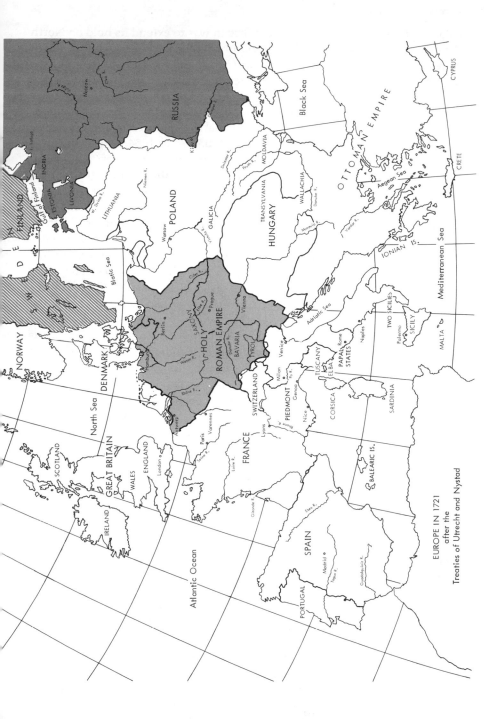

EUROPE IN 1721
after the
Treaties of Utrecht and Nystad

colonial clauses of the treaties. Great Britain was to extend its hold on North America and improve its trade with South America, from which the French were excluded. On the other hand, both Spain and the Holy Roman Empire now became dissatisfied powers, as they had failed to gain all they hoped from a long and exhausting war.

What of France? In the end its King had managed to preserve the honor of his dynasty and of his kingdom. But that was about all. The apogee of French power in Europe had been reached in 1678 or 1684, when Louis was still in his middle age and his armies had created the menace of "a universal monarchy." Philip V's presence on the Spanish throne brought no real advantages to France, and when he married as his second wife an Italian princess, his French advisers were chased away. Economic concessions were granted to the British and Dutch, and the transfer of the southern Netherlands to the Austrians deprived the French of easy military access to Germany. Moreover, the series of devastations in Germany by the French had made the name of France hated in Germany as a whole, however much petty princes might like to imitate the artistic tastes of Louis XIV. Thus, Franco-German enmity, which did not end until after 1945, can be dated back to the seventeenth century. The barrier erected by the Dutch was not to prove of much significance; so in the centuries to come Frenchmen and Germans continued to fight each other on the plains of Flanders. Lastly, the next two Bourbon rulers of France were unable to build on the territorial gains of Louis XIV, and were to dissipate their resources mainly on wars in the New World. The dreams of neither merchants nor soldier-adventurers were to be realized.

How far the internal situation of France was damaged by the far-flung European wars is disputed among French historians. There is no question that these wars were paid for by ministers like Colbert, Chamillart, and Desmarets only by debasing the coinage and piling up national debt. By 1715 the Treasury was practically empty, a large annual deficit existed, and the debt had reached fantastic proportions. The population had been reduced by famines and epidemics, though it remained the biggest in Europe. A series of good harvests followed the notably bad ones of 1709–1710 and 1713–14. The prices of grain, wine, and olive oil became reasonably low, and commerce and shipping revived. It was the Government rather than the country which was bankrupt.

Louis XIV, like his predecessors, Richelieu and Mazarin, was not especially concerned over public finance; he left it to his ministers to pay for his foreign policy as best they could; and it has been argued that it was the very poverty of the people during the years 1709 and 1710 which drove young recruits to fill the French armies and enabled Villars to win victories when his opponents were wearying of war. To Louis finance was a bore: the King was concerned with saving the rags of his *gloire* and ensuring the uniformity of his Church and the safety of his own soul. During the war the struggles between the Gallican Church and the Huguenots and Jansenists lingered on. For a time the Huguenots were left more or less alone, but at the end of the reign "a series of instructions recalled the most severe measures (and the least respected) which had preceded or followed the revocation of the Edict of Nantes." For example, doctors were prohibited from visiting the sick unless they had been provided with a certificate by the confessors of the sick that they had confessed. In 1713 the Pope, Clement XI, promulgated the bull *Unigenitus* aimed at the Jansenists, and the King even claimed the right to excommunicate the many who disobeyed it.

On the whole, then, modern French historians tend to equate the period of successful foreign policy with that of comparative stabilization at home. The years 1660–80 were those of "Colbertism." This did not mean, as has been shown, dramatic reforms of the financial machine, nor did it anticipate state socialism. Colbert, write Georges Duby and Robert Mandrou, "stimulated the faltering economic life in order to increase exports and consequently the influx of precious metals." By dint of getting rid of some of the worst abuses of tax farming and the like, Colbert provided the money for the King's wars, his insatiable taste for building, and his patronage of the arts. But after 1680 came the dragonnades, the revocation of the Edict of Nantes, the razing of the Port Royale, the center of Jansenism, the burning of the Palatinate, while taxation became constantly heavier and was even extended to the nobility, though they evaded their obligations as far as they could and the bulk of the burden still fell directly on the peasantry. A harsher spirit of government prevailed during the two wars that France had fought and lost.

Because the monarchy seemed so powerful and the exertions of the French war machine and French diplomacy so remarkable, it is easy to assume that during Louis XIV's personal reign his kingdom was strong and united. Although there was some paring down of local privileges and a growth in the bureaucratization of government, in fact discontent lay near the surface, but, as Robert Mandrou points out, revolts due to misery or economic stagnation, though not widespread, were constant, scattered, and genuine. In a few villages, in a suburb or a marketplace, or in some large forest royal troops would be beaten up and tax collectors robbed. These popular risings belonged to a long tradition of despair, and occasionally surfaced as in a rebellion in Brittany in 1673–75, in the sporadic risings in the 1690s, and finally in the great crisis of 1709, when the weather was so ruinous to the crops that many villages were depopulated.

After Blaise Pascal died in 1662, leaving his answer to scepticism unfinished, after Racine had given up writing his magnificent tragedies, and after Molière had died in 1673, the genius of the age of Louis XIV declined; the King himself became pious and even more warlike. Before he died the whole system of government came under criticism from men like Fénelon, who pleaded for more liberal government, and from Boisguillebert, an early economist, who exposed the fundamental errors in the French systems of taxation and mercantilism. These open criticisms reflected the underlying discontent of all classes with the later policies of the Sun King.

Louis met his death with stoicism and left behind him a variety of advice for his great-grandson, Louis XV. He urged him never to draw upon himself the wrath of God by any disorder in his morals (this to the future lover of Pompadour and Du Barry), and he told him to try to remain at peace with his neighbors and not to indulge in overspending. It was very different advice from that which he had written for the benefit of his son half a century earlier.

10.   The Achievement of Louis XIV

In attempting to measure the achievement of Louis XIV, one has to be careful to avoid the trap of condemning absolutism in itself as reprehensible. Most of the European rulers of the late seventeenth century and early eighteenth century were absolute. The ministers or higher officials who served absolute monarchs preferred a monarch like Louis XIV, who knew how to make up his own mind, to a weakling like Carlos II of Spain. But however hard-working a king might be and however willing he was to accept responsibilities, both his knowledge and his interests were bound to be limited. So too in fact was his power. The great French historian Lavisse wrote that the absolutism of Louis XIV was always tempered by disobedience. Professor Goubert has pointed out how even in Beauvais, less than fifty miles from Paris, Colbert's economic regulations were violated daily. Attempts at centralization and unification in the France of Louis XIV were generally resisted with success.

Louis concerned himself little with economic affairs; partly owing to a European shortage of metal currency, however, recession or stagnation prevailed throughout much of his reign. Nor did he devote his attention to the world outside Europe, where the Dutch and the British had been settling and expanding their wealth. Thus, he failed to support Colbert in his efforts to strengthen the French navy and mercantile marine. The King took little notice of Louisiana or Canada. Even in Europe he misunderstood the British, the Dutch, and the Germans. Finally, though he patronized the arts, he was unaware that Europe was moving into an age of science, reason, and toleration. His outlook was circumscribed by his palaces at Versailles, the intrigues of his courtiers, and the diplomatic maneuvers of his ambassadors. Though he left France militarily better defended, he continued his wars too long. But in the end, when victory deserted the old monarch he died in an aura of unpopularity. The villages of France had been pillaged to feed his armies and their young people dragged off to become unwilling soldiers. (That was why there were large-scale desertions from the French armies.) Population declined and stagnation set in. The King's glory faded before the eighteenth century began; the glitter of Versailles could not conceal the discontent felt by the masses. Under Louis XIV's feebler successors this rising discontent prepared the way for revolution.

11.   The Rise of Prussia

While Louis XIV was fighting to extend the frontiers of France and was fashioning his absolute if not arbitrary form of government, most of the countries in northern and eastern Europe were engaged in external and internal struggles for the same ends. In the case of Brandenburg-Prussia there was an additional factor in political evolution: that was the need for its widely scattered territories, bestriding northern Germany from the Meuse to the Niemen, to be unified and to accept equally the direction of their ruler in Berlin. The Great Elector, Frederick William, who had come to the throne in 1640, was to reign for forty-eight years, and during that time by facing each problem as it arose and not following any preconceived pattern in either domestic or foreign affairs he strengthened the Electorate. When he succeeded at the age of twenty, each of the three parts of his dominions contained nobility (or Junkers) who were exempt from paying taxes, and a Diet or *Landtag* which was supposed to be consulted about foreign affairs. Frederick William felt his way cautiously, and by a recess of 1653 after a General Diet had refused to grant fresh taxes, confirmed the privileges of the Junkers, and conferred new ones upon them. In return for this he obtained a large sum of money and was able to raise a small army.

With this army at his disposal the Elector sided first with Sweden and later with Poland in the war then in progress: as a reward at the Peace of Oliva in 1660 he acquired East Prussia as an independent duchy. During the war he insisted that he was entitled to levy taxes without the consent of the Estates in any part of his dominions if they refused to give them voluntarily. Since the Junkers did not have to contribute, they did not resist these demands; after the war, by keeping a standing army and by playing off the different Estates against one another (for example, an excise was levied on towns and not on the countryside), he gradually undermined the free institutions of Brandenburg. In 1663 he visited East Prussia to take over the sovereign power, and he introduced excise there and in other provinces. He satisfied the Junkers by upholding their privileges and by taking small contributions of money from them instead of requiring feudal service from them in wartime.

By such means Frederick William became the founder of Prussian absolutism and the patron of Junkerdom. After 1660 he devoted ten years of his reign to internal reform. He took a keen interest in sculpture and architecture, and built up the city of Berlin, although his Court was simple. He promoted agriculture and supervised guilds; he controlled exports and imports in mercantilist fashion. He had a canal constructed between the Oder and the Spree. He laid it down that no bridegroom might marry until he had planted six fruit trees. Government was through a Privy Council and the different parts of his dominions—though often violently separatist in feeling—were obliged to pay taxes for the good of the whole.

Just as he played off his different Estates or classes against each other, so in foreign affairs he rang the changes with his alliances. During Louis XIV's war against the Dutch of 1672–78 he three times changed sides. But as he gained nothing from this war because the French insisted on protecting their Swedish allies, Frederick William concluded a secret treaty with France which lasted for five years. But he disapproved of the repeal of the Edict of Nantes, and before he died in 1688 he had thrown in his lot with the Emperor and William of Orange (William III of England), to whom he was related by marriage.

Frederick William's successor, the Elector Frederick III, was of a different type. He was more interested in arts than in arms. Nevertheless, he was involved in the Nine Years' War, but to little advantage. Yet he considered his position strong enough to call himself King Frederick I, placing the crown on his own head at Königsberg in January 1701. He founded the Prussian State Library, the Royal Academy of Arts, the Berlin Academy of Sciences (of which Leibniz, the friend of the Queen, Sophie Charlotte of Hanover, became the first president), and the University of Halle. He also built himself several palaces and an opera house. But in 1701 Brandenburg-Prussia was caught between two wars raging in Europe, the War of the Spanish Succession and the northern war in which the King of Sweden was attacked by his neighbors. King Frederick I decided to join the Grand Alliance, and at the peace of Utrecht obtained Upper Guelderland and the general recognition of his title of King. His kingdom emerged from the war as the foremost German Protestant state in the Empire.

Frederick I was an extravagant ruler, and when King Frederick William I succeeded him in 1713 he inherited a bankrupt administration. Frederick William was no patron of culture; he was nicknamed the Drill Sergeant. His Court was a barracks and his kingdom a parade ground. The Junkers were encouraged to send their sons to a cadet school in Berlin to be fashioned into officers. The size of the army was doubled. By entering into the war against Sweden, Brandenburg-Prussia acquired western Pomerania and Stettin by the Treaty of Stockholm *(1720)*. At home the King fortified the absolutist powers of the monarchy, ruling no longer with a Privy Council but from a Cabinet, centralizing his administration under a general directory of officials working through departments or "colleges." Local diets of Estates were superseded. He left to his son, Frederick II, an army of eighty thousand men (conscription had been introduced in 1733) and a full treasury with the national revenues doubled. Though he starved the universities to pay for his army with its fantastic contingent of giant Potsdam grenadiers, he continued the Great Elector's policy of promoting foreign immigration, repeopling the wastelands, and stimulating agriculture and industry. Prussia was in the process of becoming a power in Europe.

12. The Rise of Russia

While the Great Elector and his two immediate successors transformed the scattered and disunited territories of Brandenburg-Prussia into an important kingdom, Peter the Great was converting the sparsely populated areas under the rule of Muscovy into a nation looking toward Europe, previously neglected but now courted and feared. Russia stretched from the Baltic to the Caspian Sea and from the borders of Poland-Lithuania to Okholtsk on the Pacific Ocean. Pioneers had crossed the Urals into Siberia in search of furs. But this huge empire had only one port at Arkangel, and was cut off from the Black Sea by the Turks. The rulers of Muscovy were also faced with domestic problems ranging from half-barbarous boyars or nobility to a mass of discontented serfs; they were also surrounded by enemies stronger or more sophisticated than themselves—the Swedes, who had conquered the eastern shores of the Baltic, the Poles, and the Turks. On the west Russia's frontiers were ill defined, and on the south there was perpetual trouble from the semiindependent Cossacks of the Dnieper and the Don. Alexis the Gentle of the Romanoff dynasty, who had become Tsar in 1645, besides having to suppress risings in Moscow and the Ukraine, was involved in wars with all his neighbors. But after two more wars with Poland he gained the important towns of Smolensk and Kiev on his western frontier and held his own against the Swedes and the Turks.

During the reign of Fedor II, Alexis's eldest son by his first wife, a truce was concluded with the Turks, but after Fedor's death came a time of confusion while two boys reigned as Tsars and the government was in the hands of a regent who was a woman. Peter I assumed power in 1694. The Duc de Saint-Simon, who met him in France, wrote that

> he had a kind of familiarity which sprang from liberty, but he was not without a strong dash of that ancient barbarism of his country, which rendered all his actions rapid, nay, precipitous, his will uncertain and not to be constrained or contradicted in anything.

He was seven-foot tall, badly educated, gross in his habits and brutal in his humor, simple and frugal in private life, with an invincible appetite and a prodigious thirst. His aim was to improve the material well-being of his country and to possess an army and navy capable of fighting his neighbors and suppressing internal revolts. In 1696 he took Azov at the mouth of the River Don from the Turks, a conquest which was confirmed by the treaty of

Constantinople *(1700)*. Then he paid a long visit to western Europe, learning in particular about the problems of shipbuilding from the Dutch and the English. He had to return to Russia in 1698 to crush a revolt by the *streltsi* or palace guards, and in the following year allied himself with the Poles and Danes against Sweden.

Although Peter was humiliatingly defeated by Charles XII of Sweden at the battle of Narva *(November 1700)*, he took advantage of the fact that Charles then turned away to fight the Poles to train and strengthen the Russian army; in 1704 he retook Narva and built himself a military base at the head of the Gulf of Finland, which was to become the city of Saint Petersburg. In 1709 when Charles XII invaded Russia, Peter defeated him at the battle of Pultava in the Ukraine and continued to fight the Swedes until by the Treaty of Nystad *(August 1721)* he obtained all the Baltic provinces—Livonia, Estonia, Ingria, and Karelia—but gave up Finland, which had been successfully invaded by the Russians, and paid a sum of money to the Swedes. In 1722–23 he made war on the Persians and acquired Baku on the western shore of the Caspian Sea. His only military failure was in a war against the Turks: his army was surrounded at the Battle of the Pruth in July 1711, and he was obliged by treaty to surrender all his strongholds on the Sea of Azov. Thus, Russia's advance to the Black Sea had to await the reign of Catherine the Great.

Peter, wrote Klyuchevsky, "expended most of his energy on developing the country's manufacturing industries and in particular the mining of ores which were of such military importance." He invited foreign artisans to Russia and sent Russians abroad to learn industrial crafts. Industries were promoted by the granting of monopolies and subsidies, and he intervened in detail in his subjects' lives. For example, the working of footwear with tar was prohibited; blubber oil had to be used instead. Passengers who traveled on the Neva were to do so by sailing ships only and not by rowboats. Army officers were instructed to shave and wear German clothing.

Peter reformed both the central and the local government. He instituted a system of boards or "colleges" at the center. In the provinces burgomasters locally elected were instructed to collect the taxes in order to protect the peasants from the ravages of the *voevodi* (local governors). New administrative units were created in the provinces largely for fiscal purposes. The army and navy were reorganized and strengthened. The capital was moved to Saint Petersburg, to which the traffic to Arkangel was diverted, and a naval base was established on the island of Cronstadt. These were expensive undertakings. Klyuchevsky says, "it would be difficult to find anywhere in military history a massacre which accounted for more men than St. Petersburg and Cronstadt." Peter called his new capital "paradise," but for many Russians it was a mass grave.

Modern Russian historians differ about the achievements of Peter the Great. On the one hand, they admire, as Stalin did, the single-mindedness with which he subsidized factories and foundries to supply his army and defend his country. On the other hand, they blame him for his cruelty and ruthlessness, for his Oriental despotism, for his neglect of anything but technical education, for burdening the national economy with the cost of his endless wars. Peter, writes P. I. Lyashchenko, a modern Soviet historian, was

> incapable of changing the existing social conditions. Therefore, while he was fully capable of seeing the negative features of serfdom, he was powerless before his own serf-holding nobility.

Thus, he is admired as a patriot but condemned for failing to be a social revolutionary.

13. The Decline of Turkey

Like Russia, the Ottoman Empire in 1648 covered part of Europe as well as Asia, and much of North Africa as well. With a population of 25 to 30 million and an army of at least a hundred thousand men, the Turks were expansionist and aggressive; they controlled most of the Balkans, Transylvania, and over half of Hungary; they directly threatened Russia from the Black Sea and the Ukraine; and they made war on the remains of the Venetian Empire. The Ottoman Empire was highly centralized, with its beys and valis in command of its provinces and its Sandjak beys, who were responsible for recruiting. It lived by war, and in spite of the importance of the Mufti as head of the Muslim religion, it tolerated Christianity—indeed, nearly half its subjects were Christians. The princes of Moldavia and Wallachia (modern Rumania) were semi-independent, and their states were not subject to Turkish occupation.

But the power of the Ottoman Empire had declined somewhat since its greatest days. There were two reasons for this: first, the high degree of centralization that existed meant that when the Sultan and his chief minister, the Grand Vizier, were not capable men, this weakness reverberated throughout the Empire; secondly, the army had not kept up with developments in the west. The Janissaries or infantry were no longer recruited from carefully chosen and well-trained Christian subjects, but tended to form a state within a state rather like the *streltsi* in Russia; the cavalry or *spahis* were raised by feudal methods under the supervision of the Sultan's slaves and so tended to vary in quality. The artillery was backward by European standards. So was the navy. Nevertheless, huge armies of brave soldiers that the Turks could raise were always to be feared.

In 1648, after a period of misgovernment and local rebellion, the Sultan was deposed and succeeded by his ten-year-old son Mehmed IV. Law and order were restored through the drastic measures ordered by a new Grand

Vizier, Mehmed Kiuprili, who at the age of seventy-one showed himself to be as ruthless as he was able. He and his son Ahmed held their own in eastern Europe against the Austrians, the Poles, and the Venetians. Ahmed died in 1678 and was succeeded by his brother-in-law, Kara Mustafa. Although the Sultan Mehmed IV was now of age, he preferred hunting to government, and left the interminable wars to be managed by his grand viziers. A large army was gathered in Belgrade with the intention of advancing into western or Austrian Hungary where Prince Emeric Tekeli had rebelled against Habsburg rule (he was a Protestant and the Austrians had been attempting to convert Hungary to Catholicism) and where the fortresses of Gyor and Komarom barred the route to Vienna. Whether or not it was Mustafa's original intention first to assault these fortresses is disputed. But during 1682 the Austrians had shown themselves to be conciliatory (Leopold was still concerned with French aggression to his west), and that may have tempted Mustafa to higher aims. The operation, known as the Red or Golden Apple—the conquest of Vienna itself—had always been the dream of Turkish expansionists. They were encouraged to this end by a message received from the French ambassador in Constantinople that no French troops would take part in the defense of Vienna; at the same time Leopold experienced difficulty in finding other allies. He believed that his own forces were insufficient to stem the advance of the Turkish hordes. So in the spring of 1683 Kara Mustafa set out from Belgrade with an army estimated at two hundred thousand men collected from all parts of the Ottoman Empire. The siege of Vienna began on July 17 after the Emperor had fled from the city, leaving its defense to Count Starhemberg with a garrison of sixteen thousand.

The siege of Vienna is one of the epics of European history. The Turks surrounded the city but, because they did not possess heavy siege guns, had to proceed by sapping and mining. The garrison, with the aid of better guns, bombs, and grenades and ample supplies, was prepared to hold out for four months, but was required to do so for only eight weeks. Relieving armies blessed by the Pope and commanded by Charles of Lorraine, the Emperor's brother-in-law, and by John Sobieski, King of Poland, arrived outside Vienna in the second week of September. A battle took place on September 12 and the Turks were defeated, with ten thousand casualties and the loss of their entire camp. They retreated across Hungary, and when Kara Mustafa got back to Belgrade he was strangled by the orders of the Sultan.

Delighted by the victory, the Emperor Leopold concluded the truce with France and, with his allies, the Poles and the Venetians, planned a great counteroffensive against the Ottoman Empire. The Russians also promised to invade the Crimea. At first all went well for the coalition. In 1686 the Duke of Lorraine captured Buda, the capital of Turkish Hungary; in 1687 the Turks were again crushed at the Battle of Mohacs; and in 1688 the Austrians captured Belgrade. On the other hand, John Sobieski failed in the Balkans and the Russians in the Crimea. But Francesco Morosini, who had earlier gallantly defended Crete against the Turks, had his revenge by invading the Peloponnesus and taking Athens. It was then that Venetian guns shattered the Parthenon.

But after this the Turks staged a recovery. Mehmed IV, who had the utmost difficulty in giving up hunting even in time of crisis, was deposed, and in 1689 Mustafa Kiuprili, a brother of Ahmed, became Grand Vizier. In a counteroffensive the Austrians were driven from Serbia. The Emperor Leopold was obliged to turn his main attention to the war against France, and so stalemate developed on Europe's eastern front. Peter the Great captured Azov again, which, as has been noted, he was forced to surrender in 1713; and in 1715 the Turks reconquered Greece. But meanwhile the western European war had ended, and Prince Eugene was sent to the eastern front. He defeated the Turks in Hungary, and by the Treaty of Carlowitz (1699) the Austrians recovered Croatia, Slavonia, and almost the whole of Hungary. Thus, by 1715, when Louis XIV died, the Austrian Habsburgs had reached a peak of triumph both in the east and the west. But the Turkish wars lingered on until the Emperor Charles VI decided to make peace because of fresh complications in the west. By the Treaty of Passarowitz (1718), Austria obtained the remainder of Hungary, most of Serbia, and part of Wallachia and Bosnia.

14. The Scandinavian Kingdoms

While during the century after 1648 the absolute monarchies of France, Prussia, and Russia expanded their territories and consolidated their gains, the two Scandinavian countries—Sweden-Finland and Denmark-Norway—suffered from declining fortunes, fought against each other, and were often torn by internal dissensions. After the treaties of Copenhagen and Kardis, Sweden, thanks to the fighting qualities of its kings, reached the zenith of its power. But Charles X died at an early age and his son, Charles XI, was only a four-year-old. The government of the Regency fell into the hands of the nobility, which was divided into two hostile sections. No consistent foreign policy was followed, and the army and navy suffered from neglect. The Swedish army in fact had either to be subsidized from abroad or to live off the land of its enemies in time of war. The kingdom gained nothing and lost nothing from its alliance with France. But by 1679 "the power which thirty years before had terrified and astonished Europe had been reduced to a position of considerable ignominy."

Charles XI *(1656-97)* had come of age in 1672 and had fought gallantly against the Danes. The ruling nobility were discredited by the events of the war. In 1680 the King summoned a Diet and asked its members if he was obliged to rule with the advice of the *rad* or Council and whether the *rad* was an Estate of the realm. He received the answer that the King was responsible only to God. This meant that the Diet agreed to the introduction of absolute monarchy. By 1682 the *rad* had become the King's Council instead of a Council of State, and its members servants of the King instead of advisers to him. Later the Diet surrendered its power over taxation and only met occasionally to offer advice.

It is said that the readiness of the Swedes to institute an absolute monarchy was influenced by the examples of France and Denmark. The Danes had rewarded Frederick III, who had come to the throne in 1648, for his courageous defense of Copenhagen by declaring that the monarchy, which had hitherto been elective, should now be hereditary. Immediately after this the Estates had released him from the obligations of the *Handfaestning* or Royal Charter to which kings had been expected to swear on their accession, and substituted the *Kongelov* or King's Law (1665), which gave him wide powers. He was therefore able to establish a bureaucracy with "colleges" and a Privy Council which met at the King's pleasure.

The Danish nobility resented the royal absolutism and plotted against it. The Norwegians saw some advantages in the new regime, as Frederick III claimed equally to be King of Denmark and King of Norway instead of Norway remaining a subjected province. This advantage was somewhat illusory, but at least a land commission was set up in Norway which carried out reforms, including the abolition of the nobility's immunities from taxation. In Denmark itself it was not constitutionally possible for the Government to abolish immunities, and in order to pay off the public debt much royal land had to be alienated; but a land survey was carried out, and by means of its findings taxation was in fact increased. However, quarrels broke out with Sweden over Schleswig-Holstein, about which the Danes were sensitive, as their kingdom could be invaded from the south through these independent duchies. Fighting was endemic until the Great Northern War broke out at the end of the century.

Charles XI of Sweden was a pacific King who concentrated on strengthening his absolute powers, notably by a vast and ruthless resumption of alienated Crown lands and revenues from his nobility (the *reduktion*). Though the political influence of the ruling classes was damaged by his policies, in the words of Professor Michael Roberts,

> the nobility's loss of so much land went far to deliver the peasantry from the very real threat of social degradation and political extinction which had been hanging over it for half a century.

The number of yeomen farmers and Crown tenants doubled, and as a whole the Swedish peasants were better off than the Danes. Charles XI was exceptionally economical, so that when he died of cancer at the age of forty-one he left to his son, Charles XII, a boy of fourteen, absolute power, sound finances, and a newly trained army.

Charles XII, King of Sweden
DAVID VON KRAFFT
National Museum, Stockholm

The accession of this young prince in November 1697 excited the cupidity of all his neighbors. The Danes hoped to gain control of Holstein-Gottorp and to win back Scania; Augustus II, the elected King of Poland, aimed to obtain Livonia; and Peter the Great of Russia wanted all the Baltic provinces of Sweden lost to Gustavus Adolphus. But the youthful Charles XII proved himself a soldier of genius. He crossed the Sound from Elsinore in Scania and menaced Copenhagen. By the Treaty of Travandal *(1700)* Frederick IV of Denmark recognized the independence of the Duke of Holstein-Gottorp and withdrew from the war. Charles now turned his army back eastward across the Baltic and defeated the Russians at Narva. During the next six years the Swedes concentrated their attentions on Augustus II: in 1701 Courland was occupied, and thence an advance made south toward Warsaw. The Poles were defeated, and the Swedes proceeded to recognize Stanislas Leszczynsky, a Polish patriot, as King of Poland. In September 1707 Augustus II capitulated to the Swedes, signed the Treaty of Alt-Ranstadt, and resigned the Crown of Poland.

The western world was astonished at the victorious career of the young King of Sweden. The western powers vainly competed for his alliance;

instead he marched to his doom at Pultava and became an honorable prisoner of the Turks. It was not until 1714 that Charles escaped and found his way back to Sweden. The kingdom was now menaced on all sides. Brandenburg and Hanover joined in the coalition against it. After Stralsund in western Pomerania, at which Charles stopped on his way home, fell to his enemies, he decided to concentrate his efforts against Denmark. In 1716 he invaded Norway but was killed in December 1718 at the age of thirty-six while laying siege to the fortress of Fredericksten.

The story of Charles XII's reign is purely one of war. Although his wars were not as costly to the Swedish population or its economy as once used to be thought, modern Swedish liberals tend to feel ashamed of their absolutist warrior-king of the early eighteenth century. Unquestionably he was a dedicated man, who did not drink, ate sparsely, and told his friends he knew how to keep his passions under control; but his dedication, as his latest biographer shows, was to war. He left no direct heir. The choice for the Swedes lay between his elder sister, who had married the Duke of Holstein-Gottorp, and his younger sister, Ulrica Eleanora, who was married to Frederick of Hesse. Ulrica was chosen Queen, but soon abdicated in favor of her husband, who became King Frederick I. After nearly twenty years of perpetual war Sweden was exhausted and its Empire dispersed. Moreover, the Swedes were disillusioned with absolutism. They compelled their new King to become a constitutional monarch, and all power was vested in the *Riksdag* or Diet, which consisted of four Estates. The *rad* or Council exercised executive power when the *Riksdag* was not sitting. The King received only the right to a double vote in the Council and the authority to create peers on his accession. Count Arvid Berhard Horn, who had been one of Charles XII's generals, became in effect the chief Minister, and he pursued a pacific policy in friendship with Great Britain and France. This era of Swedish history is known as the Age of Freedom; during it two parties evolved. One party, which was known as the Hats, favored an alliance with France and hoped to recover Sweden's losses to Russia. They dubbed their opponents Night Caps or Caps because they were more pacific.

After the exhaustion of the Great Northern War both Sweden and Denmark settled down to the role of minor powers. Frederick IV devoted himself to improving education and showed sympathy toward the problems of the Danish peasants. In 1734 he concluded a fifteen-year treaty with Sweden. This was the beginning of a Scandinavian entente which has endured with a few interruptions until modern times.

15.   The Road to Revolution

Is it possible to detect any political or social pattern in the history of Europe during the second half of the seventeenth century? It has already been suggested that the relationship between the monarchs and aristocracies, which almost everywhere were the ruling groups, was ambivalent. To put it another way, the two parties were in a state of disequilibrium. No precise pattern can be seen in the more advanced societies—that is to say, France, the United Netherlands, and England. In France the King deliberately withheld power from the hereditary aristocracy "of the sword," but he also created a new aristocracy out of his bureaucracy. After Louis XIV's death in 1715, however, the regency for the child King welcomed the princes of the blood and the ancient nobility back to power. In the United Netherlands, following the death in 1702 of King William III of England, who was also the Dutch Stadholder, the regents resumed the kind of authority they had exercised after William II's death in 1650. This period in Dutch history is known as the second Stadholderless period: it was in fact government by oligarchy. Because the Dutch Netherlands was ruled by families sympathetic to trade, modern research suggests, the economic decline there did not set in until late in the eighteenth century. In England William III's supplanting of his father-in-law, James II, as King in 1688 was in fact a triumph for the English Protestant aristocracy, which resented James's heavyhanded methods of acquiring civic equality for his Roman Catholic subjects. The aristocracy continued to rule England during the reigns of the first two Hanoverians (George I and George II), although it must be remembered that two of the most effective prime ministers of the eighteenth century were Sir Robert Walpole, who came from a minor county family in Norfolk, and William Pitt the Elder, who earned the reputation of being "the Great Commoner." Moreover, the English victory over France stimulated commercial enterprise; and the Whigs, who commanded majorities in both houses of Parliament, favored the merchant class. English commerce advanced more rapidly during the rule of Robert Walpole.

Elsewhere in Europe it is difficult to see anything other than the swing of the pendulum. Professor Palmer has written of the nobility being either "segregated" or "assimilated." In Russia one might speak of their being assimilated under Peter the Great, but later in the century the Russian boyars acquired much more freedom than they had enjoyed under the masterful Tsar. In Prussia the same thing happened. Frederick William I kept the Junkers in their place by means of a bureaucracy, but his son restored their privileges. In Spain the grandees were given a new lease of life after the Bourbon victory over the Habsburgs. While in Denmark the monarchy became absolute, the Swedes drastically pared the powers of their kings after the death of Charles XII.

What can possibly be detected in European history during this period is the emergence not of democracy—there were no significant movements toward democracy either in thought or action at that time—but the gradual evolution of a conscious nationalism. The dynastic wars which were to pulverize Europe in the first half of the eighteenth century were to leave the subjects of monarchies indifferent. But the examples of the United Netherlands and Portugal shaking off the imperialism of Spain were meaningful. In the hour of his greatest danger in 1709, Louis XIV was able to appeal to the patriotism of Frenchmen to prevent his enemies from overrunning his kingdom. The long-postponed unification of England and Scotland in 1707 created some sense of enhanced national unity. In Spain (apart from Catalonia) Philip of Anjou was able to inspire a feeling of national purpose. In Poland and Russia, however, national passions were not to be fully aroused until later in the eighteenth century: that was also true of Prussia, and to a lesser extent of Austria. But these passions may be said to have been latent, and were to be aroused by the aggressions of Catherine the Great and Napoleon I. Thus, of the three strands that contributed to the revolutionary outbursts of the later half of the eighteenth century—social discontent, aristocratic revolts, and the spirit of nationalism—the last can most clearly be detected after the revolutionary wave in the mid-seventeenth century had subsided.

FIVE

---

*"Enlightened" Governments
and
Enlightening Philosophers*

1. Monarchs and Aristocracies

In the seventeenth century monarchs had governed by divine right and claimed to be responsible solely to God for their actions. The famous preacher Bossuet, compared King Louis XIV to "the image of God who seated on his throne in the highest heavens sets the whole of nature in motion." Even of King William III of England, who had usurped his father-in-law's throne by force supported by revolution, loyal clergy could write that the transference of power from one king to another was "an act of God" and that Christians must submit to a de facto King. On the other hand, at the start of the century monarchs were often restricted by coronation oaths and established local privileges as well as by the existence of diets or parliaments and groups of Estates; moreover, publicists, lay and clerical, argued that a ruler who disobeyed the law of God or the law of nature might be deposed. The two revolutions in England showed the way.

But in the eighteenth century monarchs mostly became absolute not by divine right but by political necessity (although an admirer of Peter the Great "actually hung the Tsar's picture among the holy ikons in his house and burned candles before it"). In several countries—in Prussia and Spain, for examples—diets and Estates had virtually ceased to meet, and monarchs governed with the aid of a disciplined bureaucracy and a trained army. On the whole, however, monarchs were judged by their effectiveness as rulers capable of maintaining law and order and as military leaders; in countries where their expansionist ambitions had ended in defeat on the field of battle, as in Louis XIV's France and Charles XII's Sweden, opposition reappeared and the nobility demanded a share in decision making. Some political philosophers, notably Hobbes and Spinoza, argued that a strong government must be based not on moral or "fundamental laws," appeals to the Bible, or implied contracts, but on human nature as it actually was. In fact, the absolute monarchs of Europe were still subject to ingrained traditions and provincial privileges with which they were hesitant to tamper. They disliked (as Oliver Cromwell had done) the accusation of being called arbitrary. They were not really "despots" as were the Turkish sultans or Persian shahs or the dictators of the twentieth century. They had to exert their authority within a recognized social framework. Thus, their success in the eighteenth century was coming to be determined by purely utilitarian considerations.

At the outset of the century most European countries were ruled by monarchies. The only exceptions were Venice and Genoa, whose previous importance had been undermined by economic change; Switzerland, a small federation; and the United Netherlands which, after the death of William III, ceased to have a Stadholder exercising quasi-monarchical powers. In Sweden, as has been noted, the rights of the monarchy were drastically reduced, while in Great Britain parliaments met every year and by their control over public revenues could check policies with which they disagreed; nevertheless, the authority of the British monarchy remained considerable even after the issue of the somewhat vaguely worded Declaration of Rights in 1689, and King George III, when he came to the throne in 1760, was able to demonstrate how extensive were the royal prerogatives that still remained.

At the other end of the scale, in Russia and Prussia, both expanding states, monarchs were able to exert far-reaching powers; in Denmark the King was virtually absolute; and in Spain, France, and Austria-Hungary the monarchies held a central position in the constitution and were generally able to resist obstruction by classes and institutions. In Spain the cortes of Aragon, Catalonia, and Valencia, which had opposed the establishment of the Bourbon dynasty, were swept away; only the Basque provinces and Navarre retained some of their traditional rights: the Council of Castile became a supreme authority; if they wished to express their views, Aragonese, Valencians, and Catalans had to go to Madrid, while *corregidors* or royal governors were established in the principal cities to take care of fiscal matters. Thus, the Bourbons imposed a degree of centralization in Spain which had never been attained by the Habsburgs. In France Louis XV, after he assumed personal power, claimed to be as absolute as his great-grandfather had been and was able to exert control through his intendants. In general, during the first half of the eighteenth century monarchies became more bureaucratic and more centralized.

In spite of this in most countries the nobility continued to play an important part, although it was no longer necessary for monarchies to crush them or bribe them as had happened two hundred years earlier. The nobility were usually divided into two groups: an upper group, which was wealthy and owned much land and looked to the Court for offices and sinecures, contrasted with a lower nobility who might be obliged to live on their estates and had only modest incomes. In France, wrote La Bruyère, "a nobleman, if he lives at home in the province, lives free but without substance; if he lives at Court he is taken care of but enslaved." The upper-class nobility, *"les Grands,"* held high offices in Church and State, and usually provided leading officers for the army and ambassadors for the diplomatic service. They generally exercised jurisdiction over their tenants, whether they were tenants or serfs, and still exacted seignurial dues and rights. In England the titled nobility not only filled the House of Lords but occupied most of the Cabinet offices. Because, as Habbakuk has written, they were both in the localities and at the center the politically effective class, "they felt a responsibility for the way things went and were even prepared during the great wars against France to tax themselves heavily."

But that was unusual. Not only in France but in most other kingdoms the nobility were exempt from taxation, although they no longer furnished the services to the Crown for which this exemption had been awarded. In France, after the death of Louis XIV, the nobility laid a claim to resume the political power from which it had previously been excluded. Louis XV summoned the princes of the blood to his councils; of Louis XVI's thirty-six ministers, all but one were noble. In Spain, on the other hand, the King's ministers were often adventurers from abroad, and the aristocracy became an urban rentier class. In Prussia and Russia the nobility actively served the State; although King Frederick William I boasted that he was "ruining the authority of the Junkers and establishing Prussian sovereignty like a rock of bronze," his more famous successor, Frederick the Great, put an end to such antagonism. Under the Emperor Charles VI it has been said "the hereditary dominions of the Habsburgs were in some ways rather an aristocratic republic, a federation of great noble families than a genuine monarchy." It was not until the reign of Joseph II that their power was reduced. In Hungary it has been estimated that one subject in twenty was a nobleman, and only nobles could own land. Poland, like Hungary, was a society of nobles. They chose their kings and exerted a veto over everything the Executive wanted to do. Thus, Poland has been described as an "aristocratic anarchy." In Sweden, where a constitutional monarchy was established, the members of the first Estate enjoyed double representation on all committees, and "the Riddarhus where the nobility held their debates was the real centre of Swedish political life."

In Russia, writes Professor Max Beloff, the "noble class was distinguished from the aristocracy of other countries by the enforcement upon it of obligations to the State especially in the military sphere." By an edict of 1722, promulgated by Peter the Great, all the servants of the Tsardom were divided into fourteen orders, of which the top eight carried with them the rank of hereditary nobility. Thus, bureaucrats who successfully climbed the ladder of promotion automatically became members of the nobility (or *dvorianstvo*). Services to the Tsar began at the age of fifteen and were nominally for life. "The Russian nobility of the eighteenth century" was thus "separated not only in law but in outlook, habits, dress and even language from the remainder of the people." Later rulers were less strict with their nobility. The Tsarina Anne, who came to the throne in 1730, abolished entails (introduced by Peter I), and no longer obliged the nobility to enter the ranks before becoming army officers. In spite of the subdivision of their estates, the Russian nobility reached the peak of privilege under Catherine the Great.

Although the monarchical system appeared to be predominant, the eighteenth century was therefore broadly an aristocratic age. In most countries noblemen held all the high offices under the Crown and possessed far-reaching privileges. Only in one or two countries, notably Great Britain, France, and the United Netherlands (and to a lesser extent certain Italian and German towns) was there a significant bourgeois class emerging through the development of commerce and industry. Even there its members preferred for the most part to attend to their own concerns rather than to enter politics. In some countries there was virtually no middle class at all. Only in England did much intermarriage take place between the aristocracy and the bourgeoisie. The mass of the people were of course peasants or serfs with hardly any political rights. Poland had 7 or 8 million serfs; in Russia 60 percent of the peasants were not free. In England, France, parts of the Scandinavian countries, and western Germany the countrymen were better off. But even there they had economic grievances. Their consciousness of these was to contribute to the revolution which was to engulf Europe later in the century.

If one keeps clearly in mind the structure of society, it becomes plain that a phrase which was once commonly used in some historical textbooks about the prerevolutionary period that it was an age of "enlightened despots" is not really applicable, for two reasons: first, the sphere of radical reform open to monarchs (even if one calls them absolute) was limited by unwillingness to interfere with aristocratic or provincial privileges; secondly, the governments of the larger European states were too frequently involved in wars to pay attention to any peacetime reforms except those that promised administrative tidiness. As Anderson has observed, "Most European rulers . . . could not afford the luxury of close adherence to an ideology, even one so loosely defined as that of the Enlightenment." Even in Great Britain, where Parliament offered a platform for the airing of new social and political ideas, the deadweight of existing interests and later involvement in world war prevented their being developed. Sir Robert Walpole, who managed to keep the kingdom at peace for twenty years took, as his motto *Quieta non movere* ("Let sleeping dogs lie"). It was not until after the American War of Independence that schemes for economic and political reform were brought forward in the House of Commons. It was only in a few smaller states which managed to keep out of European wars, such as Baden and Tuscany, that enlightened ideas were tried out. In Tuscany the Grand Duke Leopold *(r. 1765-90)*, who was a Habsburg, pushed through many reforms; yet when he succeeded his enlightened brother, Joseph II, as the ruler of Austria-Hungary and other Habsburg possessions, he reversed his brother's policies as being too radical.

What the monarchs of the eighteenth century aimed to do for the most part was not to introduce radical reforms but to improve the efficiency of government, particularly in fiscal matters. Here they often followed in the footsteps of their predecessors. For example, George I's Prime Minister Walpole inherited the excise from Charles I's revolutionary Parliament and, under Louis XV and Louis XVI, French finance ministers attempted to do what Sully and Colbert had tried and failed to do. The bureaucratic machinery that was created by rulers like Peter the Great and Frederick William I was developed so as to provide "increasing administrative specialization at the centre and increasing effectiveness of government in the provinces." Let us consider how much in fact was achieved.

2.   Russia after Peter the Great

At one time it was fashionable to refer to Catherine the Great of Russia and Frederick the Great of Prussia as the outstanding European "enlightened despots." Absolute they certainly were, but most of their enlightenment was to be found in their writings rather than in their deeds. Both of them strengthened the privileges of their nobility and depressed the conditions of the peasantry. They maintained their authority more by victories in war than by wise government in peace.

Catherine II was one of the most remarkable figures in eighteenth-century Europe. She was the daughter of an unimportant German prince: born Princess Sophia of Anhalt-Zerbst, she was invited to the Court of Saint Petersburg by the Tsarina Elizabeth *(r. 1741–61)* with a view to marrying her nephew, Peter, the grandson of Peter the Great, who was destined to succeed to the throne. Sophia was fifteen when she arrived in Russia with her mother in 1744. A Lutheran by birth, she was received into the Orthodox faith and christened Catherine; in August 1745 she was duly married to Peter, who was both moronic and impotent.

Catherine occupied her time during the early years of her marriage by learning Russian, by reading books ranging from the works of Tacitus to those of Montesquieu and Voltaire, and by taking the first of a series of lovers. This plain little princess with a sharp nose and a projecting chin once declared: "the trouble is simply that my heart cannot be content even for an hour without love." After nine years of marriage she gave birth to an illegitimate son named Paul who was taken out of her care and accepted as a genuine Romanoff. (As he succeeded his mother, the Romanoffs who fell from power in 1917 were not Romanoffs at all.) In spite of her sexual extravagances (she had at least twenty-one lovers altogether) Catherine was popular at Court and found a way of living with the Tsarina Elizabeth, who regarded her nephew as an imbecile.

The reign of Elizabeth, which lasted for twenty years, was by no means a complete failure. Although she inherited some of the less pleasing characteristics of her father, she managed to find generals who distinguished themselves and statesmen who kept her finances afloat. During her reign the first Russian university was founded in Moscow and an Academy of Arts was established at Saint Petersburg. When Peter III succeeded, his behavior outraged the army, which failed to respect a Tsar who was perpetually drunk, and insulted the national religion; as an adult he still enjoyed playing with toy soldiers. A coup d'état took place at the end of June 1762; the Tsar was imprisoned and later murdered; and his wife—"our little mother," as the troops called her—was acclaimed Autocrat of All Russia. It seemed inconceivable that her reign would endure; but in fact she was to rule for thirty-four years.

So far as Catherine's domestic policy was concerned it was not in the long run to differ fundamentally from that of her predecessors. Peter the Great had insisted that it was the duty of the nobility to serve the Government either in a military or civil capacity. If they failed to do so, they were liable to have their hereditary estates confiscated. But the old nobility resented this obligation and during his brief reign Peter III ruled that service was not to be compulsory on the nobility except in time of war. Catherine did not reverse this trend. On the contrary, when Count Nikita Panin, her principal adviser, proposed that a Council of State consisting of leading nobles should be set up, she saw to it that it was powerless; the nobility who came to Saint Petersburg during her reign did so for the most part in order to live a life of splendor and luxury at Court, as the French aristocracy did at Versailles, while the poorer nobles were content to stay in the provinces and pick up such offices as might be going.

Later in her reign a reorganization of local government in fact opened opportunities for the provincial aristocracy, while a Charter of Nobility published in 1785 confirmed and extended the rights of nobles, granting them freedom from personal taxation and compulsory state service. They alone were allowed to own serfs and to supervise local government. Catherine, wrote Professor Blum, "identified herself with the nobility—'je suis aristocrate,' she said, 'C'est mon métier,'" and her long reign turned out to be the Golden Age of the *dvorianstvo*.

Catherine continued Peter the Great's policy of subordinating the Church to the State. But unlike her husband, who had ordered the removal of ikons from the churches and beards from the priests, she was careful to maintain an outward attitude of deference to the Orthodox religion. Nevertheless, she pursued the policy of impounding ecclesiastical wealth. By a ukaz of 1764 all Church property was nationalized and the clergy henceforward paid by the State. Over half the monsteries in Russia were closed and hundreds of thousands of serfs transferred to imperial ownership. Abroad Catherine's policy was represented as a triumph for the Enlightenment; at home coffers were enriched, while she kept up the stance of a devoted servant of the Orthodox Church.

There is some evidence that at the beginning of her reign Catherine was genuinely influenced by the liberal ideas wafted over from France and Italy, and that she even contemplated easing the lives of the serfs. In August 1767 she created a sensation by summoning to Moscow a conference of 564 deputies to consider the reform of the laws. She herself drew up a draft code, institute, or instruction *(Nakaz)* based largely on the teachings of Montesquieu and Beccaria. Voltaire wrote to her sycophantically: "Lycurgus and Solon would have signed your work, but they could not have performed it." So radical was its character that copies were not allowed into France. But nothing much came of it; Catherine herself described it as "a garment of peacock's feathers"; the code was slashed to pieces and the conference or commission, which was in fact dominated by the nobility (though it contained 200 urban representatives), never passed a single resolution and was abruptly suspended at the end of 1768. Western diplomatic representatives in Russia were cynical about the whole business and thought that the real object of the conference was to enhance the loyalty of Catherine's subjects, over whom she insisted that she was absolute—"the great and all-wise mother" of her dominions.

Besides her efforts at legal reform, Catherine attempted to improve the education and manners of her subjects. During her reign schools for orphans were set up in Moscow and Saint Petersburg, as well as one or two schools for the daughters of the nobility. In 1786 the Tsarina approved a statute which aimed to establish schools in provincial and district capitals. Thus, more education became available, although it was possibly not of a high standard. To improve manners Catherine herself assumed the role of an instructress. In 1769 she published a journal called *Omnium Gatherum*, in which she told women how to behave themselves in public. But Catherine's most important reform was of local government. Proposals put forward in her predecessor's reign were put into effect. The country was divided into a larger number of provinces, and powers previously exercised in Saint Petersburg were transferred to provincial governors. The provinces in turn were divided into districts, with elective boards dealing with administration and justice. She also issued a Charter of the Cities in 1785. But these changes did not create genuine self-government, nor even a large degree of centralization. The provincial governors were in fact supreme and were directly responsible to the central government, while the cities remained largely under the control of bureaucracy. This system with its enervating effect on provincial life (reflected later in the plays of Chekov) remained in existence until the revolution of 1917.

It seems clear that if Catherine began her reign with wide-ranging reformist ideas, she was disillusioned when in the midst of a long war against the Turks she was confronted with a massive peasant rebellion headed by the Don Cossack Emilian Pugachev. Pugachev claimed to be Catherine's husband, Peter III, risen from the dead, and avowed that he intended to fulfil his promise of liberating the serfs and sharing the land between them. Although many of his men were armed only with scythes, they created havoc, murdered landlords, and threatened to march on Moscow. But as soon as the peace with Turkey was concluded, Pugachev's forces were broken up and he himself was beheaded in January 1775. This rebellion put an end to most of Catherine's ideas of reform; the rights exercised by the nobility over their serfs were extended; and the reform of local government in 1775 was principally designed to avert another outbreak of social unrest. Modern Soviet historians rightly reject the idea that the Tsarina was enlightened. In her old age Catherine became more and more autocratic and susceptible to flattery. She never forgot Pugachev, and when the French Revolution began she blamed it on the lack of a strong hand like her own. But she foresaw with uncanny accuracy that in the end the French Republic would dissolve into dictatorship.

3. The Prussia of Frederick the Great

Like Catherine, Frederick II of Prussia was an indefatigable autocrat. He preferred to lead his armies in person and when he was not fighting to govern. Undisturbed by family life or other human weaknesses, he was a genuine polymath, and could talk about almost any subject under the sun. But whereas Catherine devoted her mornings to personal interviews and relied on her favorites to carry out her policies, Frederick absorbed himself in paperwork and rarely saw his ministers. In most of his domestic policies he was a typical ruler of the century. Like Catherine, he promoted education and, in theory at least, established universal primary schools. But shortage of teachers and the unwillingness of poor parents to send their children to school diminished its reality. In economic development Frederick was a thoroughgoing mercantilist who involved the State not only in overseas commerce but in the promotion of industry, banking, and insurance. He did everything he could to stimulate the growth of population and encouraged immigration; he even allowed Jesuits expelled from Roman Catholic countries to settle in Silesia.

Frederick's kingdom was a patchwork of ancient domains, each with its own customs and institutions. The King had inherited from his father a realization of the need to reform the laws. Trials for witchcraft had been abolished, and he himself put an end to torture. He thought that the laws should be equitable, simple, and few; but he seems to have relied unduly on his Chancellor, Cocceji, to supervise the working and revision of the laws. Cocceji adumbrated an elaborate scheme of Germanic law but did not live to complete it, and his successor became immersed in routine. It was not

Frederick the Great
The Bettman Archive

until 1794 that a Prussian code was promulgated. Prussian autocracy was essentially bureaucratic, but the King conferred much authority on the Junkers in the localities with the aim of offsetting the power of ordinary officials. Toward the end of his reign Frederick neglected the true welfare of his army on which his strength depended. His soldiers were expected to bask in past glories but to receive no improvements in pay or conditions of service. Hence they were unable to meet the first hammer-blows of Napoleon.

The truth was that the overcentralization of the administration in the King's own hands gave undue influence to a bureaucracy increasingly recruited from the Junkers. The middle classes were frustrated and the intelligentzia disappointed. Writing in 1799, a professor at Königsberg said that Prussia had become a "thinly veiled aristocracy." Throughout his reign Frederick had deliberately favored the Junkers, given them new offices and privileges, and enabled them to benefit from regressive taxation. The peasants in his dominions were little better off than they were in Russia or Poland. As Wangermann has recently observed, Frederick II's practice "fell short of his theory, and resembles that of an unenlightened petty tyrant more often than that of the enlightened despot." Even freedom in thought and writing was taboo except about religion. The German intellectuals had to await their emancipation in the period of *Sturm und Drang* after Frederick the Great was dead.

4.   Enlightenment in Austria-Hungary

Possibly the most enlightened rulers in eighteenth-century Europe were to be found among the Habsburgs Maria Theresa, Queen of Hungary, and her two sons, Joseph and Leopold. Maria Theresa felt sympathetic toward the peasants, and was convinced by her Minister, Haugwitz, that the nobility

The Empress Maria Theresa with her Family on the Terrace of the Castle at Schönbrunn
Kunsthistorisches Museum, Vienna

and clergy should pay their fair share of taxation. Unlike the absolutisms of Catherine II and Frederick II, that of Maria Theresa was bureaucratic rather than personal; she depended on the loyalty of all her subjects, and by separating justice from administration she hoped to protect the poor from oppression by the rich. The provincial diets, manned by the nobility, resisted the spread of bureaucracy. Nevertheless, the lot of the peasants was eased in the 1770s both in Austria and Bohemia, especially those on the Crown domains.

Maria Theresa was an enthusiast for educational reform; her adviser, Gerhard van Swieten, was particularly successful in expanding the curriculum of the University of Vienna. In 1774 a general regulation was introduced aiming at setting up a complete educational ladder stretching from the primary schools to the training colleges. Educational progress was undoubtedly more rapid in eighteenth-century Austria than in either Prussia or Russia. It was because these educational opportunities were created that efficient bureaucrats could be recruited from outside the nobility. Maria Theresa, however, resisted pressure brought to bear upon her by her eldest son and by her Chancellor, Kaunitz, to attack the Church in order to achieve educational reforms. The Queen was a devout Roman Catholic and disliked the general trend toward religious toleration in eighteenth-century Europe.

After the death of her husband, the Emperor Francis I, in 1765, Maria Theresa made her eldest son joint ruler with her and he was duly elected Emperor Joseph II. Joseph was intelligent and austere, but also impatient and inflexible in his determination to gain his ends. He has been described as "the Ignatius Loyola of the idea of the absolute State"; he once declared, "I have made philosophy the legislator of my empire." But it was not until after the death of his mother in 1780 that he was able to put all his plans into effect. He felt extremely sympathetic toward the peasants, and when as a young man he visited Bohemia at a time of famine, he paid for their relief out of his own pocket. As Emperor he limited the lord's rights to punish his tenants and he abolished the *corvée*, compulsory unpaid work on roadmaking. "By two great reforms," wrote Friedjung,

> Joseph II earned the gratitude of the peasants of his Empire: by abolishing serfdom (bondage to the soil) in 1781 and by decreeing that even those peasants who did not have full property rights could no longer be evicted.

In 1789 he introduced a far-reaching scheme of reform. His idea was to abolish all labor services (known as the *Robot*), tithes, and feudal dues. Instead, after a census had been completed, the peasants in Austria and Bohemia were to pay their landlords a fixed percentage of their gross yearly income in money and also to contribute a fixed amount to the general land tax. All landholders, noble or other, were expected to pay this tax. But the land tax and the destruction of feudalism did not apply to Hungary. Although Joseph sent troops into Hungary to enforce a census, the Magyar landholders obstructed all attempts at reform, refusing to pay their share of taxation or to invest their capital in economic improvements. The Hungarians were thus backward economically and politically; for their part they maintained that they were being exploited by the Habsburgs.

During his mother's old age and after her death, Joseph II mounted a campaign against the monopoly of the Roman Catholic Church. The clergy were subjected to taxation, tithes were abolished, monasteries were closed, and Church courts were brought under the supervision of the State judiciary. Joseph also wanted the Jews to be emancipated throughout his dominions, although in fact toleration was only conferred upon them in Lower Austria. From 1781 all kinds of Christianity were permitted, and Protestants were allowed to take degrees in the University of Vienna. Finally, Joseph tried hard to reduce the influence of the Catholic Church in the Austrian Netherlands.

It can be argued that Joseph II drove too fast and too furiously. He met with resistance not only from the privileged classes of nobility and clergy, from the Magyars, the Lombards, and the Flemings, but from the very peasants whose welfare he had so much at heart. Many of them resented the standardization of their commuted feudal dues and the amount of their tax obligations. Some of them were actually ungrateful for the commutation of their labor services on the ground that their money burdens had become heavier; others thought that the reforms were not radical enough and that feudalism should be abolished completely. Before the end of his reign Joseph II, in order to sustain his reforms, had to revoke some of them, to establish a secret police force, and to impose censorship on the press. The years 1789 and 1790 were indeed dangerous years in which to try to enforce a social revolution from above. The privileged classes feared that they would suffer the fate of the French; the peasantry hoped that the whole of the old regime would be overthrown. Joseph died a disappointed man. It appeared as if absolutism and social reform were incompatible.

In 1790 Joseph II was succeeded by his brother, the Emperor Leopold II, who as Grand Duke of Tuscany had acquired a remarkable reputation for enlightenment. Not only had he unified the administration of the city-states which comprised his duchy, but he had abolished tax farming and internal tariffs and had shaped his economic on physiocratic (liberal) rather than mercantilist lines. He even planned representative institutions and aimed at perpetual peace. But as a ruler of the wide-flung Habsburg dominions, he realized that his brother had gone ahead too swiftly and too drastically with his reforms, and Leopold deliberately canceled many of them, including the controversial land tax, which had caused such excitement not only among the landlords but also among the peasants. Leopold wrote: "It is useless to do good to people by force, if they are not convinced of its usefulness." Thus, the work of the most sincere and genuine of the so-called enlightened despots was largely undone.

5. Stagnation in England and France

In western Europe England and France were at the opposite end of the scale from Russia or Poland. The peasants were much better off and serfdom did not exist. Governments were inclined to leave things alone except when engaged in preparations for war, and monarchs were not notably enlightened. British monarchs took an active part in government: William III attended meetings of his Cabinet whenever he could; Queen Anne attended more Cabinet meetings than any monarch in British history; George I and George II were kept fully informed about all the business of government. At the center of affairs there was a vast expansion in the number of public servants, particularly in the Treasury. As Professor Plumb has written, "the immense achievements of the Civil Service between 1689 and 1715 are only just beginning to be recognized." But no radical reforms were introduced either in administration or by legislation. It took nearly fifty years before the social evils created by cheap gin were brought under control. Robert Walpole had "an elephantine complacency" and little imagination. His successors were also devoid of ideas for reform. The actual day-to-day life of the country was still under the control of the justices of the peace, who were administrators as well as agents of the law. Almost without exception these justices belonged to the landed gentry: for the most part they aimed to be benevolent despots, but were not in practice always benevolent to their inferiors.

The chief difference between England and France was that the King who succeeded Louis XIV was, as he himself boasted (not entirely convincingly), the possessor of "untrammelled legislative authority." But, like Walpole, he did nothing positive to ameliorate the conditions of the society over which he ruled because he regarded all social evils as being incurable. Where there is a parallel between Great Britain and France in the so-called Age of Enlightenment is that the representatives of the Bourbon governments in the French provinces were, like the English justices of the peace, "to a considerable extent decentralized and independent of the royal power." Even the intendants, who under Richelieu and Louis XIV had been the recognized agents of the central Government, became more and more inclined to identify themselves with the interests of the people over whom they ruled, or at any rate to bear in mind provincial needs, just as the justices of the peace did in Great Britain.

6. Absolutism in Portugal, Spain, and Italy

The monarchs of Portugal, the Braganzas, sought to imitate the glories of Louis XIV, and intermarried with the French Bourbons. John V, who came to the throne in 1706 at the age of seventeen and ruled for forty-four years, benefited from a gold rush which took place in Brazil. But just as the flood of South American silver had only temporarily stimulated the economy of Spain, so much of the Brazilian gold had to be sent abroad to pay for imports. John V, to celebrate the birth of his son, built a huge basilica and palace at Mafra, twenty miles from Lisbon, somewhat on the lines of the Escurial and as architecturally unimpressive; more distinguished was the library he gave to the University of Coimbra. After John's death in 1750 the new King, who was nothing if not lazy, handed over power to a member of his nobility, Sebastian Carvalho e Melho, known as "the Pasha" and later created first Marquis of Pombal. Pombal ruled by terror and successfully sought to repress other members of the nobility and to uproot the Society of Jesus, of whose influence in Brazil he disapproved. On the constructive side, he forwarded secular education and encouraged the study of natural sciences at Coimbra. In economic affairs he strove to imitate the discredited policies of Colbert, creating State industries and monopolistic commercial companies in an attempt to undermine British and Dutch commerce. Pombal's achievement as an "enlightened despot" has often been exaggerated, possibly because after the terrible Lisbon earthquake of 1755, which was interpreted by the Church as a punishment for national sin, he was first to set the example of suppressing the Jesuits, which was afterward followed by Spain in 1766

Ruins of the City of Lisbon after it was Destroyed by the Earthquake of 1755
©Lisbon Tourist Office

before Pope Clement XIV was persuaded to extinguish the Society altogether in 1769. But there is no evidence that Pombal was affected by the contemporary theorists of political, legal, or economic reform. After the fall of this dictator in 1777 most of his policies were reversed and his victims released from prison.

The Spain of Philip V, like the Portugal of John V, sought to imitate the procedures of Louis XIV's France. Philip—who was, after all, the grandson of the *Roi Soleil*—at first had French advisers and began to employ ministers, as in France, to direct policy instead of using the old Spanish councils. As in Portugal also, the various cortes ceased to have much significance; power was centralized in Madrid. But Philip was exceedingly uxorious, and when in 1714 he married as his second wife an Italian princess of twenty-two with "a Lombard heart and a Florentine head," who was strong-willed and ambitious, the Spanish monarchy concerned itself with intrigues to win dynastic advantages abroad more than with domestic reform. It was not until Elizabeth Farnese's son succeeded to the throne in 1759 as Carlos III *(d. 1788)* that something approaching enlightened despotism can be detected. Carlos III aimed at a benevolent and centralized absolutism; his ministers were intended to carry out his policies, and his provinces came under the rule of intendants on the French model. His agrarian policy was enlightened in spite of the opposition of the Mesta (representing the big sheep owners), and he tried to help industry without setting up State manufactures as in Portugal. On the other hand, he followed the Portuguese lead in suppressing the Jesuits and limiting Papal interference with the Church. By the time of his death Spanish industry had developed considerably, especially in Catalonia. But in spite of all his efforts the mass of the Spanish people remained both poor and ignorant.

Before Carlos III succeeded as King of Spain he had become, through his mother's efforts, King of Naples and Sicily where, though he had thought himself "the most absolute monarch in Europe," he had labored to reduce taxes and, with the aid of the Minister of Justice, Tanucci, to reform the criminal law. He also founded an Academy of Art and built an opera house in Naples. Both in the Sicilies and later in Spain Carlos did much to stimulate culture and education. He was undoubtedly one of the few genuinely enlightened monarchs who profited indirectly from the teaching of the French *philosophes.*

It has already been noted how Leopold II, when he was Grand Duke of Tuscany, carried out an enlightened policy both in economic and political affairs. But elsewhere in Italy (except in Lombardy, which came under the rule of the Emperor Joseph II) social and economic progress was impeded by the power of the nobility and the Church. It was hardly to be expected that improvements would take place in the Papal States, which were in any case poverty-stricken and where long-established clerical privileges impeded reform. Both in Venice and Naples many feudal rights persisted. The whole of Italy was fragmented economically as well as politically. Whereas rich soil was to be found, for example, in Lombardy and in Sicily, the Pontine and other marshes wasted land and bred malaria. However, during the eighteenth century parts of Italy recorded notable achievements. The silk industry, which had declined in the seventeenth century, revived, and raw silk, oil, and grain were exported. Internal customs barriers were reduced or abolished, even in the backward Papal States. Distinguished scientists, economists, and jurists emerged. Cesare Beccaria, who was born in Milan in 1728, wrote a book on crime and punishment which made an impact far beyond Italy. Neither Bourbons nor Habsburgs proved to be reactionary rulers, and after 1738 a long period of peace in Italy contributed to the beginnings of the Enlightenment.

7. The Blight on Absolutism: Dynastic Ambition

If peace had prevailed throughout Europe in the first half of the eighteenth century, it may be that greater social and economic progress would have been achieved. But the fact that most European states were ruled by absolute monarchies meant that dynastic ambition was at a premium in foreign affairs. From the tangle of treaties and minor wars which occupied the twenty-five years between the signature of the treaties of Utrecht and Rastatt and the outbreak of the War of the Austrian Succession in 1740, two main causes of disturbance may be discovered, both dynastic in character. These dynastic questions have sometimes been defended as important by historians on the ground that they could benefit the countries concerned with them since they resulted in their acquiring new territories which enhanced their strategic positions. But it is doubtful if this argument can be seriously applied to the dynastic policies pursued by eighteenth-century monarchs.

The two dynastic ambitions which determined the political history of Europe after the War of the Spanish Succession (which itself had been fought by Louis XIV for dynastic reasons) related to Spain and Austria. These two countries were dissatisfied powers. Spain had lost Gibraltar and Minorca, the southern Netherlands, and much of Italy, while the Emperor Charles VI had been expelled from Spain. It was with the utmost reluctance that they had stopped fighting each other; the other powers that had been engaged in the recent war therefore realized that the terms of the treaties would be difficult to maintain. Thus was constituted a rudimentary Concert of Europe with the object of upholding the balance of power.

In Spain King Philip V had been reluctant to hand over to the Emperor and Duke of Savoy (now converted into the King of Sicily) the former Spanish possessions in Italy. It was the representative of the Duke of Parma in Madrid, Giulio Alberoni by name, who had suggested the marriage of Philip V to his master's daughter, the formidable Elizabeth Farnese. After she had chased the French from Madrid, the new Queen bore her husband a son, the future Carlos III. But since Philip's sons by his first wife had best claims to succeed to the Spanish throne, Elizabeth Farnese was resolved that her own son should have a throne in Italy. As Philip V and Alberoni were also determined to restore Spanish influence in Italy, their desires all chimed together.

The second main dynastic ambition that colored European politics was that of the Emperor Charles VI, and it also concerned a princess. Unlike Philip V, Charles had no sons, only a daughter, Maria Theresa. Austria had never been ruled by a woman, nor could a woman be Holy Roman Emperor. Charles VI was afraid that after his death his Empire would fall to pieces. Charles was a conscientious ruler as well as a father who tried to put his finances in order by the creation of a supreme financial authority for the whole realm (the *bäncalitat*); he also aimed to extend his authority in the Balkans and to improve his Empire's general economic situation. It was obvious that a clash between the Habsburgs and the Bourbons over Italy was likely to take place. But Charles was also anxious from 1719 to obtain international approval for a "pragmatic sanction" guaranteeing his daughter's right to succeed to all his possessions. This weakened his bargaining power in diplomatic negotiations.

Although they were the most significant, the Spanish ambitions in Italy and Charles VI's Pragmatic Sanction were not the only dynastic questions troubling Europe. In England the Elector of Hanover, in accordance with the Act of Settlement passed during William III's reign, succeeded Queen Anne as King George I in 1714; the son of the late King James II, known as the Old Pretender, was a rival claimant to the throne, although as a Roman Catholic he was not really eligible. Thus, Great Britain was in danger of facing a dynastic war, should the Old Pretender find among Great Britain's enemies funds and forces to support an invasion. The Hanoverians were not popular and the Stuarts were good Scottish stock. Finally, there was the question of the future of the dynasty in France. The French Regent, the Duke of Orleans, hoped that if the child Louis XV should die, he would take his place. On the other hand, Philip V of Spain, who had superior hereditary claims, longed to return to France; though he knew the other powers would never consent to the union of France and Spain, he was prepared to abdicate the Spanish throne if he could obtain the succession in France.

Lastly, in 1733 a European war broke out over the succession to the throne of Poland, which was elective. The Russians and Austrians took the side of the late King's son, known as Augustus III, and the French backed Stanislas Leszczynski, who happened to be the father-in-law of Louis XV. The French obtained the alliance of Spain and of the King of Sardinia (Charles Emmanuel). After fighting in Germany and Italy and kaleidoscopic diplomacy, a settlement of all these dynastic questions was finally reached in 1738 by what was called the Third Treaty of Vienna. By this treaty

Stanislas Leszczynski renounced his claim to the throne of Poland and was compensated by being made Duke of Lorraine. It was also agreed that when he died Lorraine should become part of France. The actual Duke of Lorraine, Francis Stephen, became Duke of Tuscany. He was in fact married to Charles VI's daughter, Maria Theresa, and seven years later was to become Holy Roman Emperor. Elizabeth Farnese's son, Don Carlos, became King of Naples and Sicily (known as the two Sicilies), while Parma and Piacenza (over which Don Carlos had ruled for a time) were restored to the Austrian Empire. Part of the Milanese was awarded to Charles Emmanuel of Sardinia. Both he and the French King guaranteed the Pragmatic Sanction. Thus, the Emperor Charles VI was left with only part of the Milanese, Parma, and Piacenza in Italy, while in the following year he surrendered all that he had gained by war in the Balkans to the Turks. So the Austro-Hungarian dominions had contracted even before he died in October 1740, and the guarantees of the Pragmatic Sanction, which he had collected and for which he sacrificed so much, were not to be honored by any of the guarantors except Great Britain. As the late David Ogg wrote,

> the generation between the conclusion of the Utrecht settlement and the death of Charles VI was a period of diplomatic futility and inconclusiveness probably unmatched in European history.

8. Frederick the Great and the War of the Austrian Succession

Warfare in the middle of the eighteenth century, at any rate in western Europe, was generally considered by contemporaries to have become less ferocious than it had been before. Various explanations may be offered for this change. One is that the element of religious fanaticism had been eliminated. Wars were dynastic in character, and the armies of professional soldiers who served ambitious monarchs preferred to maneuver, to jockey for positions, to undertake sieges, and to avoid head-on battles as far as possible. The monarchs themselves thought that the bulk of their subjects were best employed in agriculture and commerce and thus able to supply the sinews of war; they therefore created their armies for the most part out of the dregs of the people, out of the poor and unemployed, criminals and debtors released from prison on condition that they enlisted, prisoners or deserters from the other side, mercenaries hired from smaller countries, and the like. Officers were generally recruited from the younger sons of the nobility, who were thought to have a higher sense of personal honor and less concern with calculations of profit and loss than the middle classes.

In view of the low character of the soldiery, three things were necessary: severe training, strict discipline, and the discouragement of all temptations to desertion. Frederick the Great laid it down that in order to prevent desertion troops should not camp near large woods, night marches should be avoided, and men should be led in ranks by officers when going out to forage or to bathe. Substantial magazines were established and big baggage trains organized so that the troops should not run riot or try to live off the country; soldiers were therefore well clothed and fed and the peasantry protected from depredations, though all this meant that an army was expensive to maintain and could not be squandered in useless battles. But when a battle came a soldier must do his duty. "If a soldier during an action looks as if to flee," ordered Frederick, "or so much as sets foot outside the line, the non-commissioned officer standing beside him will run him through with his bayonet and kill him on the spot."

No very notable changes were made in the techniques of fighting. But the general use of the flintlock musket and bayonet and iron instead of wooden ramrods to push down the powder made the infantry into the queen of the battle which it had not been in the seventeenth century. But musket fire was still inaccurate and of short range. Thus, to achieve effective fire-power the infantrymen were ordered to stand shoulder to shoulder in solid lines and usually in three ranks so that the front rank could let off its volleys while the other ranks were reloading or preparing to fire. In most armies light infantry, more mobile than the slow-moving regiments, were employed for skirmishing and scouting. The cavalry were usually placed on the flanks and used for shock action, but firepower had so greatly increased that the infantry was not likely to be overrun as in the past. Artillery tended to become lighter and was drawn by horses with their own trained drivers, so that it was more mobile than in the days when heavy guns could only be shifted by oxen supplied by civilians. Frederick, however, regarded the artillery as auxiliary rather than as an arm of war. Artillery was expensive, and it was not until the time of Napoleon, himself an artillery officer, that it played a major part in battles. Because of the need for long lines of closed ranks and the importance of preventing desertions, wars were fought by armies consisting of regiments or battalions and not of divisions; and these armies could not be too big, for then they became unwieldy. Forty-five thousand to seventy thousand was regarded as about the right size for an army.

The relations between Frederick II and his father had been ambivalent. Frederick William I was proud of his army and wanted to bring up his son as a soldier who would maintain the glory of the Hohenzollerns. He supervised his education, forbade him to learn Latin or to study the ancients, and obliged him to drill from the age of six. Frederick William was anxious to be loved, but his unmerciful bullying turned his son against him, and when he was eighteen Frederick planned to escape to France and thence to England, where he had relatives. But the plan was discovered; he was placed in a military prison, and a Prussian officer, in whom he had confided, was shot before his eyes. Thenceforward he learned to dissimulate and to obey his father. On his father's instructions Frederick married a plain and insignificant German princess when he was twenty-two. This enabled him to set up an establishment of his own. There he surrounded himself with congenial friends, read voraciously, and educated himself. But if he played the flute and wrote poetry, at heart he wanted to be a successful statesman and general. Women meant little to him—possibly he was a homosexual—and after he succeeded to the throne in May 1740 he put his wife away from him. Though he studied the *philosophes* and became a sceptic, the book that impressed him most was Voltaire's life of Charles XII of Sweden. Like his father, Frederick believed in absolute monarchy and that a king who was not a soldier was nothing. But he considered that his father had gone wrong in failing to utilize his resources to aggrandize his kingdom, to knit it together, and to expand its frontiers. Though the first steps he took as King were liberal ones—he abolished judicial torture and the censorship of the press and proclaimed religious toleration—his intention was, as soon as the chance came, to adopt an aggressive foreign policy and win a name for himself if possible by diplomacy, if not by war. His opportunity came at once, for in October 1740 the Emperor Charles VI died, leaving his daughter as his heiress; and most of Europe, ignoring the Pragmatic Sanction to which its governments were pledged, prepared to divide up Austria's dominions. Frederick struck first and in November invaded Silesia. The next twenty-three years of European political history were largely colored by this event. Before they ended Frederick had to struggle for his own survival. He triumphed because he proved himself a military genius.

In what did his genius consist? Unlike Marlborough or Napoleon, Frederick was not essentially a battle general. Battles, he thought, depended too much on chance. He believed that a victorious general should be a master of geography, should engage in a war of maneuver, and should achieve his ends through compelling his enemy to move by constant attacks. "To gain small successes," he wrote, "means gradually to heap up a treasure." The art of war consisted in surprise: short and lively wars were to be preferred to long, drawn-out contests. That at least was his theory. Indeed, it was forced upon him, because how otherwise could a kingdom with some 2 million inhabitants and which was not rich hope to overcome more populous and wealthier neighbors? In time, however, he was thrust upon the defensive. Once much of Europe rose in arms against him neither surprise not short and sharp wars were practicabilities; so he was driven to building fortresses and undertaking sieges. His strategy indeed was quite contrary to that of Napoleon, who seldom undertook sieges and whose winning of great victories in the field was decisive for making a good peace.

Queen Maria Theresa was a beautiful and strong-minded young woman who determined to fight for her inheritance. Her strength of mind was the only thing she had in common with her enemy, Frederick II. She had been educated by Jesuits, but she had been in no way prepared for her tasks as Queen. Though she loved her husband dearly, she was to find that he was useless either as a statesman or a soldier. Her father had left her neither a trained army nor a well-filled treasury nor even qualified advisers; his main interest had been in conducting operas and composing music.

The Pragmatic Sanction guaranteed to Maria Theresa not only the possessions of the House of Habsburg but the kingdoms of Bohemia and Hungary, the Austrian Netherlands, and Austrian Italy. The Pragmatic Sanction had excluded the two daughters of Charles's brother Joseph from any share in the inheritance, but as they had been married to the electors of Bavaria and Saxony, their husbands were soon putting forward claims. Nor was it certain that Maria Theresa's rule would be accepted by the Hungarians, for Hungary was an elective monarchy. Finally, as Maria Theresa could not succeed her father as Emperor, a movement was put on foot to make Charles Albert, Elector of Bavaria, the new Emperor; but how could he uphold such a position without an extension of his own territories? Thus, he became one of the Queen's chief enemies.

The French had not forgotten their ancient dynastic rivalry of the Bourbons against the Habsburgs. A war party won the ear of King Louis XV; Frederick II's easy military occupation of Silesia (to part of which his house had shadowy claims) was followed in the spring of 1741 by the mission of the Marshal of Belle-Isle to Germany, where he announced that France would support Charles Albert's territorial claims and by threats or bribes induced other German princes to offer their assistance in the partition of the Habsburg Empire. Meanwhile, Maria Theresa had managed to scrape together an army and sent it to expel the Prussians from Silesia. A battle was fought at Mollwitz on April 9, where the Austrian cavalry shattered the cavalry on the Prussian right. Frederick II, little experienced in war and thinking all was lost, fled the field and narrowly escaped being taken prisoner. It was not until 2 a.m. in the morning of the following day that he learned that the Prussian infantry had stood firm and beaten off all Austrian attacks.

The victory of Mollwitz inspirited Maria Theresa's other enemies. France, Spain, and Bavaria concluded an agreement whereby Charles Albert was to obtain French aid in an attack on Bohemia and Philip V of Spain was to take the Austrian possessions in Italy for his second son by Elizabeth Farnese, provided he could seize hold of them. In June Frederick II joined in the conspiracy, promising to give his vote to Charles Albert as Emperor in return for the recognition of his own claim to Lower Silesia. The only kingdom that remained true to its guarantee of the Pragmatic Sanction was

Great Britain, which promised to pay Maria Theresa a subsidy and provide twelve thousand soldiers as auxiliaries. It was to the interest of the British Government to support Austria, for Great Britain was then at war with Spain through commercial reasons, and fully expected France to join with Spain against it. Though the British war with Spain was chiefly a naval one, if the Bourbons were kept occupied in Germany and Italy, this would help the British cause. British policy was in fact to support the Germans against the French; and Maria Theresa was strongly pressed to come to terms with Frederick II.

In July 1741 Charles Albert seized Passau on the borders of Bohemia and Upper Austria; in August a French army crossed the Rhine; in September the Franco-Bavarians overran Upper Austria. Though Vienna was thus directly threatened, Maria Theresa appealed to the loyalty of the Magyars and in that same month was crowned Queen at Pressburg. The Hungarian Diet in return for concessions enthusiastically promised assistance. She now turned to try to save Austria and Bohemia. To help achieve this she even concluded a secret convention or armistice with Frederick II conceding to him Lower Silesia and the fortress of Neisse. But this treaty proved abortive. In December Charles Albert was crowned king at Prague and in January 1742 was elected Emperor. Meanwhile, Spanish forces landed in Italy and Frederick took Olmütz in Moravia, thus completing the occupation of Silesia. So at the beginning of 1742 Maria Theresa appeared to have reached the nadir of her fortunes. But Vienna remained intact, and Hungarian troops were quickly rallying to the young Queen's aid. Before winter was out the French and Bavarians were driven from Upper Austria and Bavaria itself invaded. In February, while Charles Albert was being crowned at Frankfort, his own capital of Munich fell to Maria Theresa's soldiers.

During 1742 and 1743 the ripples of the war gradually spread until all Europe was engulfed. France and Great Britain took a hand in all the conflicts and negotiations, although nominally France was a mere auxiliary of the Emperor and Great Britain of Maria Theresa. In France Cardinal Fleury died in January 1745 and Louis XV announced, aping his great-grandfather, that he would be his own Prime Minister; a year before Sir Robert Walpole, who, like Fleury, had been a pacific statesman and committed to the war with Spain against his own will, handed over power to the Pelham brothers (also Whigs), and the conduct of foreign policy was directed by Lord Carteret, a confident aristocrat, who was determined to thwart the ambitions of France and Spain.

The war continued until 1748. The Swedes and the Sardinians were brought into it on opposite sides, and the British and French officially fought one another. The Austrians, supported by British sea power, gained victories in Italy, while Frederick II continued to hold his own in Silesia and in Saxony. After confused fighting all over western, central, and southern Europe, at the end of 1745 a treaty signed at Dresden between the Austrians and Prussians again confirmed Frederick in his conquest of Silesia.

By the Treaty of Aix-la-Chapelle, finally concluded in October 1748, Maria Theresa retained the whole of her inheritance except for Silesia, and Parma and Piacenza, which were surrendered to Elizabeth Farnese's second son, Don Philip. The acquisition of Silesia almost doubled Prussian territory and population, and it might claim to have become a Great Power. Neither France nor Great Britain gained much from the war, and its cost was resented in most countries.

9. The Limits of Enlightened Despotism

It has sometimes been argued that it was only in "great monarchies" that administrative, social, and judicial progress was possible in eighteenth-century Europe. "An intelligent and determined ruler," it has been said, "would be able to overcome tradition, disregard the past, and use his authority to introduce necessary changes in many aspects of people's lives." Peter the Great of Russia has been instanced as such a monarch, but it is dubious whether he should be called enlightened. Moreover, in practice enlightenment is most easily detected in small states—such as Baden and Tuscany—rather than in "great monarchies."

Nevertheless, certain characteristics of eighteenth-century government—that is to say, the government of the ancien régime—may be said to have been common. First came the strengthening of government at the center through an increase of bureaucracy and administrative specialization. It did not much matter whether central government was run by ministers with clearly defined functions or by boards, often called "colleges." These enabled absolute monarchs to take rapid decisions; a proliferation of councils, often with overlapping functions as in Habsburg Spain, was not conducive to efficiency. Secondly, a clear administrative relationship between the central government and the provinces was essential for effective rule, especially in the days when transport and communication were slow. It did not matter much whether (as with central governments) the provincial power was concentrated in the hands of intendants (France and Spain) or in the hands of provincial boards (such as the Prussian *Kreise*). To help proficient government there seems to have been in most countries a slackening off in the sale of offices, which was so characteristic of the seventeenth century, though this point has not yet been clearly established. Moreover, good administration was often weakened by the fact that bureaucratic servants of the monarchies were insufficiently paid; and it was significant that enlightened monarchs found financial and judicial reforms the most difficult. For the law courts and fiscal bodies (for example, the tax farmers) had long been riddled by bribery and corruption which was so deep-rooted that it was hard to abolish quickly.

Where reform was most easily possible was in the regulation of trade. As has been pointed out already, the abolition of internal customs barriers (except in France) went ahead pretty rapidly. Foreign trade was also liberalized and commercial treaties frequently negotiated. The case for leaving merchants to their own devices was more generally recognized; the importance of simplifying customs and excise duties was accepted; and (except in Portugal) the idea of establishing State industries on the lines which Colbert had attempted was disapproved. But the liberalization of trade was not an expensive process. Educational and legal reforms tended to be so. Absolute rulers were inclined to pay lip service to the value of increasing education in schools, but many of their schemes remained on paper. Frederick the Great, who is sometimes regarded as outstandingly enlightened, was half-hearted about universal education, and once observed about the education of young children that "in country parts it is enough if they learn a little reading and writing, but if they learn too much, they will be running to the towns and want to become clerks and so forth." In most countries the people themselves were not enthusiastic about the idea of universal education, and invariably there were not enough trained teachers to go round.

One difficulty about the promotion of education was that much of it had long been in the hands of the Church. The Society of Jesus had taken a prominent part in it; with its suppression a huge gap was left to be filled, even in largely Protestant states like Bohemia. Furthermore, it was still being argued that education must primarily have "a moral purpose." It is notable that in England stimulus to school education came from Evangelical Christians and Wesleyans. Even Pestalozzi *(1746-1827)*, the famous Swiss educationist, experimented when he was teaching the very poor with subordinating reading and writing to the inculcation of morality. If educational progress went on slowly in schools (except perhaps in Austria) after the suppression of the Jesuits, universities were beginning to become modernized. King George I of England established regius professorships in modern history at Oxford and Cambridge, and during the eighteenth century twenty chairs in scientific and mathematical subjects were set up in these universities. By the end of the century both English universities had introduced written examinations, and degrees became more meaningful. The reputations of Scottish and Dutch universities remained high. Throughout Germany and Austria the study of subjects like jurisprudence was introduced; the classics no longer exerted a dead hand on high education.

Some modern historians (such as Lefebvre) have gone so far as to reject the whole concept of "enlightened despotism" in the eighteenth century. It has been demonstrated how difficult it is to define or apply such an idea. Were King Frederick William I of Prussia and the Emperor Napoleon I enlightened despots? Could not as much be said for Solomon or Marcus

Aurelius? The Marxist view of enlightened despotism is that it was "the effort of moribund feudal absolutism to keep alive by exploiting bourgeois doctrines and achievements and thus to retain the control exercised by the feudal class." It is interesting that the French Physiocrats are believed to have been the first to employ the phrase; and the Physiocrats were essentially advocates of laissez-faire, not of government intervention in the running of society. It can be argued—and has been argued—that such efforts at enlightened government as were practiced in the eighteenth century merely marked the waning phase of absolutism and that it was in fact the French Revolution that stimulated new and radical reforms.

Again, other historians, such as M. S. Anderson, take a somewhat middle line. He has recently urged that although administrative progress took place during the century as well as the gradual liberalization of economic policies, "enlightened despotism" was "always largely superficial and contrived." Much that was done was simply following in father's footsteps: administrative progress was begun in France under Richelieu and was continued by Louis XIV; Frederick William I set the pattern for his son in Prussia. In fact, one may conclude that the monarchs in the larger European states were neither enlightened nor despotic nor even novel in their methods of government, though they liked to convey the opposite impression. For example, both Frederick II and Catherine II claimed to have been guided by the instruction of the French *philosophes,* but their appeal to them (in Anderson's words) was "essentially spurious." Consideration will now be given to what the *philosophes* actually taught and what they really achieved.

10.   The Teaching of the *Philosophes*

Who were the *philosophes?* It has been denied that they were really philosophers. In a recent book about them they are in fact called "anti-philosophers." They certainly did not constitute a school of philosophy, and they preached few or no common doctrines. Nevertheless, four things can be said about them. The first is that in general they were popularizers of philosophers' ideas. The second is that they were sceptics: they did not accept the teaching of the Roman Catholic Church; they were usually deists—that is to say, they believed in the existence of a God, but not the God revealed by the Bible: their God was remote, a creator who had established the universe but did not interfere with it. Thirdly, they were empiricists, not metaphysicians. Empiricism is the doctrine that all knowledge is derived from experience; metaphysics involves building up a logical structure on the basis of a few simple assumptions as Descartes, Spinoza, and Leibniz did. Lastly, the *philosophes* advocated specific liberal ideas, such as the reform of the criminal law, which could be put into practice by enlightened absolute monarchs. Voltaire hoped to influence Frederick the Great, Diderot to convert Catherine the Great by giving her his advice.

The first example of popularization of scientific ideas tending to undermine faith was *Les Entretiens sur la pluralité des mondes* published by the Abbé Fontenelle in 1686. These took the form of conversations with a young lady about the nature of the universe. Fontenelle hinted that there were other inhabited worlds beside their own which might not be aware of Roman Catholicism or even Christianity. God had created a mechanical world which He wound up and set into motion. After that He left it alone.

Pierre Bayle was another Frenchman who contributed to the literature of dissension and doubt through a dictionary which he compiled in Holland. In his *Dictionnaire historique et critique,* which he wrote in Rotterdam between 1690 and 1697, he used a vast armory of learning to undermine much of the Bible both on historical and ethical grounds. He was particularly severe on miracles and saints. This dictionary, in which many of Bayle's most telling arguments were expounded in enormously long footnotes, was nevertheless one of the most influential books in eighteenth-century Europe. By 1750 it had gone through many editions in France (as had Fontenelle's book also), England, and Germany, as well as numerous abridgements. Embodied in it were pleas for complete religious toleration and the impartial writing of history. Bayle asked a number of questions which remained unanswered. Can the existence of God be proved? If so, has He endowed men with free will or not? Why does He permit the existence of injustice and evil in the world? Though Bayle did not expound a philosophy of history, he exposed the limitations of historical knowledge and threw doubt on many traditional stories.

Both Fontenelle and Bayle were popularizers, the first of science, the second of history. Voltaire *(1694-1778)* too was a first-class popularizer as well as a universal genius whose enormous output of essays, plays, poetry, novels, articles, and letters swept right across Europe. Though educated at a Jesuit school, Voltaire (his real name was François Marie Arouet and he was the illegitimate son of a songwriter and of the wife of a debt collector) soon absorbed the sceptical outlook of Montaigne and Bayle. Before he was thirty he won a reputation in Paris as a poet and playwright. But after quarreling with a member of the French nobility, he was assaulted and beaten up by the nobleman's servants and subsequently thrown into the Bastille, the State prison in Paris. This decided him to visit England, where he stayed for two years *(1726-28);* here he admired "the philosophic modesty" of Bacon, Newton, and Locke, and was "impressed by a humane, tolerant, open society where the arts were honoured and rewarded." He recounted his experiences—or rather the conclusions he drew from them—in his *Lettres philosophiques,* which was first published in England and afterward secretly in France, where it was publicly burned as subversive. Voltaire became the energetic propagandist of British empiricism and the enemy of rationalism

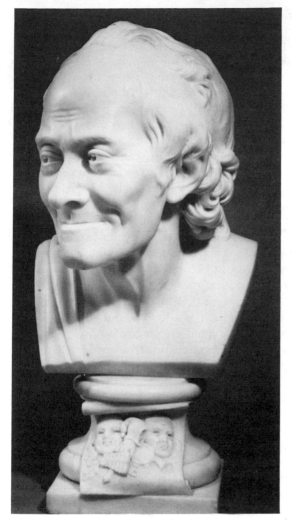

Bust of Voltaire
JEAN ANTOINE HOUDON
M.H. de Young Memorial
Museum, San Francisco. Gift
of Mrs. E. John Magnin.

and system building. He claimed that metaphysics is for philosophy what novels are for women. He stood for religious toleration, the rule of law, and freedom of opinion. In this he defied the Government of his country. Consequently, all the best books that he wrote up to 1748 were published secretly: for censors existed in France who were required to testify that books contained nothing contrary to religion, public order, or sound morality. It was not until he was sixty and had settled in a safe refuge at Ferney, near the border of Switzerland, that Voltaire launched his famous attack on Christianity: *"Écrasez l'infame!"* ("Wipe out the infamous thing!"). He equated the Roman Catholic religion with superstition, and thought superstition the cause of fanaticism which led to cruelty and injustice. Neither as a philosopher nor as a political thinker was Voltaire consistent. But he was always the enemy of intolerance and a lover of justice.

When Voltaire lived in England he imbibed the ideas of John Locke and Isaac Newton. The discoveries that they made penetrated Europe only slowly. Newton's *Principia,* being abstruse—though it had refuted Descartes's view of the universe by analytical methods—did not make its mark until forty years after its publication when Voltaire produced his *Elements de la philosophie de Newton.* But Locke's sensational psychology (that is, related to the senses) was easier to understand. He maintained that the mind was a blank sheet on which experience could write. He taught in his *Essay Concerning Human Understanding* that there are two fountains of knowledge "from whence all the ideas we have, or can naturally have, do spring. First . . . sensation, . . . secondly . . . reflection." Locke's sensational psychology led to the view that the opinions of mankind can be governed by education and by good laws. Progress could therefore be attained by enlightening opinion; if the rulers of nations were persuaded of the need for the reform of institutions, the world would become a better place. The *philosophes* rejected the view of Leibniz that this was the best of all possible worlds (a view ridiculed by Voltaire in his novel *Candide*) and accepted the idea of progress. Thus, the *philosophes* aimed to wipe out superstition, to show mankind as it really was, and to extend the range of knowledge. They published a great many books on subjects stretching from geology to esthetics, mostly with the overt approval of the French censorship; but the principal instrument of their teaching was the *Encyclopédie,* the first volume of which appeared in 1751 and aroused criticism.

The original idea of the *Encyclopédie* was a very modest one: the intention was to produce a translation into French of the two volumes of Ephraim Chambers's *Cyclopaedia or Universal Dictionary of the Arts and Sciences.* But in the hands of the two editors it blossomed into a far more elaborate scheme: it took fifteen years to complete and consisted of seventeen volumes of text and eleven volumes of plates. The original editors were Denise Diderot, born in Langres in 1713, the son of a master cutler, and Jean Le Rond D'Alembert, the illegitimate son of an artillery officer and a nun, who proved to be a genius at mathematics and physics. Both of them were at one time intended for the Church: Diderot was educated by Jesuits and D'Alembert by Jansenists; both were self-made men; and both welcomed the regular pay promised by the publishers of the *Encyclopédie.* D'Alembert gave up his editorship after a tactless article which he wrote about Geneva caused offense; Diderot stuck it out to the end.

The *Encyclopédie,* which was published as "an analytical dictionary of the sciences, arts and crafts," dealt in alphabetical order with a vast variety of subjects. It concentrated particularly on science and technology; according to Voltaire, Louis XV sent for it when he wanted to find out how gunpowder was made and when his mistress, Madame de Pompadour, wanted to know

Portrait of Denis Diderot
JEAN HONORÉ FRAGONARD
Louvre

about the manufacture of rouge. It also contained a good deal about literature, philosophy, political theory, and religion, but little history or biography. The Middle Ages were studiously ignored: this was a book for an Age
of Enlightenment, and was not concerned with a priest-ridden past.

On the face of it the *Encyclopédie* seemed harmless enough. Why, then,
did the Jesuits try to suppress it or even take it over? The answer is that a
good deal of subversive material was elaborately wrapped up in it. Under
obscure headings attacks were made on religious fundamentalism. Authors
writing about religion kept their tongues in their cheeks. In an article on
"autorité politique" in the first volume, Diderot wrote that "no one man
has received from nature the right of commanding others." All the weapons
of irony, scepticism, and rationalism were employed to destroy superstition
and to stimulate thought.

The critics of the *Encyclopédie* were not deceived by its subtleties of
presentation, its carefully worded articles, or its ingenious cross references.
After an abbé named de Prades, who had managed to get a heretical thesis
questioning the chronology of the Bible and the reality of miracles past the
Sorbonne and happened to have contributed an article on "certitude" to the
Encyclopédie, was exposed, a public row developed, and the first two volumes were suppressed. However, the Encyclopedists had friends at Court,
and the director of publications or chief censor, a young member of the
noblesse de la robe named Chrétien de Malherbes who was to perish in the
French Revolution, held liberal views: even when he felt he could not give

books his positive approval, he frequently conferred upon them his tacit consent. Far from the suppression of the first two volumes of the *Encyclopédie* damaging its reputation, it went from strength to strength. Its subscription list lengthened, and authors like Buffon the famous biologist, Rousseau (with whom Diderot later quarreled), and Voltaire contributed to it, although Voltaire once wrote that it was "built half of marble and half of mud" and later, from the safety of Ferney, was to compile his own *Dictionnaire philosophique,* which was also widely condemned.

With all its shortcomings the *Encyclopédie* was a magnificent and revolutionary achievement. It taught that reason does not consist in the possession of innate or transcendant ideas, but in a force of mind which compels the discovery of truth. It was at once dynamic and progressive in its outlook. Diderot, it has been said, aimed to make philosophy and science useful. He was consistently iconoclastic, but he believed in the immutable morality of man. In his preface to the third volume, D'Alembert explained that it was "principally by the philosophic spirit that we seek to distinguish the dictionary" and that that was why the lives of saints and the genealogy of rulers were omitted. Articles in it urged social and economic improvement, and its contributors included Quesnay, the leader of the Physiocrats, who advocated a laissez-faire economy and a single tax on land, and Turgot, another Physiocrat, who was the ablest Finance Minister of Louis XVI. In his foreword to the last volume Diderot wrote:

> We shall have obtained the recompense we expected from our contemporaries if we cause them to say, some day, that we have not lived altogether in vain.

The *philosophes* held no generally agreed views about political theory or social science. A recent writer has stated flatly that they "contributed little to political thought, certainly nothing new or original," but he goes on to add that they were attracted by the ideas of "academic Whiggery" derived from Locke and Montesquieu.

Voltaire had helped to convey the ideas of Locke on politics to the French reading public. His *Lettres philosophiques* contained by implication praise for an open middle-class society ruling through the British House of Commons and condemnation for the caste-ridden aristocracy of France. He saw a "happy balance" in the government of Great Britain. But this was a young man's book reflecting his immediate enthusiasms. Later in life Voltaire was to become a strong upholder of the French absolute monarchy against the nobility, *parlements,* and clergy. Montesquieu, whose *Lettres persanes (1721),* a satirical work critical of French politics and administration, was the only book of social criticism to appear before the *Lettres philosophiques,* aimed in his *Esprit des lois (1748)* to produce a treatise on political science. His book was an investigation into social behavior, but was also an exposition of social morality. He hated despotism and thought that constitutional government depends on balancing the powers of the executive, the legislature, and the judiciary. Like Voltaire, he praised English liberty.

The social sciences began to establish themselves in the eighteenth century, especially political economy. In France there were the Physiocrats, in Germany Cameralists, in Spain neomercantilists, and in Great Britain the laissez-faire teaching of Adam Smith, whose famous work, *The Wealth of Nations,* was published in 1776. In Italy two men of genius appeared: Giambattista Vico *(1668-1744)* and Cesare Beccaria *(1735-94).* Vico offered a philosophy of history in advance of his age, Beccaria advocated law reform; Vico worked in Naples and Beccaria in Milan. It has been suggested that the removal of these two states from the government of Spain gave a stimulus to independent thought.

Neither the mechanistic teaching of Descartes nor the sensational psychology of Locke had the same impact on Germany as it had on the French *philosophes.* Thus, the German *Aufklärung* ("Enlightenment") took a different course. Mostly, German thinkers such as Christian von Wolff *(1679-1754)* followed the teachings of Leibniz. They believed that it is the energies of the mind or the faculties of the soul, such as feeling, understanding, and approval, which shape the universe. The mind is a living mirror of the universe, a whole composed of many formative forces. The task of the philosopher is to explain the nature of these forces. Wolff attempted to reduce all knowledge to a system known as vitalism, in which nature is permeated by a life-force.

This concept of nature was compatible with deism. One of the most effective German apologists for deism was Lessing *(1729-81),* who was influenced by the writings of both Spinoza and Leibniz. Like Spinoza, he rejected the reality of biblical miracles, but like Leibniz, he considered that the miracles of reason are evidence for the existence of God. Religious truth, he thought, becomes manifest in history; there are thus both empirical and subjective proofs of the existence of God. Like Leibniz, Lessing believed that the mind is "an image of divinity, a representation of the universe."

While the *philosophes* and European thinkers in general believed that the lot of mankind could be improved by wiser laws, the destruction of superstition, and the application of scientific knowledge, Jean-Jacques Rousseau, who was born in Geneva in 1712, maintained in a prize essay which he wrote in 1750 that the arts and sciences are enemies of true morality. In his *Discourse on Inequality,* which was published four years later, he urged that man is naturally good and that inequality is caused by privileges authorized by convention. Thus, the "noble savage" is the happiest man. Education should therefore be based on "natural principles," and "natural religion" on individual emotions. Education should aim at training a natural man who could discover everything for himself and be confident in his power to use natural forces. Girls should be educated to serve the natural man. Rousseau's most famous book, which appeared at about the same time that he expounded his educational theories in *Émile* and the *La Nouvelle Héloïse,* was *Le Contrat social,* which attacked despotism and advocated self-government. Although Rousseau thought that "true democracy" could only be practiced in a small city-state, he believed that good government could be achieved through enlightened public opinion. He wanted social conventions and social morality to be cast aside and all men made free and equal before the law. But Rousseau was more of a poet than a philosopher, and his political theories, which appeared at first to be clear-cut, were in fact capable of many interpretations. The great importance of Rousseau was that just as Pascal had reacted against Descartes's mechanistic world, so Rousseau rejected the realism of the *philosophes* and paved the way to the romantic spirit which inspired nationalist revolutionary ardor.

11. The Scepticism of the Philosophers

It has been noted how while self-educated men like Diderot and Rousseau drew on the teaching of philosophers, particularly Descartes and Locke, they were not philosophers themselves. But the eighteenth century produced a number of great philosophers. Locke, who died in 1704, was extraordinarily influential. His empiricism, his sensational psychology, and his utilitarianism—the doctrine that actions are right because they are useful—gave him a variety of disciples. Pierre Coste, a French philosopher who was forced into exile as a victim of the revocation of the Edict of Nantes, translated Locke's *Essay Concerning Human Understanding* into French in 1700, through which it became known in the United Netherlands, Italy, and Germany as well as in France. George Berkeley *(1685-1753),* an Irish Bishop, pushing Locke's theories to a logical conclusion, reached the astounding view that there is no such thing as matter. Human existence, he thought, derives from the mind of God, who perceives everything. Berkeley's teaching was to have a profound effect on nineteenth-century idealists; but immediately it caused philosophers of the eighteenth century to stress the relative quality of truth.

In David Hume the scepticism of Locke and Berkeley about mind and matter reached a point of no return. If Berkeley believed there is no such thing as matter, Hume maintained that there is no such thing as a general idea. He also argued that the mind cannot grasp causal relationships: there is nothing in cause except invariable succession. He concluded that

> in all the incidents of life we ought still to preserve our scepticism.
> If we believe that fire warms or water refreshes, 'tis only because
> it costs us too much pains to think otherwise.

Thus, there can be no rational beliefs.

If eighteenth-century thinkers for the most part never reached the ultimate scepticism of Hume, it was because they were optimistic in their belief that the discoveries of science and the destruction of blind religious creeds would lead to an improvement of mankind. They gradually abandoned the doctrine of innate ideas taught by Descartes, and agreed with Locke that the mind is a white sheet upon which experience could write. They rejected metaphysics and assaulted superstition. They severed the bond between theology and natural science. To the astronomical discoveries of the previous century, which showed that the earth is one of many worlds and not the center of the universe, they added scientific researches into the stories of the Bible, which exposed improbabilities. On the other hand, they accepted from the reasoning of Descartes and Newton the idea that a Supreme Being exists; for a clockwork universe implied a clockmaker and the laws of science a lawmaker. Both Voltaire and Rousseau were deists. And in most cases deism was linked with "natural religion": religion shorn of its anthropomorphic and irrational elements. However, not all the leading eighteenth-century thinkers were deists. Hume thought that natural religion is a sick man's dream and the universe an inexplicable mystery; the Baron D'Holbach, a wealthy German who settled in Paris in the 1740s, was a convinced atheist who believed that if men allow themselves to be guided by superstition and idols they will be prevented from creating a better world on earth: the application of scientific principles must not be frustrated by the supernatural. Julien La Mettrie, a French surgeon who became a member of the Berlin Academy, published in 1748 a book entitled *Man a Machine,* in which he urged that a man's mental state depends on his bodily condition, and that morality cannot be based on the assumption that there is a supreme being: "What folly then it is to torment oneself so much in searching after what is impossible to know."

The Germans were less sceptical and more idealistic than the majority of the French and English philosophers. In Herder and his master, Immanuel Kant, one sees a break with the prevalent outlook of the eighteenth century. Sir Isaiah Berlin considers that Herder was the most formidable of the adversaries of the French *philosophes.* Unlike them, Herder attached major importance to the lessons of history. He had faith in the value of belonging to a group or culture. He became one of the leaders of the romantic revolt against classicism, rationalism, and belief in the omnipotence of scientific method. Although he began as a humanitarian, cosmopolitan, and pacifist, he evolved toward more reactionary views of nationalism. He thought that the German mission was to become a nation of thinkers and educationists. He glorified folk poetry and the folk spirit. Above all, he was convinced that language expresses the collective experience of a group. He therefore appealed to the German people to know themselves. With Fichte, Gentz, and Hegel he inspired the German nationalism of the nineteenth century. Thus, in the French *philosophes* with their religious scepticism and their belief in equality and in the German idealists with their stress on deism and nationalism one detects a bifurcation of culture in eighteenth-century Europe.

Kant *(1724-1804)* tried to reconcile the philosophical methods of the Cartesians (that is to say, logical deductions from a few simple assumptions) with the empirical methods of the British school (observations based on experiments). He taught that the right use of reason is to achieve moral ends. Thus, like Rousseau, Kant believed in democracy and the rights of man. He also taught that moral worth exists only when a man acts from a sense of duty which is compelled by his own will: this Kant called "the categorical imperative." Kant was an idealist and, like Herder, he condemned war completely. But although his outlook was liberal and democratic, his philosophy, with its emphasis on the importance of the will, was developed in many different ways by his successors: in Hegel it emerged as state absolutism and in Schopenhauer as nihilism. Thus, the romantic revolt initiated by Rousseau and refined by Kant had many strange consequences for the history of European thought. It contributed to the idea of the absolute State, whether Marxist or Fascist.

12. Philosophy and Religion

How great was the influence of European thought on the development of political history? It is clear that the writings of men like Herder and Fichte contributed to the evolution of German nationalism. But did the writings of the French *philosophes* and the *Encyclopédie* in particular play an important part in the coming of the French Revolution? It used to be thought that the *Encyclopédie* was a subtle weapon that helped to destroy the ancien régime, but this view is no longer generally accepted. In the first place it may be said that it is difficult to conceive of the *philosophes* as a group of conspirators, or as a party, or even as "the intellectual spearhead of the bourgeoisie." These authors came from different levels of society, ranging from aristocrats to self-made men. They held many different views about political organization. Even on the subject of religion the most influential writers were neither consistent nor united: some preached atheism, some deism, while Voltaire, despite his vicious attacks on superstition, thought that a popular religion was necessary so that statesmen might keep their peoples in order. "If God did not exist," he wrote, "it would be necessary to invent Him." Rousseau advocated the introduction of a civil religion and banishment for those who did not accept it.

If there were differences over religion, there were even more pronounced differences over politics. Montesquieu, as has been observed, genuinely hated absolutism and believed in the virtue of constitutional government based on a balance of powers. Voltaire, after he had been employed by Frederick II of Prussia, became disillusioned with his master: he wrote to

D'Alembert in 1752 that at the Prussian Court "there are a prodigious number of bayonets and very few books. The King has greatly embellished Sparta, but he has transported Athens only to his study." Condillac and Helvétius put their faith in a privileged oligarchy like Plato's Guardians. Even outside the circle of the *philosophes* European political thinkers were not yet advocating democracy. Locke, who had many followers, was not committed to any particular form of government, holding only that it must be based on consent, that its duties should be minimal, and that its main objective must be to protect private property by a rule of law. This political philosophy has been described as that of a possessive class. Kant, like Voltaire, hoped that the Government of Prussia might be liberalized, while Fichte and Hegel, who were both professors in Berlin, were satisfied with it as it was. Only Rousseau, although he rejected true democracy as an impracticability, condemned "enlightened despotism" and thought that absolute government of any kind turned the State into a conscript army.

"The reformism of the Philosophes," wrote R. J. White,

> might lead one to imagine that the Revolution was the harvest of what they had sown. It was in fact rather an arrest upon it, for reformism is often the enemy of revolution.

By the time the Revolution took place nearly all the *philosophes* were dead, and the moderate reforms which they had advocated were swept aside by more far-reaching ideas. Though the French Attorney General Seguier declared in 1770 that "the philosophers have shaken the throne and upset the altars through changing public opinion," it is doubtful if the new ideas penetrated as far as one Frenchman in five. The mass of the people were more concerned over their long-endured economic grievances. But, on the other hand, it may reasonably be argued that the *philosophes* did have one thing in common: the spirit of scepticism about existing institutions and in particular about the Roman Church. The destruction of the Society of Jesus, whose members had exerted a powerful hold over European education and earlier on specific monarchs, was due at least in part to the doubts about established religion spread not merely by the *philosophes* but by deists and rationalists and by philosophers like David Hume. Thus, traditional faith was undermined at any rate among many who belonged to the educated classes. Scepticism about traditional faith could easily be extended to scepticism about the value of absolute monarchies which, if they were not divinely inspired, had little obvious raison d'être. The enlightenment of the European rulers was, as has already been argued, largely a myth, a pretense at reforming society which was intended as much as an opiate for the masses as State religion. But the European peoples could not be hoodwinked indefinitely. The peasants of western Europe increasingly resented the remnants of feudalism and the privileges of the big landowners: in eastern Europe the serfs grew more and more restless. Also, a spirit of ardent nationalism was aroused by the German idealists. The most that can be said for the *philosophes* specifically is that they contributed to the stream of liberal thought such ideas as the need for the abolition of torture and slavery and the value of the codification of the laws. At the turn of the century the largely negative and sceptical attitude of the *philosophes* gave way to the positive if less reasonable approach of the romantic movement, begun by Rousseau, developed by the German idealists, and inspired by a new school of English poets.

SIX

*Roads
to Revolution*

1. Intertwining Wars (*1738-1748*)

In the mid-eighteenth century two great conflicts intertwined. One was that between Great Britain and France for dominance in the New World; the other was the dynastic struggle between Frederick II and Maria Theresa for supremacy in Germany. Before Maria Theresa took over her father's throne in Vienna or Frederick invaded Silesia, Great Britain had become involved in a naval war with Spain. Since the conclusion of the Treaty of Utrecht British commerce had forged ahead. It has been estimated that between 1714 and 1750 the value of British exports doubled; and as its imports had not increased proportionately, it enjoyed a favorable balance of payments. At the same time shipping had expanded, and thus there were also invisible exports. No precise figure of the favorable balance can be reached because the volume of smuggling both in and out of the kingdom was considerable. But undoubtedly the commercial revolution which had begun in the second half of the seventeenth century had continued and probably accelerated. To this the monopoly of the export of slaves from Africa to Spanish America, which was known as the *asiento,* conferred on the British by the Treaty of Utrecht, also contributed.

It was British commercial interests that compelled the Government to go to war with Spain in October 1739. A series of grievances had provoked them into doing so. Profitable smuggling had been interfered with by *guarda-costas* licensed by Spanish colonial governors. British ships and cargoes were seized, confiscated, or pillaged. It was in fact a war between Spanish pirates and British smugglers which the two governments were unable to stop. The "despairing British merchants" and the British West Indian planters were powerful in the House of Commons and insisted upon war. One reason why Walpole had been reluctant to go to war was that he believed that owing to the existence of a "family compact" between the Spanish and French Bourbons a war with Spain would sooner or later mean a war with France as well. In the twenty-five years of peace which followed the Treaty of Utrecht the efficiency of the British navy had declined, and the total number of warships was less than that of the combined Spanish and French fleets, while the army was small and had deteriorated. Though Admiral Vernon captured Porto Bello on the Isthmus of Panama in November 1739, subsequent attempts upon Cartagena in South America and Santiago in Cuba were dismal failures, while the home fleet suffered from the fact that it was under the command of an admiral eighty years old.

In March 1744 the event that Walpole feared came about; the British navy then had not only to fight the Spaniards but also to protect the British West Indies against the French, to support the British settlements in North America, and to succour the East India Company in India. Although, owing to the enterprise of the Governor of Massachusetts, the fort of Louisburg, which guarded the entrance to the Saint Lawrence river, was seized from the French in 1745, in the following year the French admiral La Bourdonnais captured the port of Madras while Joseph Dupleix, the able French Governor of Pondicherry, successfully withstood a British siege. When the Peace of Aix-la-Chapelle was signed in 1748, Madras was restored to the British East India Company and Louisburg was given back to the French, but the objects for which the British had originally gone to war with Spain were not realized. Although the *asiento* was continued for another four years, the advantages which British merchants had possessed in the Spanish overseas empire virtually came to an end. Only Frederick the Great (who retained Silesia) and King Charles Emmanuel III, ruler of Savoy, Piedmont, and Sardinia, who had been bribed by the British to aid Austria against France, gained much from the war out of the many countries sucked into it. The idealist view that Frederick aimed at the unification of Germany and Charles Emmanuel at the unification of Italy is no longer accepted. But the opinion that the European war which began in 1740 was but a part of a more than a hundred years' war between Great Britain and France is more plausible. It can be dimly discerned amid the fog of dynastic struggles and was to culminate in the foundation of the British Empire and the break-up of the Bourbon ancien régime in the French Revolution.

2. The Diplomatic Revolution and the Seven Years' War (*1756–1763*)

The tangle of diplomatic negotiations which was to be seen in Europe in the years before Frederick the Great again attacked Maria Theresa in 1756 is called the Diplomatic Revolution. The author is often conceived to have been Kaunitz, who pressed on Maria Theresa in an elaborate state paper the argument that if she wanted to regain Silesia she must seek an alliance with France. But although the Queen sent Kaunitz to Paris as her ambassador in order to test the ground there, it was the British Government headed by the

Duke of Newcastle, who succeeded his brother Henry Pelham as First Lord of the Treasury in March 1754, which set the ball rolling.

After long wars allies generally fall out. Maria Theresa had little reason to be grateful to the British, who constantly pressed her to come to terms with Prussia in order that the combined forces of Germany should resist the French, while the French felt that Frederick had let them down by twice opting out of the war when it suited him to do so. Consequently, Austria was ready to search for fresh allies in a renewed contest with Frederick, as Kaunitz had suggested, and Frederick's nightmare was a combined onslaught by the Austrians, Russians, and French against him.

Great Britain's interests at this time were to safeguard the neutrality of Hanover and to occupy the French as much as possible in Europe while extending its own overseas possessions. Even under Louix XV the French were still a Great Power in the world, and by 1757 were engaged in a war with the British in North America, India, West Africa, the West Indies, and the Mediterranean.

At first Newcastle toyed with the idea of hiring an army of Hanoverians, Austrians, Saxons, and Poles to defend Hanover, Saxony, and the German possessions of Maria Theresa. But opposition developed in the British Parliament to so grandiose a subsidy policy, and Newcastle then turned to Russia with an offer to pay out subsidies if the Tsarina Elizabeth would keep an army near the frontier of East Prussia ready to intervene if Hanover were attacked. This treaty was concluded in July 1755. A Russian army, however, could not reach Hanover without trespassing on Prussian territory. Frederick II was alarmed. He was aware that now that the Swedish war was over the Russians contemplated a western advance; so he feared a triple assault by Russians, Austrians, and Saxons supported by British and Russian fleets in the Baltic. He therefore welcomed an approach from the British for a defensive treaty. This has been described as "a mere *ad hoc* agreement to preserve the neutrality of Germany." The two parties promised not to attack one another's territories and to do their best to prevent their allies undertaking hostile action. They also agreed jointly to resist the entry into Germany of the troops of any foreign power. Frederick did not regard this treaty, which was signed at Westminster on January 1, 1756, as being incompatible with his alliance with France, although Newcastle thought of it as a step toward including Prussia in the British sphere of influence.

The French retorted by reaching similar terms with Austria in a treaty signed at Versailles on May 1. The French aimed to isolate Great Britain in Europe, while the Austrians hoped for a military alliance against Prussia. But neither the Treaty of Westminster nor the Treaty of Versailles had openly offensive aims. Yet, as has often happened in the history of Europe, the mere existence of two power blocs created a dangerous situation. Again it was Frederick who lit the flame by leading his army into Saxony in August 1756—whether out of recklessness or to wage a preventive war is still debated. At any rate, in consequence of their treaty obligations Great Britain and France were once again at war.

When the news arrived in London that the French had taken Minorca, the Duke of Newcastle was attacked for the failure of his foreign policy. Though King George II was reluctant to do so, William Pitt, one of the most outspoken critics of the Government, was called to office in November as Secretary of State for the Southern Department and was soon taking measures that helped to build the first British Empire.

Although Pitt once declared that "America had been conquered in Germany," British intervention in the European war was regarded by him simply as a containing operation. The French coasts might be assaulted, a British-subsidized army sent to fight in northern Germany, and Frederick II sustained by British money, but it was through command of the seas, the dispatch of reinforcements to Canada and India, and the genius of men like James Wolfe and Rober Clive that the first British Empire was won.

In Europe Frederick II managed to hold his own against the Austrians, Russians, and French. He was attacked on two fronts. While he fought the Austrians in Saxony and Bohemia, the Russians came into the war against him and overran East Prussia. Yet in spite of his inferiority in numbers he had several advantages. He enjoyed unity of command and the possession of inner lines. Thus, through the use of mobility he managed to prevent his enemies from joining one another or concerting plans of campaign. Nor did they ever discover a general equal to Frederick. In battle he invented an oblique order of attack which enabled him to employ either offensive or defensive tactics. If the assault by his forward wing was successful, his other wing could be used to reinforce it. If it was not successful, then the wing held in reserve could cover a retreat.

In the summer of 1757 Frederick entered Bohemia and laid siege to Prague. But the Austrians raised the siege and the Prussians were driven out of Bohemia. Meanwhile, the Russians were entering East Prussia and a British-Hanoverian force capitulated to the French west of the Elbe. However, toward the end of the year Frederick struck back and defeated the French at Rossbach in Saxony and the Austrians at Leuthen in Silesia.

By 1760 both sides were growing exhausted. Maria Theresa, virtually deserted by the French, tried to encourage the Russians, promising them that they should retain East Prussia if she regained Silesia. Although the Austrians were again defeated, the Russians occupied Berlin. In 1761 stalemate continued. Neither the Russians nor the Austrians were in a hurry to try another battle, and Frederick was able to spend much of his time reading history and literature. But in October William Pitt resigned from the British Cabinet, and Frederick was left practically without an ally. He decided he must seek peace, but as he was hopelessly outnumbered, he did not see how to attain it. "The more I reflect on events," he wrote to his brother, "the more I conclude how right the Romans were to consecrate a golden statue to Fortune."

In the very next month Fortune smiled upon him. His inveterate enemy, the Tsarina Elizabeth, died and was succeeded by her nephew Peter III, who had a passionate admiration for Frederick, whose bust he kissed and before whose portrait he knelt. Not only did Peter withdraw the Russian troops from Prussia, but in June 1762 he entered into an offensive alliance with the King, promising to regain Silesia for him. Maria Theresa, also deserted by all her allies and appalled by the ravages of war, gave in. The Treaty of Hubertusburg between Prussia, Austria, and Saxony restored the position as it was before the war began. Maria Theresa finally lost Silesia and Frederick II did not gain Saxony. Thus, another futile European war came to an end.

3.   Europe and America

In Europe the importance of the War of the Austrian Succession and of the Seven Years' War was that Prussia doubled the size of its population and became a Great Power, the future nucleus of a united Germany. But outside Europe French involvement in these wars gave an opportunity to the British to build up an empire at the expense of France and other European nations.

By the 1750s, although Spain still managed to maintain its hold on Central and South America, Cuba, and other West Indian islands, the Dutch Empire was in decline, mainly because its East India Company was unable to establish a genuine Dutch colony in Asia. The climate of places like Java, Ceylon, and Formosa was hardly conducive to European settlement, and Dutch women were unwilling to go there. The Dutch colonists were encouraged to intermarry with native women, but the higher-class native women were forbidden by their religion to do so. Thus, when the Dutch settlers married it was usually with Eurasians or lower-class natives. "Batavia," writes Professor Boxer, "thus presented the curious spectacle of a Dutch Calvinist male society welded uneasily with a largely Indo-Portuguese female society." So the New Netherlands in the tropics was alienated from the homeland. In any case, the Dutch Republic itself was becoming stagnant; its population declined; and it grew less warlike. The fact that the New Netherlands in North America never had a population of more than a few thousand, although the climate was suitable for Europeans, suggests that the Dutch in those days were not successful colonists. Their Empire was one of trade rather than settlement, and the Dutch capitalist was satisfied if his prosperity lasted his own lifetime. Thus, the main struggle outside Europe was between Great Britain and France.

During the middle of the eighteenth century, it has been pointed out, the British and French faced each other in four different parts of the world and fought for the control of four different commodities: Negroes, sugar, tobacco, and indigo. The colonial trade of both countries increased and enhanced the activity of their Atlantic ports. The French exercised close control over their colonies, while the British were more concerned with treating them as monopolistic business ventures. But restrictive policies rarely worked. The Navigation Acts were extensively evaded. It was difficult to exercise control across three thousand miles of sea. The smuggler had superseded the buccaneer. Local officials had no wish to uphold monopolies which they did not think were for their benefit. For example, the Molasses Act of 1733, which aimed to prevent the American colonies from buying French sugar, was a dead letter. Similarly, the Spaniards had difficulty in preventing the British from cutting logwood in Honduras.

The West Indies were generally considered to be the most valuable of the European colonies. Their main output was sugar. The French had Saint Dominique, Martinque, and Guadeloupe; it is said that the output of sugar from Saint Dominique alone exceeded that of all the British islands put together. Jamaica was the principal British sugar island, but there were other industries in the Bahamas and Bermudas. Moreover, the British possessed excellent naval bases at Port Royal in Jamaica and English Harbour in Antigua. Although the French sugar undersold British in New England and other markets, sugar was protected in the British home market; thus, the plantation owners in the British West Indies were not keen for the British Government to gain further islands by war as they feared that this would result in a reduction of the prices obtained for their sugar.

If the French were better at selling sugar, the British were more successful in the slave trade. Slaves were thought essential to the economy of the West Indian islands, and were also transported from West Africa to North and South America. It has been estimated that the British sold twelve thousand Negroes a year against seven thousand sold by the French, and that between 1680 and 1786 some 10 million slaves were exported from Africa by the British, French, Dutch, and Portuguese. Slaves were the most valuable African export: the only significant European settlement in Africa was Cape Colony, the property of the Dutch East India Company. By the end of the eighteenth century it contained fifteen thousand Europeans and seventeen thousand slaves, and pioneers had penetrated as far as the Orange River.

As in the West Indies, the main European rivalry in eighteenth-century India was between the British and French. India was constantly torn by war. The old Moghul Empire was conquered by the Mahrattas. The Europeans therefore concentrated chiefly on the seaboard, the British settling in Bombay, Madras, and Calcutta, the French at Surat, Pondicherry, and Calicut, the Portuguese at Goa, and the Dutch in Cochin. The principal Indian exports were cotton and silk piece goods as well as raw cotton and silk. European manufactured goods were in little demand, though some broadcloth was sold there as well as metals such as lead, copper, and tin. Thus, both the British and Dutch East Indian companies had to pay for most of their imports with bullion. Sea power was needed to establish political control in India, but the East India companies also had miniature armies in order to defend their trading posts.

It was in North America, however, that the rivalry between the British and French was most fierce. By 1732 thirteen British colonies had been established along the Atlantic seaboard. These colonies had different economic characteristics—in the North fishing and timber cutting were the principal occupations, in the middle colonies cereals were grown, and in the South tobacco, rice, and indigo—but they all had much the same form of government, a governor and council appointed from England and local assemblies of a representative character. The Hudson's Bay Company covered a wide area to the north of Canada, while Newfoundland and Acadia had been acquired by the Treaty of Utrecht.

The French occupied Canada, their main settlements being along the banks of the Saint Lawrence river. Louisbourg was built as a fortress on the Ile Royale in 1714. At the extreme south of the North American continent the French founded New Orleans in 1718, and in 1722 it became the capital of a vast area known as Louisiana, abutting the Spanish possessions of Florida and Mexico. Along the huge length of the Mississippi River were isolated French trading posts, but there was some development of Illinois and Ohio by the French during the first half of the eighteenth century. The extensive French possessions were divided from the British seaboard colonies by the line of the Allegheny Mountains and the settlements of the five Nations of Iroquois Indians. Nevertheless, the French Canadians and New Englanders were in contact south of Lake Ontario; and as the population of the British settlements expanded, the pressure grew for a movement in search of land to the west. Thus, a clash between the British and French in North America was hard to avoid even when the two nations were not at war in Europe.

The French were saddled with three disadvantages in North America. The first was that they were largely dependent on the export of one commodity—fur—and they had to buy much of their food from outside. Secondly, the French Government was centralized at Quebec and was unable to exert much control over the vast area of New France. Moreover, the French at home valued Canada far less than the West Indian islands. Thirdly, the French never had a population of more than about fifty thousand in Canada, while Louisiana suffered because it was owned by a number of different organizations during the first half of the eighteenth century. Just as the English South Sea Company was imperiled by overoptimistic investors, so Louisiana was the subject of big and equally optimistic speculations associated with the name of John Law.

The peace in Europe in 1748 made little difference to the undeclared war between the British and French in America. In 1749 the then French Governor General determined to prevent the British from penetrating the Alleghenies and establishing themselves on the Ohio. His policy was continued by his successor, the Marquis Duquesne, who was resisted by the Governor of Virginia, Robert Dinwiddie. The French, who outnumbered the Virginians commanded by young Colonel George Washington, managed to erect a fort at the forks of the Ohio, which they named Fort Duquesne. This was the beginning of what was known as the French and Indian War. For when it was learned in London that the Virginia militia could not oust the French regular troops, the Government reluctantly decided to send out two thousand regulars under the command of General Braddock. But Braddock was ambushed and killed in 1755, so that the Ohio was left under the control of the French and their Indian allies. Such was the position until the Seven Years' War broke out in Europe in May 1756. The settlers were temporarily demoralized by Braddock's defeat and by the swift dispatch of French reinforcements to Canada. It was not until William Pitt took charge of overseas operations in 1757 that the British colonists in North America were able to make use against the French of their natural advantages in their larger population and the support of British sea power.

Pitt the Elder is one of the strangest of the great figures in British history and an example of the saying that genius is to madness near allied. Grandson of a fabulously rich East India merchant and governor, Thomas Pitt, a man with a terrible temper who once said his wife should be locked up in Bedlam, William came of a family in which much insanity existed and which died out scarcely a hundred years after Thomas Pitt's death. While still a relatively young man William was subject to manic-depressive fits and prolonged attacks of gout. Educated at Eton and Oxford, he was originally intended for the Church but instead secured a commission in the army, and at the age of twenty-eight was elected member of Parliament for the "rotten borough" of Sarum (Salisbury). Ambitious to make a name for himself and a natural orator, he attacked Walpole for his "un-English measures" and Carteret as "sole and execrable Minister." He was associated with the opposition group that centered on King George II's son, "poor Fred," to whom he became Groom of the Chamber in 1737. But seeing he was getting nowhere, in 1746 he changed sides, resigned as Groom of the Chamber, and accepted the lucrative but uninfluential office of Paymaster of the Forces under the Pelhams. After some kaleidosopic changes he had by June 1757 risen by sheer ability to become in effect both Minister for War and Minister for Foreign Affairs.

Pitt's outstanding gifts were unrelenting hard work and a definite policy. At heart he was an imperialist and regarded the expulsion of the French from Canada as his principal mission. The French were to be contained in Europe, first by the subsidy methods which he condemned in Carteret, secondly by bottling up the French navy in their chief bases, and thirdly by amphibious attacks on the coast of France: none of these "side shows" was a success, but they served their purpose in distracting the French Government. Later in the war the French statesman the Duke of Choiseul returned the compliment by threatening to invade England.

It took Pitt time to reorganize the army and navy. He created a militia force to guard the homeland while he sent his regular forces to America. He also enlisted the help of an American army by promising that its officers should have the same status as British regulars. In 1758 he launched a triple attack on North America; an amphibious force was sent to capture Louisbourg, General Abercrombie with the main British army was directed against Canada from the south, and a third military force under the veteran General Forbes was dispatched from Pennsylvania into the Ohio valley. Though Abercrombie was defeated by the French General Montcalm at Ticonderoga, south of Lake Champlain, Louisbourg was reconquered in July and Forbes, though a dying man, took Fort Duquesne, which was renamed Fort Pitt and later Pittsburg. These victories were sustained by British command of the sea. The French navy was unable to save Louisbourg, and the food supplies of Canada were reduced by the British blockade. In 1759 there was another triple campaign, but in fact it was left to James Wolfe to win a victory over Montcalm on the Plains of Abraham, in which both generals were killed, on September 13. Montreal surrendered a year later.

Although Pitt's principal military effort was directed against the French in Canada, British superiority at sea helped secure victories in West Africa, in the West Indies, and in India, where Robert Clive, a clerk turned soldier, regained Calcutta, which had been captured by the French ally, the Nawab Siraj-ud-daulah; in 1757 Clive easily defeated an overwhelmingly more numerous army of Moghuls at the battle of Plassey. Pondicherry surrendered to the British in the following year.

Because of the resolute direction of the war and the superiority of British sea power, the French were thus defeated in every theater of war. But they still had one shot left in their locker: that was to bring in the Spaniards. Pitt tried to persuade the Cabinet to strike against Spain before the annual treasure ship from South America reached home. When he was overruled, he resigned and his "Great Ministry" came to an end in October 1761.

By the terms of the Treaty of Paris (1763) the French surrendered the whole of Canada to Great Britain and yielded Louisiana west of the Mississippi to Spain in return for Florida, which also became British. The only rights retained by the French in North America were in the fishing off Newfoundland and a couple of small islands to the south of it. There was considerable discussion in Great Britain whether Canada was of more value than the islands of Martinique, Guadeloupe, and Saint Lucia, which were restored to France, or Cuba, which was restored to Spain. Although Great Britain gained Grenada, Tobago, and certain smaller islands, the British West Indian sugar planters did not want to acquire new rivals in the protected British market. In Africa the French ceded Senegal and retained Goree. In India the two companies returned to their position before the war began, but in fact the British victories meant that if there was to be a European successor to the Moghuls it would be Great Britain.

Again in opposition, Pitt criticized the peace terms. He said that "our conquests in North America are of very little detriment to the commerce of France," whereas the surrender of the French and Spanish West Indian islands was both a strategic and an economic loss. He also thought that the King of Prussia had been betrayed. What he wanted, in fact, was that France should be irretrievably crushed both in a military and a commercial sense. It does not seem that he recognized the illimitable possibilities in North America, where the 2 million settlers and their slaves could now march from the Atlantic seaboard to the Mississippi and consolidate their territory from Hudson's Bay to Florida. He did, however, feel strongly that by giving up the conquests in the West Indies British naval communications had been dangerously exposed, and that by failing completely to destroy the imperial power of France Great Britain had left an enemy, by no means disarmed, which would one day take revenge.

Although, looked at from a world point of view, the conquest of Canada by Great Britain was the most significant event of the Seven Years' War, in Europe the exhaustion of the combatants, particularly of Prussia and Austria, contributed to the strengthening of the Russian Empire and the contraction of Poland and Turkey. France by turning its thoughts westward opened the opportunity, which was to be seized by Catherine the Great of Russia, to dominate much of eastern Europe, while the Dutch, no longer afraid of French aggression against the southern Netherlands, retired into neutrality. The enmity of France and Great Britain was exacerbated and was to continue until 1815.

4. The American War of Independence and Europe

The American War of Independence only belongs to European history strictly through its influence on the constitutions and diplomatic relationships of the European powers. It has recently been argued by Professor R. R. Palmer in a brilliant book and by others that the war not only excited democratic revolutionary aspirations in Europe, but also contributed to a general revolutionary movement that covered many parts of Europe during the last thirty years or more of the eighteenth century. In the 1760s and 1770s, it has been suggested, the radicals in Great Britain and America believed that they had a common interest in sustaining each other's political demands. Certainly the American revolution had its repercussions both in Great Britain and in France. "Riots and disorders," writes Steven Watson, "were part of the way of life in 1760." Efforts made before William Pitt's time to raise a native militia provoked lively agitation. In 1762 the first number of the radical magazine edited by John Wilkes entitled *The North Briton* was published and in its forty-fifth issue was highly critical of the

King's Speech defending the Peace of Paris. In 1770 Edmund Burke, a brilliant Irishman, published his book called *Thoughts on the Present Discontents,* and in due course the Wilkes-and-liberty riots were to follow. A year earlier the Society of Supporters of the Bill of Rights was organized to press for parliamentary reform.

The origins of the American war need not be discussed in detail here. But the event that sparked it off—namely, the attempt by the British Government to impose taxation on the colonists—was, as has already been remarked, one of the principal causes of revolutions both in the seventeenth and eighteenth centuries. To that was added a second cause which has already been stressed: the demand for national independence. It was not that the Americans could not afford to pay taxes. Indeed, a tide of prosperity had swept over the continent and led to both economic and political maturity. Already before the Treaty of Paris was signed the American colonists had resented trading restrictions to which they were subjected by the mother country and had evaded them as much as they could.

To these commercial restrictions were now added fiscal impositions. The British national debt had nearly doubled as a result of the Seven Years' War, and British governments thought it right not that the colonists should repay the cost but that they should help toward the upkeep of forces still needed for their own security. These taxes ranged from a stamp duty to a tax on tea. When it was realized in London that such taxes were deeply disliked, they were abolished, though the principle that it was the right of the British Parliament to tax the American colonists was maintained. In 1766 a Government, of which William Pitt, who had been elevated to the House of Lords as the Earl of Chatham, was the effective head, was faced not only with unrest in America but with bread riots at home—"there is nothing but riots and insurrections over the whole country," it was said, "on account of the high price of provisions, in particular corn"—and although Chatham's aim had been to pacify the colonies, a Mutiny Act imposed on the Americans led to fresh troubles.

Chatham, physically and mentally ill, soon retired from responsibility, and the reconstituted administration under the Duke of Grafton, after vainly attempting to increase the land tax in England, tried to raise a modest sum of thirty-five to forty thousand pounds sterling a year by introducing taxes on certain commodities, including tea, imported into North America. These duties were resisted by nonimportation and nonconsumption; and when regular troops were used in Boston in support of the customs officials, riots took place and blood flowed. Again the offending duties were repealed except for that on tea.

The Tea Act of 1773 gave a monopoly to the British East India Company, which was allowed to export directly to America on payment of an import duty there of threepence a pound. But the colonies were still outraged and at Boston a cargo of tea was thrown into the sea. The British Government, now under Lord North, closed Boston as a port and prepared to quarter troops on the town. At the same time the Quebec Act, also passed by Lord North's Government, appeared to limit the aspirations of the thirteen colonies to expand westward. In September 1774 a Continental Congress met in Philadelphia and decided to oppose all British legislation passed since 1763 and to defend themselves if attacked. Thus, in the following spring the War of Independence began.

It was never likely that the 2 million English-speaking people in America, with a tradition of individual freedom behind them, once united by political action would want to remain subject to Europe. The distinction that had been drawn by some speakers on both sides of the Atlantic between internal taxes (like the stamp duty) and external taxes (like the tea duty) was never a significant one. "A Parliament of Great Britain," declared John Adams in 1765, "can have no more right to tax the colonies than a Parliament of Paris." Once this was admitted, it was but a short step to saying that Americans did not want to be governed by a British Parliament at all. As Thomas Hutchinson, Governor of Massachusetts, said in 1773, "I know of no line that can be drawn between the supreme authority of Parliament and the total independence of the colonies. It is impossible that there should be two legislatures in one and the same state." It was also argued that the colonies had never been constitutionally subject to the Imperial Parliament, but only to the British monarchy from which they received their charters. Thus, the War of Independence became a war not against the British Parliament but against King George III *(1760-1820)*. Logically, once the colonies were united, they had to become a republic.

That the Americans would sooner or later have won their independence cannot be doubted. They had many natural advantages over their enemies, but they had to fight without a trained army or navy, without complete political unity, and against the strongest single naval power in the world. Therefore, in time they sought and found allies in Europe. The Duke of Choiseul had been determined that the French should be revenged for their defeat in the Seven Years' War, and while he was Minister of Marine *(1761-66)* he strengthened the French navy: in 1766 it was estimated that the French and Spanish fleets outnumbered the British by four to three. In September 1770 the French Government had shown its aggressive spirit by seizing the island of Corsica, where Napoleon I had just been born. In that same year Great Britain and Spain were on the verge of war over a quarrel about the newly discovered Falkland Islands off South America. But neither the French King nor his other ministers were yet ready for war, and Choiseul was dismissed. Nevertheless, after young Louis XVI succeeded in 1774, he had a Foreign Minister in the Count of Vergennes who inherited Choiseul's mantle. His plan was to attack Great Britain directly or in its outlying dependencies near the European mainland. The American war, which broke out in the spring of 1775, obviously offered a splendid opportunity.

The Americans began well by forcing the British to evacuate Boston, but when in turn they were obliged to retreat from Canada, withdraw from New York, and allow the British to occupy their capital of Philadelphia, the French hesitated to intervene. After the first American representative, Silas Deane, arrived in Paris in July 1776, Vergennes wanted Louis XVI to go to war, but a policy of underhand assistance to the Americans was preferred. Turgot, the Controller General of Finance, was even opposed to that and resigned. Money and munitions were then provided and American privateers welcomed in French harbors. But after the news of the British General Burgoyne's surrender at Saratoga was received in Paris, the French Government changed its mind. A treaty of commerce and a treaty of alliance were signed on February 6, 1778: it was agreed that in the event of Anglo-French hostilities the Americans should keep any conquests on the mainland of North America, while the French should retain any islands they might conquer in or near the Gulf of Mexico.

War was declared between France and Great Britain in July. The British did not take this lying down; Pondicherry was occupied in India and Goree in West Africa. In April 1779 the Spaniards entered the war against the British, but not as the allies of the Americans. In fact, King Carlos III first tried to mediate and only became a belligerent after the promise of all sorts of satisfactions from the French. In February 1780 Russia, Sweden, and Denmark formed a league of armed neutrality to resist the British demands to search neutral vessels and to close the Baltic to British ships. The United Netherlands acceded to this league, and when Dutch merchants proceeded to supply the French and Spaniards with naval stores, Great Britain declared war on the Dutch at the end of 1780. (This is sometimes called the Fourth Anglo-Dutch War.) But now the decision, so far as American independence was concerned, was being reached. In the summer of 1781 a French fleet under Admiral De Grasse reached Chesapeake Bay in Virginia and was able to support with French troops the American land forces already there. Sir Henry Clinton, the British commander-in-chief, had unwisely divided his army between the southern states, New York, and Virginia. On October 19 General Cornwallis was surrounded and surrendered at Yorktown. Though Clinton lingered on in New York, the American war in effect ended that day.

But among European nations the war was not yet over. In April 1782 the British Admiral Rodney destroyed the fleet of De Grasse; in October Gibraltar was relieved after a long siege; and both in the West Indies and in India the British held their own. To the annoyance of Vergennes, the British were able to conclude a separate treaty with the Americans recognizing their independence, but retaining Canada, in November 1782. By the Treaty of Versailles (January 1783) France regained Saint Lucia and acquired Tobago in the West Indies, Senegal and Goree in West Africa, and an extension of fishing rights off Newfoundland. Spain recovered Florida and Minorca, but could not obtain Gibraltar. The Dutch gained nothing: they lost Ceylon and admitted the British to trading rights in the East Indies. Thus, the American War of Independence made no difference to the balance of power in Europe, though, like the Seven Years' War, it helped indirectly the expansion of Russia. Moreover, by undermining the finances of the French monarchy it paved the way for the French Revolution.

5.   The American Victory and Europe

How far did the successful American Revolution have an impact on European thought? In France in particular, accounts in the newspapers and stories related by serving officers, such as the Marquis de Lafayette, who had fought in America, stimulated attention. Benjamin Franklin and Thomas Jefferson, two great Americans, were ambassadors in Paris, and Jefferson's *Notes on the State of Virginia* was widely read. Bishop Talleyrand wrote in

Lafayette at Monmouth, Leading the Cavalry in a Desperate Charge
The Bettman Archive

retrospect in his memoirs: "We talked of nothing but America." Nevertheless, Professor Palmer, one of the advocates of the notion that the American Revolution contributed substantially to the coming of French democracy, admits that the influence was "imponderable" and that "psychological influences are difficult to gauge." It can be argued that French antagonism against England, which may be dated back at least to 1689, was what was most aroused. The British defeat was a hard fact; notions of liberty and equality are intangible. Professor Godechot suggests that the American Revolution had three main repercussions on European society: first, it made people realize that they were living in an age of upheaval; second, it proved that the doctrines put forward by political philosophers (notably by John Locke) were not mere utopias but could be put into effect; third, it showed that a democratic community, as recommended by Rousseau, had actually been created. One need not necessarily accept all these conclusions: for example, it can be argued, and has been argued, that the American Constitution was aimed at making the country safe from democracy, while it is doubtful how widely Rousseau's democratic theme had been absorbed outside the ranks of the *philosophes*. Nevertheless, it is certain that the American Declaration of Independence, with its bold assertion that the true aims of government are to safeguard life, liberty, and the pursuit of happiness, and that governments which fail to pursue these aims should be overthrown, impressed enlightened Europeans. So did the phrase, "all men are equal," though in fact the American Revolution did not make all men equal: it did not free the black slaves. For Americans the true passion was individualism; for the French it was equality.

Outside France indications of a revolutionary influence on political thought are sparse, though it had some effect on the United Netherlands and Ireland. Some European thinkers were impressed with the idea of a written constitution defining rights, but constitutions safeguarding liberties or privileges were not, after all, new: they could be found from Castile to Warsaw. Even England, which was to remain almost the only country without a written constitution at any time, could boast of Magna Carta and the Bill of Rights. What may be detected in America, as has already been pointed out, was the example of a revolution provoked by tax demands and widened into a claim for national independence. This was the same stimulus that had sparked off the Portuguese Revolution over a hundred years earlier. It may be true, though it is not easy to prove, as Professor Palmer has written, that the American revolution "inspired the sense of a new era"; that "it added a new content to the conception of progress"; and that "it gave a whole new dimension to ideas of liberty and equality made familiar by the Enlightenment." Yet against this idealistic belief may be contrasted the alternative realist view that the French Revolution was unique, owing its origins essentially to social and economic causes inherent in the structure of European society, and only to a minor degree excited by the American success.

6. The Industrial Revolution

Just as historians are not in complete accord about the complex of revolutions that is to be found in the last quarter of the eighteenth century, so there are differences over the economic changes that were taking place at this time. One recent historian says flatly: "No economic revolution preceded the political revolution that ended the eighteenth century." Yet another historian, again writing recently, speaks of a "dual revolution" that altered the shape of Europe and was responsible for its expansion throughout the world in the nineteenth century. The first revolution, according to this view, was the Industrial Revolution which took place first in Great Britain, though England had already experienced its "bourgeois revolution" over a hundred years earlier. The second revolution was the political revolution—again "bourgeois" in origin—which occurred in France. But no specific connection can be traced between the two parts of this "dual revolution": in fact, the Industrial Revolution did not really reshape society, particularly by creating an industrial proletariat, until after the French Revolution ended. The most that can be said is that the strengthening of the British economy contributed to the ultimate defeat of Napoleon.

Preliminary to the Industrial Revolution had been an expansion in population and a spectacular growth of international commerce. No precise agreement has been reached about the size of this growth. One estimate is that the European population rose from about 100 million in 1700 to 140 million in 1750, and to 188 million at the end of the century: this was out of a world population of some 900 million. Undoubtedly, population increased in the second half of the century, though it was not evenly distributed. The population of England and Wales is thought to have grown from $5\frac{1}{4}$ million at the outset of the century to well over 9 million at its close. But in the middle of the century the English population is believed to have been only about 6 million. If, therefore, the population increased by 50 percent in the latter half of the century, it may have been one of the reasons why the Industrial Revolution first began in England. The population of Russia also rose substantially, but that was due in part to the acquisition of a large part of Poland; a considerable increase in Prussia is likewise explained by the acquisition of Silesia and part of Poland. The increase of population in France between the middle of the century and 1792 was only about 20 percent. In Spain, Portugal, and Italy the increase was also comparatively small.

What explanation can be offered for this growth in population? It used to be largely attributed to a notable fall in mortality. But modern research suggests that in some countries at any rate it was owing to an earlier age of marriage and larger families: the countries where these factors had an effect included Russia, the Scandinavian countries, Ireland, and to some extent

England. But it still appears as if lower mortality was the chief cause of the growing European population. While it is true, as Dr. Lester S. King has written in his book *The Medical World in the Eighteenth Century,* that medical knowledge was still "pathetically rudimentary," nonetheless some advance was made upon the stereotyped practices of the previous century, when physicians and surgeons probably killed more people than they cured. The universities of Leiden, Padua, and Edinburgh possessed excellent medical schools; and chairs of medicine and kindred subjects were instituted at Cambridge in England. Hermann Boerhaave, who has been described, no doubt with some exaggeration, as "the greatest physician of modern times," introduced modern clinical methods at Leiden in 1714. A Swiss doctor, Albrecht von Haller, wrote an important book on *Elements of the Physiology of the Human Body* in 1766. Two Scotsmen, Sir John Pringle and William Cullen, made significant contributions to medical knowledge. Pringle stressed the value of hygiene and Cullen analyzed contagious fevers.

Among the teachings of eighteenth-century European scientists there emerged some useful medical discoveries. Boerhaave first treated anemia with iron; Stephen Hales, an English clergyman, recorded and measured blood pressure; the French naturalist Reamur invented a practical thermometer. Syphilis was successfully treated with mercury. At the end of the century the German Samuel Hahnemann, though guilty of some eccentricities, advocated homeopathy and criticized the current medical practice of giving large doses of drugs to patients. He also emphasized the importance of questioning patients in detail about their symptoms. Bloodletting, which was the commonest method of dealing with fevers in the previous century, became less used. Forceps were employed in obstetrics.

Nevertheless, one must not exaggerate the progress of medical science. If percussion of the surface of the body was introduced together with the stethescope, effective pulse watches and clinical thermometers had not yet penetrated into medical practice; while surgery was less primitive than it had been, neither anesthesia nor antiseptics were known. And although inoculation against smallpox was practiced—Catherine the Great was proud of having introduced it into Russia—it was not until the end of the century that Edward Jenner discovered vaccination.

Probably for the mass of the people the biggest advance of the century was in hygiene and diet. Surprisingly enough, a betterment in hygiene began in the towns. Countrymen's cottages were usually insanitary, but in English towns at any rate improvement acts were a common feature of the latter half of the century. Open drains were covered in, streets were paved and lighted, and sewers improved. Reformers attempted to promote sanitation in hospitals and prisons. It was found that fresh fruit and lemon juice would combat scurvy at sea. The potato, which was despised in the seventeenth century, became a common item of diet. Haricot beans and pumpkins were imported from America. If the poor rarely saw a doctor, "empirics," who included John Wesley and Bishop Berkeley, and the numerous apothecaries often suggested sensible remedies for common illnesses. Thus, though the rate of infantile mortality remained high, young people suffered less from under-nourishment or an ill-balanced diet.

Still, the progress of medicine was not rapid; it took time for discoveries to penetrate and spread. Yet it is a fact that pestilences and epidemics diminished. Biological changes helped put an end to the plague-bearing rat. Better nutrition reduced rickets, anemia, and tuberculosis. Bubonic plagues had disappeared completely by 1721. Inocculation had some effect in reducing smallpox.

It is probable that the growth of population, especially in England, played its part in stimulating the development of industry, while the opening of new markets abroad in consequence of the British victories over the French helped to raise the standard of living. It does not appear that the pure scientists did much to aid technology. Astronomy was the subject in which most progress was achieved. In England Edmund Halley and William Whiston put forward new theories about the comets; at Basel a group of scientists applied the calculus to astronomical analysis; in Paris Lagrange and Laplace (who taught mathematics to Napoleon) developed Newton's theories in detail. But astronomy was of little importance in the ordinary affairs of life. If God had emerged as a mathematical physicist, it was only the intelligentsia whose religion was shaken.

More practical were discoveries relating to chemistry and biology. Electricity was studied by two Italians, Galvani and Volta, whose names are still used in connection with modern machines. The old view that matter consists of four elements was finally swept away. Some of the discoveries of modern physical chemists about the molecular structure of matter were anticipated. Chemical elements and gases were discovered. A great French chemist, Antoine Lavoisier, found that air consists of oxygen and nitrogen, and the Englishman Joseph Priestley discovered that water is a compound of oxygen and hydrogen. Biology and zoology also made strides forward. But, as with astronomers, the immediate importance of the biologists was that they undermined traditional religious beliefs. Men were no longer, it was thought, condemned to a life of misery that could only be alievated by conversion or prayer. Lamarck, who in his *Zoological Philosophy* (1809) expounded the doctrine of the inheritance of acquired characteristics, lent weight to the growing belief that mankind could be improved by being given a better environment.

The progress of science, then, only played a relatively small and indirect part in promoting what is customarily called the Industrial Revolution of the eighteenth century. What precisely is meant by "industrial revolution"? The late Professor T. S. Ashton, who knew as much about British economic development in the eighteenth century as anyone, observed that the word *revolution* implies a suddenness of change which is not at all characteristic of economic processes, and that the changes which transformed Europe toward the end of the century were as much social and intellectual as industrial. Contemporaries were certainly not conscious that such a revolution was taking place at any specific point in time, and if the phrase must be used at all, it is wiser to think of it as a movement than as a period. Such a movement, however, did gather momentum, though at quite different times inside and outside European countries. If it can be accepted, as has generally been assumed, that it gathered momentum in England toward the end of the eighteenth century, it may be argued that it did not do so in Russia until the twentieth century.

In a recent book the Industrial Revolution has been defined as consisting of, first, the substitution of machines for human skills; secondly, the introduction of engines for converting heat into work; and thirdly, the use of new and more abundant materials. It has been suggested that among the factors stimulating invention and new technology in eighteenth-century Europe were *(a)* a will to master nature brought about by the rational approach to problems, exemplified by scientists like Descartes and Newton; *(b)* the growth of colonialism, which supplied new markets outside Europe as well as providing a source of raw materials; *(c)* the comparative freedom from devastating wars up to the time of the French Revolution; and *(d)* the impulse given to hard work and inventiveness by the Protestant ethic. None of these explanations is entirely satisfactory: for example, colonialism dates from the sixteenth and seventeenth centuries, while no general agreement exists on the significance of the Protestant ethic in economic progress. Possibly it is simpler to relate industrial and technological development in the eighteenth century to the accumulation of capital derived from commerce and the growth of banking and to an increase in population providing better markets inside Europe itself. Still, the pattern of trade was changing with the growth of imperialism which was the product of the Seven Years' War. Whereas two hundred years earlier England had been an underdeveloped country relying for such export trade as it had on raw materials like wool, by the eighteenth century it had become an advanced nation mainly importing raw materials in exchange for manufactured products. But too much stress should not be placed on the scientific revolution which was occurring in most parts of Europe. The early British inventions were comparatively simple ones; they were not very expensive to introduce, and did not require large capital investment. As to population, it can plausibly be argued that its increase was owing to economic progress rather than one of the causes of economic progress.

In fact, in trying to answer the question why industrialization made its first striking advances in England, it is not always easy to distinguish cause and effect. But, on the whole, rising population did stimulate home demand. So too did a standard of living which compared favorably with that of other countries. British industry was relatively free from State control and from wars and public disturbances. Primogeniture drove the younger sons of the nobility into industry, as it had formerly attracted them to commerce. Below the level of the gentry no barriers existed between land and trade. There was no internal customs system and thus mobility both of goods and men prevailed. Great Britain also owned valuable raw materials in coal and wool. From the middle of the century onward communications were strengthened. The country had always benefited from its numerous harbors and navigable rivers. But both coastal shipping and movements of goods by river were relatively slow and expensive. The development of canals by the second Duke of Bridgwater with the cooperation of the engineer James Brindley, a movement which culminated in the "canal mania" of 1790-94, speeded up the carriage of goods on internal waterways, while Metcalf, Telford, and Macadam began building turnpike roads. Railroads were in use before the end of the century at any rate for the drawing of trucks by horses in coal mines and iron works.

The most noticeable advance in eighteenth-century England was in the cotton industry. In 1760 2½ million pounds of raw cotton were imported; by 1787 the consumption of raw cotton was 22 million pounds. Though during the first half of the century spinning and weaving were carried out mainly in the workmen's own homes (even when a "jenny" which enabled the warp to be spun more rapidly was invented, it could be housed in a cottage), but after Richard Arkwright patented a water frame in 1770, factories had to be built to house it. By 1802 there were fifty-two cotton mills in the Manchester area alone. The industry, particularly in the manufacture of calicoes and muslins, lent itself more easily to mechanization than woolen textiles, and the demand for cotton goods was more elastic both at home and abroad. Imperial expansion stimulated the swift growth of the industry. Raw cotton was imported from the West Indies and North America, and cotton goods were sold in Africa, the West Indies, and the Americas. Because of these factors, the inventions of John Kay (the fly shuttle) and Wyatt and Paul (the spinning frame) designed for wool were first applied to cotton.

The iron and steel industries were also stimulated by technological inventions. At first the British ironmasters were handicapped by the fact that ore had to be converted in blast furnaces fed with charcoal and the supply of timber was becoming scarcer. Although as early as 1709 Abraham Darby invented pig-iron smelting with coke, it was not until many years later that this process was generally adopted. In the 1780s the British output of iron was smaller than that of France, and a substantial amount of iron was being imported from Sweden and Russia. But coal mining prospered. In 1708 Thomas Newcomen, a Devonshire blacksmith, invented a steam engine that could be used to dry out mines, while in the 1780s James Watt patented a much superior and more economical engine, though this was installed in breweries, distilleries, and tin mines rather than coal mines. The output of coal in Great Britain more than quadrupled in the course of the century. Another important industry which developed in England in the second half of the century was the manufacture of pottery. Josiah Wedgwood set up his famous business in Staffordshire in 1759. As a result of new inventions Great Britain became preeminent too in cannon founding and the building of wooden ships. Just as in earlier centuries the invention of stone castles, the long bow, the horse saddle, and banking had given an advantage to enterprising nations in making war, so Great Britain's sophisticated methods of banking, the use of factories to make soldiers' uniforms, and improvements in the building of wooden ships all contributed to the ultimate victory over

The Newcomen Steam Engine, Bristol, England
The Bettman Archive

Napoleon. It is not that the English were remarkably inventive, though maybe the Scots were. But as Hugh Trevor-Roper has said,

> the societies which look forward are not those which transmit ideas, nor even, necessarily, those which generate them: they are those which can seize them and exploit them.

Nevertheless, one must not overestimate the speed of industrial change in eighteenth-century Britain. It was not until 1784 that the British output of iron began to soar, or till later that cotton exports exceeded those of woolen textiles; in fact, France, Sweden, and Prussia were also technologically advanced at the time of the Industrial Revolution. Technology was stimulated in France by the publication of the *Encyclopédie*. The Le Creusot iron works were using the coking process for smelting in 1785, while the discoveries of Lavoisier and Nicholas Leblanc helped the chemical industry. The manufacture of Dresden china at Meissen and of hard porcelain at Sèvres anticipated the achievement of the English potteries. Not only France but Italy and Brandenburg were ahead of Great Britain in the construction of canals. The French were also pioneers of steamships. The French engineer Trésaguet invented a new three-layer system for building roads, and this method spread throughout Europe from the Mont Cenis pass to the Siberian highway.

Two points may be made about industrialization at the end of the eighteenth century. The first is that nearly all European nations were engaged in it; for technology, like science, knows no frontiers. Some nations were undoubtedly inspired by British inventions, such as the Newcomen steam engine, and John Kay introduced his flying shuttle to the French. The Austrian and Prussian governments spent money on industrial development, and Frederick the Great's conquest of Silesia gave his kingdom a valuable source of coal and iron. But to describe these changes as a European revolution is misleading. What is not misleading is to speak of a British revolution which was brought about by the accumulation of capital derived from expanding commerce, the possession of natural advantages that could be exploited, and the relatively sudden development of new markets both at home and abroad. Unlike most countries, especially in eastern Europe, Great Britain did not have a downtrodden and exploited peasantry. The commercialization of agriculture, partly through accelerated enclosure, made the country largely able to feed itself and its soldiers, while food could be imported, when necessary, in exchange for textiles and other manufactured exports.

Secondly, one needs to be careful in ascribing the reasons why Great Britain surged ahead in the nineteenth century. To some extent it is true that the kingdom enjoyed advantages over other European countries, some of which had poorer communications, experienced a shortage of raw materials, or suffered from excessive intervention by their governments and from bad fiscal systems. But it is wrong to attribute the head start obtained by Great Britain to the relatively simple inventions dating from the early part of the century. Unfettered private enterprise assisted industrial growth and the commercialization of agriculture fed it. The overwhelming advantage that Great Britain gained was that while war set fire to the whole of Europe from the Iberian peninsula to Moscow between 1793 and 1815, this small island was immune from the destruction wrought by the *levée en masse*. As David Landes has written,

> the last five years of the [Napoleonic] Empire were years of spasmodic crisis that left the economy much enfeebled and momentarily helpless to meet the rush of cheap British products that came with peace.

The golden age of the British export trade, consisting chiefly of manufactured goods carried by British ships to European markets, may be dated from 1815.

It is noteworthy that many of the scientists and technologists of the eighteenth century were men of the middle classes who were passionately anxious to unravel the truth about nature and its workings and to improve the lot of their fellow men. There were of course exceptions: the Duke of Bridgwater promoted the building of canals, D'Holbach boasted a German title. But to give a few examples: John Kay was the son of a yeoman, James Watt was the son of a merchant, Joseph Priestley was the son of a weaver. Georg Ernst Stahl, the inventor of a nonexistent substance called "phlostigon," which nonetheless paved the way to the discovery of gases, was an apothecary; and Lavoisier was a tax collector. Most of these men made their own way without much help from publishers or manufacturers. Thus, one may detect one thing in common between the Industrial Revolution and the French Revolution that was to follow it: both were triumphs for the middle classes. But the old aristocracy still had its day—or at least it took a long time dying.

SEVEN

Indian Summer
of
an Aristocracy

1. An Aristocratic Resurgence

During the twenty years or so that preceded the outbreak of the French Revolution the aristocracy was strengthening its power in most parts of Europe. In some cases—in that of Catherine the Great, for example—monarchs, recognizing that their own authority was entwined with that of the aristocracy, deliberately conferred fresh privileges upon it. In other cases— for instance, in the empire of Joseph II—the aristocracy fiercely, and often successfully, resisted reforms; it can be argued that the *révolte nobiliaire*, which took place in France and which some modern historians regard as the first stage in the French Revolution, had its counterparts elsewhere.

One uses the word *aristocracy* in preference to *nobility* because, as Professor Palmer has pointed out, the two were not necessarily the same. The United Netherlands had an aristocracy in their regents; Geneva had an aristocracy in its patricians; in Great Britain the untitled landed gentry could be considered part of the aristocracy; even in north America there were landed families, like the Washingtons, who were accustomed to regard themselves as belonging to a ruling class before and after the American Revolution.

In Chapter 5 something of the restlessness of the aristocracy in eastern Europe was outlined. In Hungary the Magyar lords who dominated the country withstood all the attempts of Maria Theresa and Joseph II at administrative reform. Here the peasants were to revolt against them in 1790, but were suppressed by troops sent in from other parts of the Empire. In Austria and Bohemia the magnates had protested indignantly against Joseph II's land tax and compelled Leopold II to withdraw it. In Prussia where the Great Elector, after the Thirty Years' War, had started reducing the influence of the Junkers, Frederick the Great had reversed this policy and increased their authority; Frederick had said as early as 1752 that "the preservation of the nobility was an object of policy of the Kings of Prussia, for the noble class were the foundations and pillars of the State." He employed the Junkers as army officers and as *Landräte* who could sway the course of provincial life. The Prussian code of law, introduced in 1791, was especially tender about the privileges of the nobility. By her Charter of Nobility in 1785 Catherine defined and extended the rights of the Russian aristocracy which had been lessened in the reign of Peter the Great. In Poland it was magnates like Prince Adam Casimir Czartoryski and Stanislas Malachowski, eager to preserve their independence, who in 1788 headed the revolt against Russia, dragging their King reluctantly along with them.

In western Europe, too, the power of the aristocrats was manifested. In the Austrian Netherlands it was the wealthy landowners, supported by the Church, who led the opposition to the attempted reforms of Joseph II. In the United Netherlands the regents of Holland, supported by some of the other provincial oligarchies, attempted in 1787 to abolish the office of the hereditary Stadholder, William V of Orange; it needed the intervention of the Prussian army (Frederick William III was the brother of the Princess of Orange) to defeat the intentions of these aristocratic "Patriots." In Geneva a long, drawn-out struggle took place between the patricians and burghers who fought for political emancipation; it ended in a victory for the patricians in 1782. In other parts of modern Switzerland what may be called class wars took place during the eighteenth century, but on the whole the oligarchs held their own. In Sweden, although Gustavus III in 1772 overthrew the constitution of 1720, which had been imposed on the monarchy by the privileged classes, he was not allowed under the new constitution to decide foreign policy without the consent of the Senate. In 1789 the officers of the army, who were members of the nobility, actually mutinied against him in time of war; Gustavus was able to take advantage of this unpatriotic behavior to exact a completely absolutist constitution from the Estates. He obtained the backing of the other three Estates (clergy, burghers, and peasants) against the nobility, but in 1792 he was murdered by a member of the nobility.

Throughout the whole of the eighteenth century Great Britain was largely governed by an aristocracy—sometimes called "a Venetian oligarchy"—and it would perhaps be difficult to show that its political influence increased during the latter half of the century. It did not possess the privileges of the French or Russian aristocracies, but it was in effect strong enough. The House of Lords played an important part in the legislature, and the House of Commons consisted mainly of landed gentry, many of whom were related to the nobility. Even though the Prime Minister might be a commoner, as was William Pitt the Younger, the cabinets of the 1780s were stiff with dukes and earls, while able commoners like Edmund Burke and Henry Dundas were excluded from them. The land tax, which had to be paid by the peers and gentry, was kept as low as possible through the vigilance of the Commons. Even in wartime when this tax was levied at the highest rate of 4 shillings in the pound, it only provided about an eighth of the revenue, the rest being raised by indirect taxes. In Great Britain countrymen were better off than most of those on the mainland of Europe. The growth of industry offered them alternative employment or provided them with a market for their products. Although small farmers and farm laborers were said to "fare extremely hard," none of them died of starvation as in France. The riots and demonstrations which took place in 1768-70 on behalf of the outlaw John Wilkes, who defied the landed classes, were backed by the London mob, not by the peasantry, who accepted the squirearchy as their natural leaders.

In 1778-79 during the American War of Independence the British Government was faced with unrest in Ireland. The Irish military garrison was then replaced by volunteers. Thus, a force was created that could be used in support of rebellion if long-standing Irish grievances were not met. The British Government, then headed by Lord North, was alarmed. Might King George III lose the allegiance of the Irish as well as of the Americans? The Volunteers were not drawn from the Roman Catholic peasantry, who constituted the bulk of the population, but from well-to-do Protestants. They were supported by landowners like the Earl of Charlemont. The Government gave way to their demands: first it granted economic concessions, then in 1782 Ireland was given full legislative independence. These favors, however, did nothing to solve the principal problems of Ireland, which were the grinding poverty of the peasants and the exclusion of Roman Catholics from all political rights. But the Catholics were apathetic and the Protestant landlords satisfied. Thus, an Irish rebellion was postponed until 1798.

Is it possible to detect any common factor in all these revolutionary or rebellious movements as new taxes imposed for the purposes of war had been a common factor in the revolutionary movements of the mid-seventeenth century? Professor Palmer has observed that between the American and French revolutions there was "an aristocratic resurgence." As has been noted, in Hungary, in Poland, in the Austrians Netherlands, and to some extent in Ireland, Sweden, and even North America, it was the aristocracy that led the resistance to the policies of monarchies. In England, though the radical hero John Wilkes was sponsored by the first Earl Temple and later in 1780 anti-Catholic riots in London were provoked by the fanaticism of Lord George Gordon, third son of the Duke of Gordon, neither of them would have made such an impact on the King's Government had it not been for the active support of a discontented London mob. The aim of the British Government in 1768 was to extinguish the "spirit of riot which . . . threatened to bring on a disrespect of all government and lawful authority." But there was little in common between these London rioters, the peasants who followed Pugachev in Russia, and the Genevan burghers. Though some of the rebels against authority appealed to democratic or semidemocratic principles, they had no mass following. The grievances of the peasants in eastern Europe and of the mobs in London or Paris were economic, not political.

Moreover, they could be repressed by the firm exercise of military strength. As Professor Palmer writes, "It was only of the aristocracy that eighteenth-century governments were afraid."

2. The *Révolte Nobiliaire* in France

Parallel with these disturbances elsewhere a conflict took place in France not so much between the monarchy and the old aristocracy *de l'epée,* but between the monarchy of Louis XV and the new aristocracy *de la robe.* The *parlements* of Paris and of other places, which had taken such a prominent part in the rebellion known as the first Fronde, had been kept under control by Louis XIV, but had achieved a considerable degree of authority during the Regency and had been appeased by the Duke of Choiseul, the Foreign Minister who served Louis XV from 1758 to 1770. Louis XV, who was bored by state business and preferred intrigue to government, had for twenty years a liberal and enlightened mistress in the bourgeoise Madame de Pompadour. She died in 1764, and the pretty but irresponsible Countess of Barry became the King's mistress. During her regime Choiseul was dismissed by the King, and the Chancellor, René Maupeou, became the most influential minister. Maupeou was determined to strengthen the monarchy by reducing the powers of the *parlements.* When the Parlement of Paris defied the King in January 1771, Maupeou sent most of its members into exile from the capital, condemned the abuses of the old judicial system, and established five superior councils to exercise the authority previously wielded by the *parlements.* Backed by Terray, the Controller General of Finance, Maupeou's aim was completely to overhaul the legal system of the kingdom, thereby crushing the *noblesse de la robe.* His intentions won the approval of Voltaire and Turgot. But the judges he appointed were corrupt, and one of the first things which Louis XVI did, when at the age of twenty he succeeded his grandfather on the throne, was to dismiss Maupeou and to restore the authority of the *parlements.* Throughout the remainder of his reign the Parlement of Paris obstructed all judicial and financial reforms. The victory of the Parlement in 1774 was, up to a point, a kind of dress rehearsal for the so-called *révolte nobiliaire* of 1787.

French participation in the American war against Great Britain is estimated to have cost 2 billion livres. French public finance was already in a bad way before the war began, largely owing to the extravagances of Louis XV. Louis XVI was genuinely anxious to reform the French financial system, and between 1774 and 1789 he made no fewer than eight changes in his finance ministers (or controllers general) with this end in view. They had to confront an outmoded system in which the main taxes were the *taille,* a land tax at a flat rate from which the privileged classes were exempt; the *capitation,* a surtax on the *taille*; and the *vingtième* a 5 percent property tax on land, offices, and the profits of industry. Although the nobility had to pay these new taxes (and had been required to do so ever since 1749), the administration of taxes, especially of taxes which did not fall on land, was so ineffective that many bourgeois as well as the wealthier privileged classes escaped heavy taxation. Indirect taxes, of which there were many, imposed on the necessities of life were farmed, and the tax farmers took a generous share of the proceeds. Indeed, it was not so much the exemptions from taxation that was the basic financial trouble in France, but a thoroughly inefficient administration and the lack of a central bank.

Louis XIV's first two controllers general of finance, Turgot and Necker (a Swiss by birth), were both capable men. Turgot reduced Government expenditure and succeeded in borrowing money at lower rates of interest; he also established free trade in grain (outside Paris) and abolished the *corvée* (forced labor employed on road making), as Joseph II was to do in Austria. The Parlement of Paris protested against these comparatively mild reforms, although they were welcomed by the less privileged classes. Louis XVI at once showed a weakness, similar to that of Charles I of England 150 years before: first he supported Turgot by forcing his edicts through the Parlement by means of a *lit de justice;* then he decided to dismiss Turgot and replace him with Necker, who financed the war against Great Britain by borrowing on a large scale. Necker demanded extensive powers from the King to carry out his policies; when these were refused Necker resigned in May 1781. He was succeeded by Joly de Fleury, who increased direct and indirect taxes.

Louis XVI's subsequent controllers general of finance were faced with annual deficits, which were the legacy of the American war. It is not true, however, to say that the Government was bankrupt. In a rich kingdom like France it had no need to be. The national debt was not overwhelming. What was at fault was the immunity of the privileged classes from paying the *taille réelle* (on land) and the *taille personelle* (on property) and their ability to evade the *vingtièmes* and *capitations* (for example, by intimidating the collectors), so that a triple burden was imposed on the peasants, who might otherwise have been prosperous, of having to pay direct and indirect taxes, a tithe to the Church, and dues to their landlords. Calonne, who became Controller General in November 1783, took some time to discover the extent of the annual deficits and the shortfall in the yield from the *vingtièmes* (which raised only about a third of what they should have done). Calonne therefore proposed far-reaching reforms involving an increase in taxation and a reduction in expenditure. He wanted to introduce a graduated land tax and to appoint new parochial assemblies to assess the value of the real property on which this tax would fall; he proposed also to abolish all internal customs barriers and to put an end to State control of the corn trade; he was determined that small landholders should be given the opportunity to reduce the amount of the *taille personelle, corvée,* and *gabelles,* though not to abolish them. These plans would have meant the ultimate end of all fiscal immunities and the extinction of feudal dues.

In order to win approval for these wide-ranging changes Calonne advised the King to call an Assembly of Notables, for which there was good precedent, consisting of members of the two nobilities and the clergy, intendants, magistrates, representatives of the provincial Estates, and urban officials. The King agreed to do so. Though the members were nominated by him, the assembly was not "packed." Calonne hoped that this assembly would act as a patriotic Council of State. He distrusted the Parlement of Paris after the failure of Maupeou's reforms, and he rejected the idea of calling a meeting of the States-General, which had not been summoned since 1614, since to do so would have been to admit that a national crisis existed and would also, he thought, involve long delays. But the Notables deliberately sabotaged this attempt to solve the King's financial problems and claimed that Calonne was both authoritarian and corrupt. He was dismissed by the King in April 1787, much as Turgot had been earlier.

After a brief interlude while the Assembly of Notables was still sitting in Versailles, Loménie de Brienne, Archbishop of Toulouse, a man of great ambitions, was appointed Controller General. It was hoped that Brienne, who was himself a Notable, would be more agreeable to the privileged classes than Calonne. But Brienne felt obliged to advocate much the same program of fiscal reform, though in a more cautious way. The Assembly, which had proved itself nothing more than a vehicle for putting forward the discontents of the privileged orders, professed it was unable to agree to such radical plans; the majority had no intention of foregoing their privileges; it advised that the scheme should be submitted to the Parlement of Paris or the States-General. Parlement was tried first, but it refused to register Brienne's decrees; and, like the Assembly of Notables, it asked for a meeting of the States-General. The King retorted with an attempted coup. He held a *lit de justice* to override the Parlement's objections and, aiming at judicial reform, exiled the magistrates from Paris. This was to imitate Maupeou's plan during his grandfather's reign. But equally it was a failure. By the autumn the Parlement had reassembled in Paris.

The struggle between the Parlement and the King, which has been called the *révolte nobiliaire,* continued into 1788. When in May of that year the Parlement took up the challenge and condemned what it called arbitrary government, the King again held a *lit de justice* to secure the registration of the edicts aiming at destroying the privileges of the *parlements.* At the same time troops surrounded the law courts in the capital. Now all classes rallied against the King in support of the *parlements.* The middle classes backed the nobility and higher clergy; hundreds of pamphlets were published condemning the edicts of May; riots took place in many parts of the country, where the *parlementaires* exploited the economic grievances of the masses. The King was again forced to yield; Brienne was dismissed and replaced by Necker; and a meeting of the States-General was promised in May 1789.

This was to toll the knell of the French King and aristocracy. But before we leave the aristocracy which had ruled Europe for so many years, let us see what kings and nobilities had done to encourage and create the arts in the eighteenth century. To reverse Tom Paine's dictum, as we watch the dying bird, let us praise his plumage.

3. The Age of Rococo

By the beginning of the eighteenth century the *style Louis XIV* was drawing to its close and baroque took on a new lease of life, spreading eastward from Italy to Germany, Austria, and Russia. At the end of his life the *Roi Soleil* himself felt that something more youthful was needed in the decoration of the Château de la Menagerie, designed for the thirteen-year-old Duchess of Burgundy, whereupon the Surveyor of the Royal Works, Jules-Hardouin Mansart, submitted drawings showing ceilings covered with a pattern of arabesques, the motifs consisting of

> acanthus leaves, garlands of flowers, ribbons, arrows, stylized rustic bowers, all spun out like filagree work, with hunting dogs, birds and figures of young girls perched among the tendrils and branches.

The King thought the drawings charming, and this was to become the keyword for the rococo style, which was to embellish and later to supersede baroque. Rococo was originally a style of surface decoration, not of three-dimensional architecture. Its features included a lavish use of S-shaped curves and C-shaped scrolls, of mirrors, French windows, and *boiseries;* it favored gold and pale colors; it paid much attention to lighting; and it used naturalistic motifs woven in a gay spirit. Though in France rococo was employed only in interior decoration, toward the middle of the century it played such an important part, especially in German architecture, that it is possible to describe it as a successor to baroque. Even if this is an oversimplification, it is generally accepted as a rough guideline that the first forty years of the century were dominated by baroque and rococo in architecture; that in the middle of the century a period of artistic restlessness occurred, which coincided with the writings of the *philosophes;* while in the closing years neoclassicism, to be exemplified particularly in Napoleonic France, again became fashionable.

It has been said that the masters of the Roman baroque regarded themselves as liberators of the human spirit—and this must also have been true of the German masters of rococo—while the roots of neoclassicism were essentially didactic. The rococo style spread speedily, so that every European court had its rococo phase. The greatest rococo architects included the Frenchmen Meissonier and Cuvilliés and Gilles Marie Oppenordt, an apprentice of J.-H. Mansart, who was sent to study in Rome. This was a time when the German princes and aristocrats had a mania for extravagant building. For example, the Elector of Bavaria, Max Emmanuel, brought François de Cuvilliés, who was a dwarf born in 1695, to Munich, where he designed the Reichen Zimmer in the Residenz and the Amalienburg, a summer house outside the city. His style of decoration, more naturalistic than the rococo in France, soon acquired admirers and imitators throughout Germany. Another celebrated architect of the time was Batholomeo Francesco Rastrelli, an Italian who came to Russia when he was fifteen and then was sent to Paris, where he obtained a taste for rococo. It was he who built the Winter Palace at Saint Petersburg and the palace of Tsarkoe Selo outside the city for the Tsarina Elizabeth, giving Russia two fantastically elongated buildings conceived and decorated in the new style. Frederick the Great and Carlos III were other monarchs who were then building themselves palaces, but the *Neues Palas* at Potsdam was influenced by the Palladianism of Inigo Jones, and the royal palace at Caserta in Naples represented the French classical style. In Piedmont Victor Amadeus II invited Filippo Juvarra, a distinguished Italian architect, to design palaces and churches in which he managed to combine Renaissance style with baroque. All these palaces and churches exemplify the architectural restlessness of the mid-century.

Many churches and palace-monasteries were also built in a variety of styles. In southern Germany, Bohemia, Switzerland, and Austria baroque churches sprang up. Brilliant examples survive in Bavaria. The interiors of all the churches were lighter and more spacious than the baroque. In Spain, notably at Toledo Cathedral, rococo reached its most bizarre.

It was only to be expected that a reaction would take place against the elaborate decoration of baroque and rococo, especially in Protestant countries, where it was hardly suited to church architecture. The reaction began in Great Britain, where a Scottish architect, Colin Campbell, and Richard Boyle, the third Earl of Burlington, who was himself an architect of distinction, urged a reversion to the classical style of Palladio and Inigo Jones. Wanstead House in Essex (designed by Campbell) and the Assembly Rooms at York (designed by Burlington) showed the new trend; when James Gibbs, who had been trained in the late baroque, designed Saint-Martin's-in-the-Fields (now in Trafalgar Square), he built it largely in the classical style. Elsewhere in Europe the reaction took place somewhat later when writers like Laugier (in France), Winckelmann (a German who spent most of his life in Rome), and Piranesi (in Venice) advocated noble simplicity and a calm grandeur. There was some dispute among the advocates of neoclassicism whether Greek or Roman models should be followed; but as at that time extremely little was known about either Greek architecture or sculpture (even the Parthenon was unfamiliar to western Europeans until the nineteenth century), the Romans had the advantage. The temple at Nîmes was considered an ideal model by Laugier, and it impressed Thomas Jefferson when he visited Europe.

The idea that architecture should be rational and functional as well as grand and noble gradually spread throughout Europe in the second half of the century. Neoclassicism produced a whole series of books on esthetics, ranging from Cordemoy to Kant. It resulted in the building of the Pantheon in Paris and Somerset House in London. It stimulated interest in archaeology. It influenced town planning, leaving to posterity the Place de la Concorde in Paris, Bedford Square in London, and the Brandenburg Gate in Berlin. No doubt it was suited to modern imperialism and capitalism; but it lacked the excitement, the color and the inventive decoration of baroque and rococo, which belonged to the aristocratic world that was to be shaken by revolution.

Painting also tended to reflect a changing climate of opinion. Religious paintings were obviously unsuited to an age of scepticism, and the only outstanding Christian painter was Giambattista Tiepolo. On the other hand, it was urged, particularly by Diderot and Sir Joshua Reynolds (the first President of the Royal Academy of Art), that the artist's duty is to promote moral education. Some painters did so, such as Hogarth in England and to a lesser extent Chardin and Greuze in France. William Hogarth *(1697-1784)* had originally wanted to be a history painter, but found there was no market for this kind of work; he also resented the activities of Lord Burlington and

Canvassing for Votes
WILLIAM HOGARTH (1757)
Memorial Art Gallery of the University of Rochester

his school, who built themselves Palladian houses and stocked them full of Italian paintings. So he turned to social satire; his series of paintings such as *The Harlot's Progress* throw a flood of light on London in his time. Greuze was also a didactic painter who depicted virtuous milkmaids and dutiful sons, but tended to sentimentalize them. Chardin, the finest of the three, specialized in edifying domestic narrative.

But the eighteenth century was most distinguished by open-air paintings, its *"fêtes galantes,"* and its portraiture. Antoine Watteau, a consumptive who died young, was perhaps the greatest painter of the century. He is sometimes described as a "rococo" painter, as Tiepolo has also been. Certainly Watteau reacted against the classical style. His own style was intensely personal and elusive. Nevertheless, his genius influenced not only French painters such as Le Moyne, Lancret, Boucher (the favorite of Madame de Pompadour), and Fragonard, but also the best English painter of the century, Thomas Gainsborough.

Gainsborough was a versatile artist who loved painting landscapes in his native Suffolk but made a fortune out of portraiture. His contemporary Richard Wilson devoted himself entirely to landscapes. They may be said to have started a line of nature painters in which Constable and Turner were to follow. In Italy tourists flocked from all over Europe to see the sights of Venice and to buy the paintings of Antonio Canaletto, Francesco Guardi, Sebastiano Ricci, and most of all Tiepolo. Venice became almost as popular a tourist center as Rome, but whereas Canaletto and Guardi were content to preserve imaginatively the beauties of their native city, Tiepolo's work was in demand from Bavaria to Spain, where he died. As Professor Ettinger has written, "Tiepolo's brush created a perfectly real world of unreality for the grandiose dreams of his patrons." The Germans also boasted their own artists, who ranged from the Asam brothers, exponents of the high baroque, to Anton Raphael Menges, son of a court painter in Dresden, who engaged with immense success in the neoclassical style preferred by Winckelmann.

4. Music Brings Romance

If architecture and, to a lesser extent, painting were dependent on the patronage of monarchs, the aristocracy, and the Church, so too, very emphatically, was music. Indeed, many operas and concerts were performed only for the benefit of courts and courtiers. This applied also to masques, ballets, and plays. In his old age Voltaire put on plays that he himself had written, and invited his friends to see them in his private theater at Ferney. Plays and operas were rarely performed more than a few times in the same theater, thus suggesting that patronage depended on a limited ruling class. The seventeenth century had discovered the opera and the concerto; Italian operas date from the beginning of that century. Then Jean-Baptiste Lully, although he himself was a Florentine, became Louis XIV's musical dictator and the founder of French opera, based on a tragical-lyrical style which differed from that of Italy. By the eighteenth century opera had spread to Germany: and while southern Germany favored Italian opera, northern Germany found a few operatic composers of its own. Most German princes and dukes, besides building their own versions of Versailles palace, had their own court musicians and court organists.

In spite of the vast output of operas or lyrical dramas and the stimulus they received from the Court of Vienna, by the middle of the eighteenth century a reaction set in against *opera seria* with its stately classical themes. As early as 1728 John Gay's *Beggar's Opera,* a burlesque of Italian opera (and also of the British Prime Minister Walpole), had a striking success in London. In the middle of the century *Le Devin du Village,* a lyrical play by the versatile genius Jean-Jacques Rousseau, and Pergolesi's *Serva Padrona,* an early example of *opera buffa,* were acclaimed in Paris and elsewhere. Two other *opera buffa, Les Troquers* and *La Fille Mal Gardée,* both written by Frenchmen, were successes in Paris, and by 1790 the Comédie Française and the Opera Comique were well established there. In the period 1762–70 Christoph Willibald Gluck, a German trained in Italy, breathed new life into the *opera seria,* his most notable innovation being the substitution of orchestral recitative for the recitative *secco.* The first of three "reform" operas by Gluck, *Orfeo and Euridice,* was well received in Vienna in 1762.

But even if experiments were not unwelcome, there was a diminution of enthusiasm for opera as the century advanced. The operas of Rameau, a highly intelligent French composer, who aimed to succeed Lully, were severely criticized. Handel, although he wrote thirty-nine operas, abandoned their composition in favor of oratorios when he had finally settled in England. Mozart's *Le Nozze de Figaro* (1786) and *Don Giovanni* (1787), two of the greatest operas that have ever been written, caused little stir except in Prague; Beethoven's *Fidelio* was withdrawn after three performances in 1805.

Apart from these last three operas, the finest musical achievements of the century were to be found in symphonies and sonatas, in church music, and in chamber music. The first four-part symphony was performed in 1740. Symphony drew for its inspiration on concertos and operas. The names of Haydn, Mozart, and Beethoven are immortally linked with the symphony. Johann Sebastian Bach, who wrote neither operas nor symphonies, was the greatest artistic genius produced by the Lutheran Church; employed for most of his life as an organist, he composed a succession of cantatas and oratorios. Handel, also a German Lutheran, wrote magnificent oratorios after he abandoned opera; this dramatic music was intended for the concert halls rather than the churches. It has been said that in Handel's oratorios, he "glorified the rise of the free people of England," of whom the people of Israel were the prototype. Beethoven was a sincere Roman Catholic whose masses reflect both his musical genius and his unshakable religious faith.

*Mozart with his father, Leopold,
and his sister, Nannerl*
Watercolor by Louis Carrogis de
Carmontelle
By courtesy of the Trustees
of the British Museum

Nearly all these splendid composers—centered for the most part in Vienna—wrote a vast amount of chamber music ranging from piano sonatas (the piano was Mozart's favorite instrument) to string quartets, in which many believe that the sublimity of Beethoven's genius was reached. But whereas the appeal of the later quartets is essentially to the trained musical intellect, his symphonies and his *Missa Solemnis* can move all men at all times.

Unquestionably these musical works, ranging from the compositions of Lully and Purcell through Handel and the Bach family to Haydn, Mozart, and Beethoven, are the noblest contributions of the period 1648–1815 to European civilization. But two things must be said about them from the historical point of view: the first is that contemporary appreciation by no means coincided with that of later generations. What the aristocratic patrons required was light entertainment and virtuoso compositions. Thus, Johann Sebastian Bach was praised as a first-class organist rather than for his original music. Mozart was insufficiently valued and his operas were mostly failures: they were even called "heavy." Though he was launched by his father as an infant prodigy, he was buried in a pauper's grave at the age of

Ludwig van Beethoven
Oil on copper by JOHANNES HEINRICH RAMBERT (1820)
The Granger Collection

thirty-five. Beethoven's music did not appeal to the aristocratic salons: his tragedy was that he had to live through the Napoleonic upheaval, and before he died he became stone-deaf. Yet his impact on nineteenth-century music was enormous. Secondly, whereas in the late twentieth century art is mainly dependent upon the State or Church (the millionaires who earlier functioned as patrons are becoming exhausted), in the eighteenth century art required aristocratic patrons; and artists who failed to please their patrons lost their way and had no real outlet for their genius. The revolutionary leaders were not to be discerning patrons of the arts. Even Napoleon had little taste. As the neoclassicism which the Revolution was to promote died, romanticism slowly began to evolve.

The revolutionary or *Sturm und Drang* period of German history, which began with the poet Klopstock's drama of that name first performed in 1776, emotionally inspired educated Germans of the time, and Rousseau projected a romantic movement in Europe. It is also possible to detect romantic elements in Beethoven, which were developed by a succession of composers from Schubert to Mahler. Poetry and music are often called the characteristic arts of romanticism. In Goethe and Schiller, in Wordsworth and Coleridge one can trace the beginnings of the movement before the eighteenth century was over. But its story, well attuned to revolutionary feelings, really belongs to the next century.

It is perhaps not wrong to say roughly that baroque stemmed from the Church, rococo from the eighteenth-century aristocracy, and neoclassicism from French imperialism victorious after revolution.

5. Long-term Causes of the French Revolution

Such were the gifts provided to European civilization by the aristocracy which had enjoyed a resurgence in the 1770s and 1780s, a resurgence which some historians have used as a curtain-raiser to the French Revolution or even as the opening stage of the Revolution itself. But what the French aristocracy hoped to do was to retain as much as it could of its old privileges and wealth against the attempts of Calonne and Brienne at radical reform, and it also hoped to dominate the States-General when it met. Professor Hobsbawm puts it this way:

> The Revolution . . . began as an aristocratic attempt to recapture the state. This attempt miscalculated for two reasons: it underestimated the independent intentions of the "Third Estate" . . . and it overlooked the profound economic and social crisis into which it threw its political demands.

What were the long-term causes of the French Revolution, and when in fact did it begin? For more than 150 years French historians have debated the subject, but there seems to be more of a consensus today than there used to be. Three main explanations of the Revolution have been favored, and of course they can be blended with one another. The first explanation is that the Revolution was brought about by "the people" as a whole, who demanded political reform; the second is that it was a conspiracy by an active minority who, fed by the teaching of the *philosophes,* had lost all veneration for ancient institutions and demanded a new deal; the third is that it was a revolt of the underprivileged classes, who were resentful of their economic disabilities and sought a social revolution that would give them authority. As in the case of the seventeenth-century revolution in England, it was sparked off by an economic crisis.

The first explanation attunes with the idea that this was an age of democracy. But as yet democracy and democratic ideas could scarcely be said to be flourishing in Europe, but only up to a point in North America. The older French historians, notably Mignet and Thiers, expounded this view; so did Michelet, writing just before the Revolution of 1848: it has been said that this version of the Revolution was a "romantic" one which took "the people" for its hero; for Thomas Carlyle, the Scottish mystic, writing about the same time but looking at it from the opposite point of view, it was a tragedy of the frenzied mob. Louis Madelin, a French academician, writing in 1911, described it as a rebellion against inequality; F. V. A. Aulard, who died in 1928 and had devoted most of his life to scholarly documentation, gave it a patriotic and democratic interpretation. For those who accepted this point of view the Revolution was inevitable. The enlightened middle class could no longer be excluded from power; yet a peaceable liberal bourgeois solution was in the circumstances of the time an impossibility. When the Republic was attacked from abroad, the people responded patriotically to the challenge. The ideals of the Revolution were embodied in the Declaration of the Rights of Man and Citizen.

The "conspiracy" version of the French Revolution is generally said to have originated with the British statesman Edmund Burke, who published his *Reflections on the Revolution in France* as early as 1790. For him the old order of things, in which the monarchy and aristocracy constituted the ruling classes, was the best. Democracy undermined authority and damaged social stability. Institutions hallowed by time were essential, though they might be gradually improved. But the *philosophes* had attacked these institutions both in Church and State and had thereby imperiled the whole of Christian Europe. A minority, poisoned by the doctrines of the *philosophes,* had conspired to fashion a revolution dragging the ignorant mob along with it. Several historians and a number of popular writers have accepted the conspiracy theory over the years. Taine, writing after the French defeat in 1870, attributed the decline of his country to the events of the Revolution. He was a pessimistic determinist. The body politic, he thought, had been envenomed by a materialist and atheist philosophy masquerading as *l'esprit classique.* The middle-class Jacobins were a minority carried away by this spirit, and they managed to infect the scum of the kingdom, who then overthrew established institutions in a mass hysteria. Though few today would accept Taine's fanatical attitude toward the Revolution, the thesis of conspiracy has found advocates more sophisticated than Taine. Cochin, a French historian killed in the First World War, whose last book was published posthumously, maintained that Freemasons and other secret societies had propogated the teachings of the *philosophes* and created a revolutionary mob.

How far is it true to say that the Revolution was inspired by the writings of the *philosophes* and of Voltaire and Rousseau? It used to be thought that the publication of the *Encyclopédie,* like that of Voltaire's *Lettres philoso-*

phiques, was a bomb thrown at the ancien régime. Contemporaries like Burke believed that an anti-Christian conspiracy had been concocted by *philosophes,* sophists, and anarchists, and that their chief weapon was the *Encyclopédie.* But it has to be remembered that the scepticism felt by most of the contributors to the *Encyclopédie* was subtly displayed and can only have penetrated to a limited readership. Many of the articles can scarcely have aroused revolutionary feelings. The main attacks of the *philosophes* were directed against orthodox Christianity, and that certainly affected the character of the Revolution. Voltaire too, especially in his old age, directed his social criticism chiefly against the Roman Catholic Church. But Diderot, the principal editor of the *Encyclopédie,* thought of Catherine the Great as an enlightened reformer, just as at one time Voltaire had high hopes for Frederick the Great. In his books on Louis XIV and Charles XII of Sweden, Voltaire found praise for absolute monarchs. Though Voltaire was not completely consistent in his political attitudes, he was opposed to the pretensions of the Parlement of Paris and, on the whole, looked to enlightened monarchs to carry out reforms. He differentiated absolutism from despotism and thought that an absolute monarchy was suited to France. The French historian Mornet, whose book on the intellectual origins of the Revolution was first published in 1933, concluded that the influence of the *philosophes* was minimal and that the literate classes were chiefly concerned over practical problems. He thought that if intelligence only had menaced the ancien régime it would have run no risk. The late Alfred Cobban considered that Rousseau's *Contrat social* had no ascertainable influence upon the Revolution and only a very debatable one upon its course. He believed that Locke's political ideas, as interpreted by Montesquieu, had a greater impact. Joan McDonald in her recent book *Rousseau and the French Revolution* asserts that the *Contrat social* was little read or even heard of; it was scarcely referred to in the debates in the Jacobin Club. *Émile* and the *Nouvelle Héloïse,* which were concerned with education and morality, were much more widely read. The Abbé Sieyè's pamphlet *Qu'est-ce que Le Tiers État?,* published in January 1789, was far more effective than the profound and abstract arguments of Rousseau. She concludes that any attempt to link the Enlightenment with the Revolution as cause and effect is unacceptable.

    The third interpretation of the causes of the French Revolution stresses its economic and class aspects: it naturally finds its most definitive form in the writings of socialist and Marxist historians. But one of the first advocates was De Tocqueville, who has been described as "the most serene and impartial of the historians of the Revolution." De Tocqueville argued, in contradistinction to Michelet, who had seen the Revolution as a crisis of famine or a war of hunger, that it was the very prosperity of the underprivileged classes that had made them all the more conscious of the injustices from which they suffered: the peasantry, generally a conservative class, became aware that they could earn a decent livelihood from the rich French soil if only it were not for the triple burden of taxation, tithe, and seignurial dues. But other classes, notably the bourgeoisie, the men of commerce, and the professional classes, were also irked by the advantages enjoyed by the aristocracy, which had actually been increased in the course of the century: the two nobilities, constituting some four hundred thousand out of a total population of 26 million, were not allowed to practice a trade or profession and lived, exempt from taxation, on rents and seignurial dues or benefited from commissions in the army, high positions in the State, such as the intendancies, and valuable offices in the Church, almost exclusively. Thus, they provided ample cause for jealousy.

It was because of these sharp class distinctions that De Tocqueville considered that the break-up of the French social structure was more or less inevitable. Actually, the argument is somewhat exaggerated; for example, the nobility had been required to pay taxes from the middle of the eighteenth century. Later Jaurès, himself a practicing socialist, also expressed his belief that the events of 1789 were brought about by an alliance between the bourgeoisie, the peasants, and the urban proletariat. Jaurès had a disciple in Mathiez, who had formerly been a pupil of Aulard but had quarreled with him. Both of them were superb examples of the scientific historian. But whereas Aulard had stressed the poetic and idealistic view of the triumph of the people over their oppressors, Mathiez thought of the Revolution in terms of classes and economic forces. His hero was Robespierre, the ruthless leader of the Jacobins (just as the rather less ruthless Danton was the hero of Aulard and Madelin), and he defended the Terror as an essential stage in the Revolution. Although Robespierre was in fact bourgeois, Mathiez considered that the people had been duped by the bourgeoisie and ultimately betrayed by the coup of Thermidor. The bourgeoisie had been prosperous before the Revolution and through the Revolution became more prosperous still. The Declaration of the Rights of Man was "the work of the middle classes," which condemned ancient abuses but upheld property and religion and "subordinated equality to social utility." To them property was as sacrosanct as it had been to the English revolutionaries of 1642 or 1688.

The work of Mathiez gave a tremendous impulse to the study of economic and class history. He himself did not study the peasantry deeply; his investigations were largely concentrated on the underworld of Paris. But the peasants represented over 80 percent of the French population, and it is realized more and more that their discontents lay behind the Revolution. The bread riots and the *jacqueries* which took place during the eighteenth century were not of course confined to France but, as De Tocqueville saw, it was because they had experienced relative affluence that grievances bit deeply into the peasants' minds. Modern research, notably that of Labrousse, has shown that from 1733 up till 1776 the French economy was flourishing. Labrousse speaks of "a revolution of prosperity." The price of farm products rose and profits grew; the expansion of commerce and industry created new markets, and there were no famines. Although during the period 1775-87 the price of grain remained stable, scattered bread riots occurred. After 1778, when France went to war, a depression began which particularly affected wine and textiles. A trade treaty concluded with Great Britain in 1786 injured the French economy except for the wine trade. Unemployment rose. Finally, the harvests were poor in 1784 and 1787 and, above all, in 1788, when the price of wheat doubled.

Although the peasants owned much of the land—figures of a third to a half have been given—they did not own much of the best land, and many of the peasants owned quite small plots. Thus, the ironic situation arose that although farming was their living the poorer peasants did not grow enough to feed their own families, and in the years of bad harvests, such as those of 1787 and 1788, they actually faced starvation. While the King was quarreling with his *parlements* in 1788 and the demand for the summoning of the States-General was being made, massive riots were taking place: this was the revolution of hunger. Before the elections to the States-General were held in 1789, the electorate was invited to put forward its grievances in *cahiers* (on paper). Many of these *cahiers* have survived. It is remarkable that whereas the nobility complained about the arbitrary acts of the monarchy and the bourgeoisie sought civil equality and freedom of speech, the *cahiers* drawn up in the rural parishes demanded a reduction in the price of bread and a lightening of the burdens of taxation, tithe, and seignurial dues. From the end of 1788 onward much of the French countryside had been disturbed by outbreaks of violence, and while in Versailles in 1789 the three Estates were contending for political supremacy, the peasantry succumbed to what was known as *La Grande Peur*—a rumor that the aristocracy and landlords were going to employ armed brigands to revenge themselves on the rural rioters. This rumor induced peasants during the high summer to burn down *châteaux* and destroy manor rolls. Thus, the revolutionaries in Paris and Versailles had the support of the mass of the people.

It is plain that all classes played a part in bringing about the Revolution: this was made particularly clear in the synthesis achieved by the late Georges Lefebvre, a great historian. The Assembly of Notables paved the way for the meeting of the States-General. The bourgeoisie dominated the Third Estate which fashioned the States-General into a National Assembly. But these revolutionary movements, which pulverized the monarchy and the ancien régime, would not have been successful if it had not been for the backing of mobs in the towns and the rebellious peasants in the country. But it is important also to understand that these classes were by no means homogeneous. A wide gap existed between the wealthy nobility living on rents drawn from their family estates or the perquisites of office and the *hoberaux*, whose relative poverty confined them to a restricted life in the country. The bourgeoisie, a convenient but greatly overworked word, might be merchants and industrialists or professional men and officials. The city mob might have been wage earners or small shopkeepers and workshop masters. The peasants could be well-to-do freeholders or landless agricultural workers living on the margin of subsistence. Lefebvre wrote that "the revolution is only the crown of a long economic and social revolution which had made the bourgeoisie the mistress of the world." But this, it has been suggested, is an oversimplification. In the first place, internal peace—the absence of disturbances of any sort—is most conducive to the interests of merchants and industrialists. The bourgeoisie who led the Revolution belonged not to a capitalist class but to professions or the municipal bureaucracy. Robespierre and Danton were both lawyers; Desmoulins was a journalist. Over four hundred members of the Constituent Assembly were listed as lawyers. The phrase *rural bourgeoisie* has sometimes been used by French historians, but it is really a contradiction in terms. Nevertheless, it appears to be true that it was the better-to-do classes both in the town and the country who benefited from the Revolution. The late Professor Cobban maintained that "the revolution was a triumph for the conservative, propertied, land-owning classes, large and small," while Lefebvre argued that the peasant proprietors, shopkeepers, and professional men—the three classes that contributed most to the Revolution—all struggled *against* the forces of rising capitalism. The Revolution was neither a triumph for the new industrial capitalism, which was winning its way forward in contemporary Great Britain, nor, on the other hand, did it mean the emancipation of the French poor. What emerged from the Revolution was a new landed aristocracy and a new bureaucracy.

Whatever the results of the Revolution may have been, its leaders had from the beginning been careful to preserve the rights of private property and private enterprise. Yet the Revolution was essentially a social one directed against the ancien régime. As Professor Hobsbawm has written, "a riotous people stood behind the deputies of the Third Estate." For this reason it is difficult to accept that the Revolution began with the so-called· *révolte nobiliaire* of 1787. Both the nobility *de la robe,* as represented in the Parlement of Paris, and the nobility *de l'épee,* who were called to the Assembly of Notables, were determined to resist "revolution from above." Voltaire perceived that they were selfish reactionaries. Their activities formed part of the "aristocratic resurgence" which, as has been seen, was taking place all over Europe in the later part of the eighteenth century. The real revolt came from the Brutuses of the States-General who took over the leadership of the National Assembly. Most of the nobility and higher clergy had withstood this political revolution as long as they could. But the Third Estate, though the bulk of its members belonged to the "enlightened middle class," had allies in the Paris mob and in the peasantry, who were resentful about shortages of food and high prices. This they blamed on the aristocracy as well as on the monarchical government.

What one sees everywhere throughout Europe in the latter part of the eighteenth century is growing resentment against the privileges of the landed aristocracy. For the modern man it can perhaps be perceived most readily in the operas of Mozart: the libretto of the greatest of them, *The Marriage of Figaro,* owed its inspiration to the French satirist Beaumarchais, who had taken an active part in helping the American War of Independence. How the aristocracy must have been hated! How the villagers must have been riled by the efforts of a Count Almaviva, as of right, to seduce Susanna, or a Don Giovanni to entice Zerlina. In what contempt they must have held their masters, such as was felt by Figaro or by Don Giovanni's servant, Leporello. But resentment could not easily be transformed into effective action. A revolution from above, such as was attempted by Joseph II, created suspicions among the peasants which could actually be stimulated by their landlords. A revolution from below, like Pugachev's rising in Russia, could be crushed by the exercise of military might. The Revolution took place in France because the peasants and the *menu* (humbler) people in the towns found leaders in the middle class, who had their own grievances but were also inspired by political ideals. Thus, the French Revolution became evangelical. The Declaration of the Rights of Man and Citizen had a universal appeal. War was to be declared not in order to "make conquests" but to "liberate peoples." French revolutionary ideals of equality were to arouse enthusiasm, at any rate among educated people, elsewhere in Europe, and in a few cases gave birth to spontaneous insurrections. But whether the French Revolution as such was part of a general democratic revolution is doubtful.

The new French regime had to withstand a counterrevolution aimed at preserving the aristocracy in the Indian Summer of its power. The counterrevolution failed. On the other hand, the old established order of European society could hardly be destroyed in a few years. It was not in fact until 1830 or 1848 that western aristocracy finally succumbed in an industrialized Europe.

EIGHT

Revolution

1. The Constituent Assembly

Whatever the long-term causes of the French Revolution may have been, little doubt exists about its immediate causes. They were compounded of the failure of the King's ministers to solve the problems of public finances; the weakness of Louis XVI himself, who was constantly changing his mind and was unduly under the influence of his wife, the indiscreet and headstrong Austrian Marie Antoinette; and the ambitions of the middle-class leaders of the Third Estate, who had previously been excluded from political power. The growing importance of the Third Estate was recognized when the Royal Council decided that it should have double representation as compared with the other two Estates. The atmosphere of unrest, which prevailed throughout most of the country during the winter of 1788-89 and showed itself in peasant demonstrations against the most privileged classes, strengthened the hands of the Third Estate. At the end of January 1789 the Abbé Sieyès, who was to prove himself to be a prolific constitution-monger, published his *Qu'est-ce que le Tiers État?* in which he claimed that the Third Estate constituted the nation. The general *cahiers de doléances* ("lists of grievances") drawn up by the Third Estate demanded not only the destruction of absolutism but the complete equality of the Estates. When the States-General met at Versailles on May 5 the Third Estate was determined that the three Estates should not meet separately as before, but should all join together to form a united assembly which could then obtain political and social reforms on a national basis.

The method of electing the deputies of the Third Estate was complicated; for whereas the nobility and clergy voted directly, the elections to the Third Estate were indirect. The deputies were, in the words of Lefebvre, "for the most part mature, rich or well-to-do, educated, industrious and honest men"; the bulk of them were lawyers or practiced other professions; there were only a few peasants. When the King and his ministers addressed the twelve hundred members of the three Estates, they offered little guidance about what they were expected to do other than to put the royal finances in order. (This was reminiscent of the English revolutionary Parliament nearly 150 years earlier.) But the Third Estate was of one mind: under the influence of the writings of Sieyès and the oratory of Honoré de Mirabeau, a renegade from the order of nobility, the members refused on May 7 to verify their powers, elect a president, or constitute themselves a separate chamber. On the contrary, after four weeks of confusion, they decided to invite the other Estates to join them so as to create one body representative of the entire kingdom. The nobility refused, but a substantial minority of the clergy (mainly lower clergy) was sympathetic. On June 17 the Third Estate, which had now been joined by a few parish priests, voted by 491 to 90 to assume the title of National Assembly. On June 19 the majority of the Estate of the clergy and some noblemen decided to take part in this National Assembly. On June 20 the National Assembly, finding itself locked out from its usual meeting hall, gathered in a nearby tennis court, where it swore not to dissolve until a new constitution had been agreed. That was a direct challenge to the monarchy.

The King's brother, the Comte d'Artois, had childishly ordered that the tennis court where the National Assembly had sworn its oath should be reserved on the following day (the Assembly met instead in a church, where the Third Estate was joined by the Estate of clergy), and it was the Comte d'Artois, together with the Queen, who persuaded the King to make his next move. On June 23 the King met the three Estates in a hall surrounded by troops, declared the decrees of the self-titled National Assembly were voided, and commanded all three Estates to separate from each other. When the Third Estate stood its ground, soldiers were summoned to the doors. Mirabeau cried out to them: "Go tell your master that nothing but bayonets will drive us from here!" The King gave way: he agreed to the amalgamation of the three Estates; and on July 7 the National Assembly appointed a committee to plan discussions about a new constitution.

Why did the King yield? In the first place, he was conscious of the growing unrest in Paris. Here the Duke of Orleans (who, like Mirabeau, had got himself elected as a deputy of the Third Estate) organized at the Palais Royal a revolutionary committee which distributed propaganda and aimed to win over the army from its loyalty to the Crown. At the same time the electors in Paris established a headquarters at the Hotel de Ville (town hall) and drew up plans for a citizens' National Guard. Secondly, Louis XVI became aware of disloyalty among his soldiers, some of whom had disobeyed orders on June 23. Henceforward the King's policy—if it can be called a policy—became one of trying to conciliate the National Assembly, seeking first the advice of Mirabeau (who took his pay) and that of another renegade aristocrat, the Marquis de Lafayette; later Louis XVI relied on the advice of three deputies—Barnave, Lameth, and Duport—who belonged to the Jacobin society, a political club originally formed in Versailles, and who were known as the Triumvirate.

But before he did this the King took what proved to be an unwise step: for a second time (on July 11) he dismissed Necker, the only minister trusted by the Assembly. Necker's dismissal had profound consequences. As Lefebvre wrote, it led to a display of three aspects of the revolutionary mentality which frequently followed one another: fear, a defensive reaction, and the will to punish. Many Parisians, already angry over the high prices then ruling (the price of a loaf of bread was double what it was normally) and influenced by the propaganda of the Palais Royal, were fearful that reactionary moves, backed by the army, had been decided upon. A call to arms was issued from the Palais Royal; demonstrators clashed with cavalry in the Tuileries gardens; the Paris garrison withdrew under mob pressure. Next the crowd turned its attention to the internal customs *(octrois)*, which they blamed for the high prices. Customs posts were burned down and customs offices wrecked. Then a hunt for arms began and continued for two days. On July 14 a mob marched to the Bastille, the royal fortress to which State prisoners were sent but was now almost empty: the intention was to obtain the gunpowder stored there and to force the governor to withdraw the guns from the battlements. An armed crowd was supported by two detachments of disloyal guardsmen led by a noncommissioned officer. The governor

Storming of the Bastille, July 14, 1789
© Giraudon

surrendered, but nevertheless he and a few of his garrison were massacred. The fall of the Bastille symbolized the end of the ancien régime and was greeted with rejoicing by liberals throughout Europe.

When the news of the fall of the Bastille reached Versailles the National Assembly was delighted: it assumed that an attempt at coercion by the army had been frustrated. The King was shaken and told the Assembly that he would visit Paris: when he did so, he was greeted by a deputy named Bailly, who had been appointed Mayor; unflinchingly the King put on a tricolored cockade which had been adopted by the Paris revolutionaries as their emblem, and later listened to lectures by orators at the Hotel de Ville. It was from the Hotel de Ville that a National Guard was being organized, with Lafayette as commandant, to maintain order and sustain the revolution. Here a Commune was set up. Towns in the provinces followed suit, appointing communes and forming national guards. The events in Paris gave a further stimulus to rural revolt. The rumor that the aristocracy was sending out armed brigands to wreak vengeance on the peasantry provoked further outbreaks, anarchy prevailing through much of the French countryside. This *"Grande Peur"* lasted from July 20 to August 6. But the truth was that the aristocracy was losing its nerve. The Comte d'Artois and other members of the nobility began in the second half of July to emigrate from France. It was assumed that the *émigrés* would seek foreign aid from their fellow aristocrats abroad. So the revolutionary leaders became sharper and more determined.

The National Assembly pushed forward with its revolutionary reforms. Stimulated by the *Grande Peur,* to pacify the peasants early in August it declared that seignurial rights, tithes and the *corvée* were abolished, and on August 27th the Declaration of the Rights of Man was adopted. Then the debate on the new constitution began. A minority of the Assembly favored an English-type constitution giving the King an absolute veto over legislation and establishing an upper chamber. But the majority was doubtful about the King and feared a second Chamber would be dominated by the aristocracy. They had good reason to distrust Louis XVI, who was again vacillating. He refused to give his assent to the August decrees, he would not accept the Declaration of Rights, and he summoned the Flanders regiment to join his Life Guards in Versailles, where it arrived at the end of September.

Once again the Paris mob came to the rescue of the Assembly. Force was met with force. Although the harvest had been good, flour was scarce and so the price of bread was raised in the bakers' shops. On October 5 a crowd of women gathered outside the Hotel de Ville demanding bread. A march on Versailles was improvised to present their grievances to the King and the National Assembly. The women (together with some men dressed as women) set forth to "fetch the baker, the baker's wife and the little baker's boy" and were followed by National Guardsmen led by the reluctant Lafayette. The King again yielded to intimidation and announced his acceptance of the August decrees and the Declaration of Rights. He also gave orders for the provisioning of Paris. But the mob was not satisfied. It compelled the King, Queen, and Dauphin to come back with it to Paris "like cattle on the way to the slaughter house." Ten days later the National Assembly also moved to Paris and on November 9 met in the riding school in the Tuileries.

During the remainder of 1789 and throughout 1790 and much of 1791 the Constituent Assembly, as it was now known, devoted itself to far-reaching work of political and social reform. It was decided that a Legislative Assembly should be elected from which the King's ministers were to be excluded and also, by a self-denying ordinance, all members of the Constitutent Assembly. The idea was that this new assembly should become supreme in the State, for the King was only to be allowed a suspensive veto. But it was to be a bourgeois assembly, because the deputies were required to have a property qualification and the electorate was divided into "active" and "passive" citizens, the active citizens being those who paid a minimum amount of taxes and were given votes. The property of the Church was nationalized; sales of Church lands began in May 1790, and in September bonds known as *assignats* came to be used as revolutionary paper money. The Church itself was subjected to the State and made more democratic by the promulgation of the Civil Constitution of the Clergy, which was accepted by the King on July 22. Henceforward bishops and parish priests were to be elected by all the "active" citizens and the numbers of dioceses reduced to equal the number of *départements* which were now being created throughout the kingdom. Clergy were required to take an oath to be loyal to the Civil Constitution on penalty of losing their benefices. But half the clergy refused to take the oath, and at length the Constitution was condemned by the Pope, Pius VI. Finally the Constituent Assembly conferred civil equality on Protestants and Jews.

Besides reforming local government, which became for the time being virtually a federation of elective *départements,* the judicial system was also radically reformed. The King's prerogative powers, the seignurial courts, and the old *parlements* were swept away. A network of tribunals was established at the head of which were a Court of Appeal and a High Court. The judiciary was declared independent of the King and dependent on the nation. Justice was to be free and the same for all.

Another egalitarian measure was the reform of taxation. The old immunities were abolished and a land tax and income tax payable by all owners of property was instituted. Indirect taxation was taken out of the hands of the tax farmers. Money was borrowed on the security of Church lands, which were put up for auction. By these means the Assembly was temporarily freed from financial difficulties. But the peasants were by no means satisfied with the new taxes; they also resented the fact that they were expected to pay compensation for the redemption of the seignurial dues, and they were annoyed that the Church lands were not allotted to them. As to the workers in the towns, they obtained little benefit from the new regime. The Declaration of Rights had upheld the sanctity of private property, a phrase which was interpreted generously. Slavery in the French colonies was not abolished; the Assembly passed in June 1791 the Le Chapelier law, which banned trade unions and strikes. Trade guilds were suppressed and public workshops closed. No provision was made for the unemployed.

Thus, the new Constitution, although it changed extensively the political organization of France and rid the kingdom of privileged classes, was of limited benefit to the masses. Essentially, it embodied ideas dear to middle-class individualism. The urban poor was given neither the right to vote nor the right to strike; the poor in the countryside were still at the mercy of the large landowners. But the principal weakness of the new order was that it had failed to construct an effective Government. The Legislative Assembly was given wide powers to become autocratic, but was obviously not a suitable instrument of government. Moreover, deputies who had acquired some political experience in the Constituent Assembly were ineligible for the Legislative Assembly. The King's ministers, also excluded, were in no position to govern. In any case they were mostly nonentities, and Louis XVI was driven to seek advice from politicians who held no official posts. Even the Legislative Assembly was largely directed from the outside by members of the political clubs which were establishing themselves in Paris, such as the Cordeliers Club, the Jacobin Club, and later the Feuillants Club. The Constitution, which was finally put into operation in September 1791, was justly described by Lefebvre as that of "a republic with no real government."

2. The Repercussions of the French Revolution on Belgium and the United Netherlands

Apart from the mutinies in the army, which had been repressed on orders from the Constituent Assembly, the year 1790 was comparatively calm in France. But the Revolution had its repercussions on Europe, though their character varied from country to country. The most violent disturbances took place in the Austrian Netherlands, which consisted of ten provinces, each with its own privileges and no national traditions. An incipient Belgian nationalism dated from 1786, when the Emperor Joseph II had attempted to impose constitutional and ecclesiastical reforms of a liberal character on all the provinces, overriding ancient privileges derived from their Burgundian past. The Estates of Brabant had risen in revolt; not until the spring of 1788 were they pacified, and then the pacification proved only temporary. In 1789 the Estates of Brabant again rebelled against Joseph II, refusing his request for subsidies and resisting his proposed constitutional changes. Henceforward every concession extorted from Louis XVI in France was an encouragement to the opposition to Joseph II. The Austrian garrison was too weak to check the rebellion, which spread from Brabant to the other Belgian provinces. In December Austrian troops were compelled to withdraw from Brabant after a successful rising in Brussels: here in January 1790 a United Federal Republic of Belgium was proclaimed. Although the French National Assembly was sympathetic, it was not prepared at this stage to intervene. The Emperor Leopold II, by abandoning most of his brother's attempted reforms and by sending a large army into Belgium, broke the rebel resistance and destroyed the Republic. But Belgian nationalism had been born.

Yet the Belgians were divided among themselves. The conservatives merely wanted to preserve the religious and social position they had enjoyed before Joseph II tried to introduce reforms. The *"Vonckists"* or "democrats," on the other hand, desired not only to throw off Austrian rule but to reduce the power of the privileged classes as was being done in France. Thus, if war were to begin between the French revolutionaries and the European monarchs, Belgium, which, as always, would become a battleground, was ripe for revolution.

The French Revolution also had a profound effect on the United Netherlands, one of the most civilized nations in Europe. But the political divisions among the Dutch, which dated back to the days of William II of Orange and John de Witt, were not really democratic. The Dutch Stadholder of the House of Orange had always been pro-British. William V of Orange (*r. 1751–95*) had an English mother, and his sympathies lay with Great Britain at the time of the American War of Independence. Nevertheless, the Dutch had gone to war with Great Britain, a war which they lost, and in 1784–87 the Dutch "patriots," who were mostly members of the upper middle classes, cooperated with the Dutch aristocracy or regents in an attempt to drive out William V and his Orangist party, an attempt from which he had been rescued by the Prussians. The French had backed the Patriots, who hoped to exact revenge upon the Orangists. A secret Batavian legion was formed of Patriots in exile in France (as two Belgian legions were also formed). But at first the French revolutionaries were not anxious to multiply enemies, and blew hot and cold on the would-be Dutch rebels.

3. The Destruction of Poland

The French Revolution also acted as a spur to a nationalist revolt in Poland, although there, as in Belgium, the character of the rebellion differed fundamentally from the radical movement against the King in France. The Polish Revolution, which broke out in 1788 and again in 1794, was neither bourgeois nor democratic and had little in common with the French Revolution. Indeed, the French revolutionaries regarded the Poles as reactionaries, although the French ambassador in Warsaw did what he could to stir up trouble and invigorate the local political clubs.

In order to understand what happened in Poland in the 1790s one must look back as far as the beginning of the century, when the Electors of Saxony were also Kings of Poland. Surrounded by the growing Great Powers of Russia and Prussia, as well as the Habsburg Empire, Poland was at the mercy of its neighbors, who were determined not to allow Poland to have a strong Government. Both in 1733 and 1763 the Russians intervened to ensure that the elected monarch was agreeable to them. But it was not in fact this constitutional and elective King who really ruled the sprawling territory of Poland-Lithuania. A few magnates had come to dominate the social and political life of the country, to whom the *szlachta* or gentry were clients. The King's powers were strictly limited by a feudal structure; and decisions taken by the *Sejm* or Diet could be wrecked by the vote of a single deputy known as the "liberum veto." Thus, Poland was an anarchical oligarchy managing a neofeudal system. The economy was weak; the silver currency was debased; the exports of corn fell in the face of foreign competition; the output of serf labor (five-sixths of the peasants were serfs) was poor; industrial processes made little headway. The King as a foreign nominee was subject to violent pressures from abroad. His army was small, and at no point were the frontiers easily defensible. Minorities of Protestants and Orthodox Christians in a largely Roman Catholic kingdom provided excuses for outside interference.

In 1763 Catherine the Great made an error. She and her army, which was drawn from a larger population than that of Poland (20 million against about 12 million), were determined to ensure that a former lover of hers, Stanislas Poniatowski, a *piast* or member of the Polish aristocracy, should be elected King. Stanislas, however, soon showed that he was no Russian puppet but a patriot after his own fashion. The Polish Government rejected an immediate demand from Russia for an offensive and defensive alliance and for concessions to its dissident or non-Catholic subjects.

But the Russians were resolved to dominate Poland. In March 1764 Catherine concluded an alliance with Frederick the Great for eight years, and every effort was exerted to control Poland. Catherine laid it down that the Polish monarchy should not become hereditary, that the "liberum veto" should not be abolished, and that the Polish standing army should not be enlarged. She also demanded that all the non-Catholic Christians in Poland should be placed under her protection. The Russian resident in Poland was Prince Nikolai Repnin, who had at his disposal ten thousand Russian troops stationed in Warsaw since 1763 and others which he could call up from the Russo-Polish frontier. He began acting like a dictator, and in March 1768 compelled the Poles to sign a treaty by which the country became virtually a Russian protectorate. When an anti-Russian guerrilla movement was formed at Bar in Podolia and spread rapidly into other parts of the kingdom, tens of thousands of Russian soldiers were sent into Poland and many Poles arrested and exiled to Russia.

Meanwhile, the Ottoman Turks had become perturbed by the Russian domination of Poland. In the autumn of 1768 a frontier incident was followed by the imprisonment of the Russian ambassador in Constantinople, and war broke out between Russia and Turkey. This was not unwelcome to the Russians, for it enabled them to pursue Peter the Great's idea of expanding the Empire southward across the Sea of Azov to the Crimean peninsula and the Black Sea. The Russians were almost universally victorious in the war. In 1770 they captured Bucharest, and a naval force that had sailed right round Europe defeated the Turks at the battle of Chesmé and menaced Constantinople. But the Russian victories alarmed other European powers, especially Austria, while unrest in Poland and the rising of Pugachev in Russia itself kept the Imperial armies fully stretched. Finally, in 1772 the young King Gustavus III of Sweden, having overthrown the constitution of his kingdom, threatened to attack Russia in the hope of regaining some of the losses of territory inflicted on his predecessors. It is the measure of Catherine II's statesmanship that she emerged triumphantly from all her difficulties.

But to gain her triumphs Catherine had to pay a price. Not only was the Sultan concerned over the Russian domination of Poland, but so was the Emperor Joseph II. It appeared for a moment as if the Austrians would ally themselves with their ancient enemies the Turks, and that the whole of eastern Europe would be consumed by war. In the summer of 1770 the Austrians began massing troops on the Hungarian-Polish frontier, and in December the Court of Vienna formally proclaimed that Zips (or Spisz), which had been Polish since 1412, was now incorporated into the Crown of Hungary. At first Frederick the Great was not worried by this seizure, which he thought had been carried out purely for defensive reasons and would later be abandoned. He was much more anxious about the aggrandizement of Russia, which, he believed, "will be able to become a dreadful and appalling neighbour for all Europe." He wanted the Turkish war brought to an end and Poland pacified. But his brother, Prince Henry, who visited Saint Petersburg in the autumn of 1770, advocated the dismemberment of Poland between its three neighbors. Frederick was induced to change his mind. Austria had set the example of dismemberment by incorporating several Polish districts into Hungary. Thus, in August 1772 treaties were signed between Russia, Austria, and Prussia for the first Partition of Poland, and in September the Polish Diet acquiesced under the threat of *force majeur.*

By the Partition Prussia gained an area situated between Pomerania and East Prussia; Russia obtained a large strip of territory to its west with part of which it had ethnic affiliations; and Austria-Hungary took a big triangle of rich land on the south and southeast of Cracow. Austria, which had begun the partition, gained the wealthiest and most populous area, containing over

2 million inhabitants. In all Poland gave up 4 million inhabitants and fifty thousand square miles of territory. In spite of its terrible losses the kingdom of Poland now tried to put its house in order by reforming its constitution and improving its economic and financial situation. Paradoxically, while the first Partition of Poland had been brought about by the country's weakness, the second Partition was to be the result of its strength.

Once the first Partition was out of the way, Russia was able to bring the war with Turkey to an end. Troops withdrawn from Poland were victorious in 1774, but the Pugachev rebellion induced Catherine to seek peace. By the Treaty of Kutchuk Kainardji (June 1774) Russia obtained the northern coastline of the Sea of Azov with access to the Black Sea, on which freedom of navigation was guaranteed to Russian merchant vessels. The Crimea was declared independent of Turkish sovereignty. The Sultan also recognized the right of Russia to protect the interests of his Christian subjects. Russia was in the process of becoming the strongest power in eastern Europe, and still aimed to expand both to the east and the west, driving the Turks out of Europe and subjecting the remainder of Poland as a vassal state.

Russian expansionist ambitions first took the shape of a plan to partition the Turkish Empire in alliance with Joseph II. But Joseph was no soldier and was thwarted by Frederick the Great (who was still a masterful ruler in his late sixties). Frederick was resolved to resist Austrian aggrandizement in either the Balkans or Bavaria. Yet though Prussia and Sweden lent their support to the Turks, Russian arms and diplomacy prevailed. By the Treaty of Jassy (January 1792) Russia became the sovereign of the Crimea and of part of the coastline of the Black Sea, where the city of Odessa was to be founded a year later.

The Poles had taken advantage of the Russian absorption in the second war with the Ottoman Empire to try to strengthen their position. After Stanislas had been refused any promises of territorial gains at the expense of the Turks in return for providing a contingent to take part in the war and had been compelled instead to agree to another humiliating alliance with Russia, he looked to the King of Prussia for assistance. Finally, in the spring of 1790 an offensive and defensive alliance was concluded between Poland and Prussia. The Poles hoped that it would put an end to the Russian domination of their kingdom; Frederick William II (who succeeded his father in 1786) thought of it as part of an elaborate plan to create an offensive coalition against Russia and Austria. But Russia was not immediately concerned over the Poles, and the alliance between Russia and Poland was dropped under Prussian pressure.

The Poles welcomed the outbreak of the eastern war as furnishing them with an opportunity to throw off the yoke of Russia, though the King himself still favored the maintenance of Russian friendship. But the opposition was led by some of the wealthiest magnates of Poland, who could draw upon the widespread hatred of the Russians. In October 1788 a Great Seym or four-year Diet, as it was to be called, met in Warsaw. This Diet was directed by the nobility, for Poland had practically no bourgeois class. By various devices the "liberum veto" was circumvented, and it was agreed that the nobility and clergy should contribute to taxation and thus double the Government's revenues. In May 1791 a new constitution was promulgated whereby the monarchy was declared hereditary instead of elective, the "liberum veto" was abolished, and something approaching parliamentary government created. An obvious comparison was made with the French Constitution of 1791, but in fact the Polish Constitution was far less egalitarian. The aristocracy remained largely in control and serfdom was retained. It was certainly no democratic constitution. There was no social upheaval as in France.

The new constitution was at first welcomed in Austria and Prussia, but caused dismay in Russia. The Austrians were anxious for political stabilization in eastern Europe because they were now preparing to intervene in France on behalf of the royal family: Marie Antoinette was, after all, the sister of the Emperor Leopold II. But Catherine II had not the slightest intention of tolerating a united and independent Poland. The invasion took place in May 1792. At the same time a Russian note was read to the Polish Diet claiming that the intervention was on behalf of Polish "liberties" and in reprobation of the "illegal" constitution of the previous May. The Polish Government had vainly relied on the friendliness of the Emperor Leopold II and the alliance concluded with Prussia to protect it against the Russian wrath. But Leopold died in March and in April the French revolutionary Government had declared war on the Habsburg Empire. Thereupon the Prussians joined the Austrians in the war against France in the belief that it would soon be over and provide agreeable territorial pickings.

Catherine II was delighted. For months she had been "racking her brains to push the Courts of Vienna and Berlin into the French enterprise, so that she might have her elbows free." She genuinely detested what was happening in France and pretended—or perhaps really believed—that she was playing her part against "the Jacobins" by crushing revolutionaries in Poland; she also asserted that she would lend her military aid against France as soon as the Polish problem was settled. Thus, the Poles were left without allies. Although they fought heroically under the leadership of Tadeusz Kosciusco, a protégé of the Czartoryskis but also a romantic who had read Rousseau, on July 24, 1792 King Stanislas surrendered, and the Russians were allowed to occupy Warsaw without resistance.

For some months Catherine II delayed her decision about the future of Poland. Eventually she resolved on a second Partition in collaboration with Prussia. This Partition, which was dictated to the Poles in January 1793, enabled Russia to gain virtually the whole of the eastern half of Poland, including its main granary, while Prussia obtained Great Poland, lying to the east of the Oder: this brought the Prussians to within easy reach of Warsaw and Cracow. Russia's increase in territory was four times that of Prussia's:

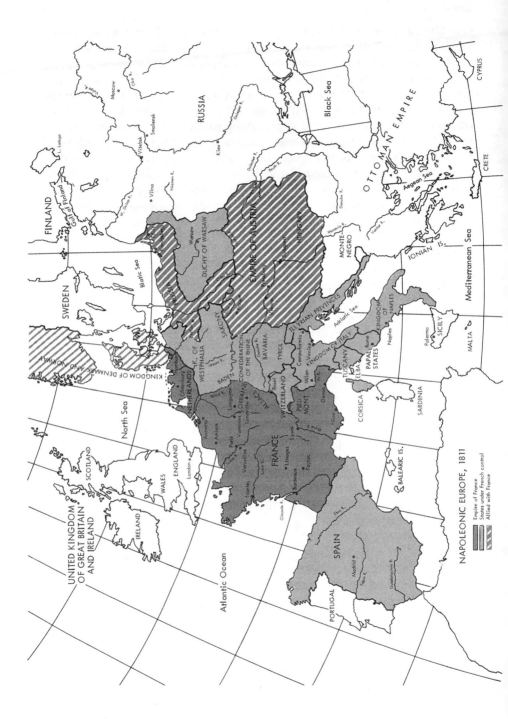

NAPOLEONIC EUROPE, 1811

Empire of France
States under French control
Allied with France

Catherine acquired 3 million new subjects. Unlike in 1772, there was no ethnic justification for the huge Russian gains. Russian troops continued to occupy almost the whole country and the Russian ambassador to act like a dictator. Austria was excluded altogether from the second Partition, but was given to understand that its acquisition of Bavaria would be facilitated.

To the surprise of the world, in the spring of 1794 the Polish nation rose from the ashes of defeat. After the second Partition Kosciusco and the leaders in the Great Seym found refuge in Saxony. When in March a Polish brigade refused orders to disarm, Kosciusco hurried into Poland and assumed the direction of a rebellion. In turn the Russian garrisons were driven out of Cracow, Warsaw, and Vilna. But this time it was the Prussians who were first to invade Poland, although in September they and the Russians were obliged to abandon the siege of Warsaw. The Austrians were determined not to be left out in the cold again and invaded Poland from the south, although they suffered formidable losses. Finally, the Russians under their able general Suvoroff entered in force during November, and the Polish resistance movement was cut to pieces and many were massacred in Warsaw. Poland was then wiped from the map of Europe—only to be revived and partitioned again in the twentieth century.

By the third and last Partition of Poland in the eighteenth century the western frontier of Russia was advanced to the border of East Prussia, then southward along the line of the River Niemen, meeting the Austro-Hungarian frontier along the line of the River Bug. Prussia obtained more territory to the north of that, which it had gained in 1772, including the towns of Cracow and Lublin. The new Habsburg Emperor Francis II gratefully accepted his share, acceded to the Partition treaty of 1793, and received more worthless promises of support over Bavaria. The Polish Revolution, therefore, had little to do with the kind of social grievances that launched the revolution in France. It was essentially nationalist in its aims and it became the victim of power politics.

Thus, when Catherine the Great died in 1796 she had extended the Russian Empire from the east of the Baltic to the north of the Black Sea and from the borders of East Prussia to Siberia. The population of Russia was nearly doubled and the prestige of the Tsardom enhanced. Catherine had not, however, succeeded in driving the Turks from Europe, nor in conquering Constantinople; "the sick man of Europe" was to be a nuisance to Russia throughout the nineteenth century. As to the obliteration of Poland, that was not a crime by eighteenth-century standards, but it could be argued that it was a mistake. For instead of having a protectorate or buffer state in Poland, Tsarist Russia was to become a neighbor of the aspiring Hohenzollerns, and was to pay the price for that in 1914. When the Austrian ambassador at Saint Petersburg, Cobenzl, learned in 1793 about the second Partition of Poland, he exclaimed: "this changes the whole system of Europe—the French revolution is child's play, compared with this event." Looked at with hindsight, it could well be said that the expansion of Russia was to mean more in the history of the modern world than the rise and fall of the French revolutionary empire did.

4. The Second Revolution in France

The French Revolution, then, had acted as a spur to the nationalist revolt in Poland, which ended in that kingdom committing hara-kiri, and in Belgium to the creation of a reactionary Republic. Apart from influencing nationalist movements in Belgium and Poland, the French Revolution contributed to agitation in Ireland, to disturbances in Switzerland, to sympathetic expressions in Italy, and in Spain to the enactment of repressive legislation. But it was only in those countries which were entered by French revolutionary armies that revolts succeeded. In 1791 the most notable result of the Revolution was that it induced the autocratic rulers of Austria and Prussia, after the end of the first Russo-Turkish War, to enter into an alliance to restore order in France.

In France itself, a reaction took place in 1791 against the speed and violence of the political changes pushed through by the Constituent Assembly. In Madelin's view the country had become sick of politics and wanted the resumption of business as usual. Whether this is true or not, it is certain that the country was divided. Some politicians thought that the Revolution had gone too far; others that it had not gone far enough. The refusal of half the clergy to take the oath to the Civil Constitution and its condemnation by the Pope had disturbed good Catholics, especially in the western departments, where the peasants looked for leadership from the priests, as in La Vendée. Louis XVI had disliked signing the decree imposing the oath on the clergy; Marie Antoinette hoped that her brother might help to restore real power to her husband; and the *émigrés* of 1789 were swollen by a fresh exodus of nobility who carried on propaganda against the Revolution from Brussels to Turin.

But Leopold II himself was reluctant to act until the French royal family had escaped from their tutelage in Paris. He therefore brushed aside the importunities of the *émigrés*. Louis XVI, restless under the fetters that had been tied upon him as a constitutional king, was in fact determined to get away from the capital. Before he died in March 1791 Mirabeau had warned Louis against this dangerous move, and in April when Louis tried to leave Paris for his palace of Saint-Cloud National Guards objected and Lafayette, their commander, was unable to overrule them. So the King was driven into deceptions. On June 21, disguised as a servant, Louis XVI attempted to take his family by coach to Montmédy on the eastern frontier. There he hoped to be joined by an army corps stationed at Metz, which he believed (wrongly) was loyal to him. (To a British historian this is all reminiscent of King Charles

I's escape in disguise from Oxford, hoping in vain to find succour from the Scottish army.) Louis does not appear then to have meant to appeal for foreign help. But he hoped to frighten the Constituent Assembly. His attempt failed; the King was arrested at Varennes on the road to Malmédy by the procurator of the commune and ignominiously brought back to Paris. Vainly Louis protested that he had not intended to leave the kingdom. He was deprived of his remaining functions and kept a prisoner in the Tuileries. A republican movement, hitherto dormant, began to bud.

But for the moment no attempt was made to dethrone the King. The right wing of the Constituent Assembly, led by Barnave (of the Triumvirate), persuaded his fellow deputies, who were understandably nervous about foreign intervention, to exculpate the King and Queen on the ground that they had been "abducted." The Cordeliers Club (which was democratic and republican) and the Jacobin Club refused to accept the decision, whereupon Barnave and his friends broke with the latter and formed their own Feuillants Club. Two days after the exculpation of the King by the Assembly a demonstration in favor of his abdication, sponsored by the Cordeliers and Jacobin clubs, was held in the Champs de Mars. Lafayette ordered the National Guard to fire on the mob: sixty were killed or wounded and two-hundred put under arrest. This "massacre" revealed the split between the right and the left of the Third Estate. For the time being the right was in the ascendant. The Triumvirate vainly tried to get the Constitution revised, making it more of a balanced monarchy. Though they only managed to obtain some minor amendments, the King was invited to give his assent to the revised Constitution and was restored to his former duties. A secret agreement was reached between the Feuillants and Marie Antoinette that in return she would use her influence with her brother to prevent his intervention in French affairs.

Leopold in fact had been alarmed by the episode of the flight to Varennes and on July 6 had addressed a circular to his fellow monarchs, known as the Padua circular, urging upon them joint action on behalf of the French royal family. It met with a tepid reception, especially from Catherine the Great, who, as has been seen, was more interested in expansion westward into Poland and eastward into Turkey than ideological crusades. However, on July 25 the Emperor concluded a defensive alliance with the new King of Prussia, and on August 27 they jointly issued a declaration from Pillnitz inviting other powers to intervene in aid of the French monarchy. It is true that they already knew that their invitation was unlikely to be accepted. But it naturally alarmed the French revolutionaries, and was the first step toward another European war.

The Constituent Assembly had in May 1790, on the proposal of Maximilien Robespierre, the ascetic deputy who was a lawyer from Arras, passed a motion that "the French nation renounced the thought of undertaking any war with the object of conquest," and in general a pacific attitude prevailed. But the atmosphere of the Legislative Assembly, which first met on October 1, 1791, was rather different. Although the voting for this assembly was upon a more restricted franchise than its predecessor, the character of its members was much the same; they were mainly lawyers, journalists, men of letters, and other professional men. Most of them were young, ambitious, and inexperienced. Of the 745 deputies the right consisted chiefly of members of the Feuillants Club and was led from the outside by the Triumvirate, while the left, mainly Jacobins, was also partly led from the outside by Robespierre and Danton; but inside the Assembly the left had also leaders in two eloquent orators, Jean-Pierre Brissot, a journalist, and Pierre-Victorin Vergniaud, a lawyer with a mania for ancient Rome. The center consisted of some four hundred deputies who could be swayed by argument or emotion. From the outset Brissot advocated an armed crusade against the crowned heads of Europe, although this was resisted in the Jacobin Club of Paris by Robespierre and Marat, a revolutionary journalist who edited *L'Ami du Peuple.* Several possible pretexts for war against the Habsburg Emperor existed, such as the shelter given to the *émigrés* in Germany, apart from the provocative threats that had been made of restoring Louis XVI to his former power. An exchange of diplomatic notes between Vienna and Paris did nothing to diminish the tension. Louis XVI's ministers were opposed to war with one exception, the Count of Narbonne, who had been appointed to take charge of the War Office in mid-December. Narbonne was an adept intriguer who wanted war and prepared for it; thus, his appointment was welcome to the Brissotins. When Louis XVI dismissed Narbonne on account of his intrigues, the Legislative Assembly condemned the King for doing so and also impeached the Foreign Minister, Delessart. Thereupon all the King's ministers resigned. Louis himself, frightened by the violence displayed in the Assembly, where Vergniaud had just made a speech attacking the Queen, in an almost fatalistic frame of mind appointed a new Ministry agreeable to Brissot. The new Foreign Minister, Dumouriez, an adventurous soldier, was intent on war against the Emperor. As Francis II, who had succeeded Leopold II in March 1792, was not averse from war, both sides presented ultimatums. On April 20 the Assembly voted by an overwhelming majority for war against the Emperor. It was on this date, in the opinion of Lefebvre, that "the second French revolution began."

5. France Invaded

The Austrians, to whom the Prussians were allied, proceeded in an extremely leisurely way to prepare for the invasion of France. Ferdinand, Duke of Brunswick, the supreme commander, had been one of Frederick the Great's generals, and was no mean soldier, but the forces assigned to him were neither numerous nor efficient. The rulers of Austria and Prussia believed that the French were so divided and demoralized that they would soon surrender. Brunswick was therefore instructed to publish a manifesto warning the French people of the dire consequences that would follow if they did not submit to their King and safeguard the royal family. The manifesto was signed on August 1. Frederick William II of Prussia was confident that Brunswick would soon be in occupation of Paris; but Brunswick himself thought that he would not get there before the following spring.

The Brunswick manifesto had precisely the opposite results from those intended. A republican movement was already in progress. On June 20 a Paris mob had invaded the Tuileries and menaced the King before he was rescued by the National Guard. The Legislative Assembly, now under the direction of the left wing, led by Brissot and Robespierre, rallied the country in the name of patriotism. In July the fatherland was declared to be "in danger." The Jacobins in Paris invited sympathizers in the provinces to send them support. A battalion was marched up from Marseilles singing a hymn of war which was to become the revolutionary national anthem. These men were republicans. Forty-seven out of the forty-eight sections of the Paris Commune voted in favor of the King's abdication, while Robespierre demanded the the suspension of the King and the summoning of a democratic National Convention to replace the Legislative Assembly. On August 9 the *"sans-culottes"* of Paris, so called because they wore trousers instead of knee-breeches, the emblems of aristocracy, elected a new revolutionary Commune, and on the following day an armed mob attacked the Tuileries, where Louis XVI and his family were sheltering with the Assembly. The new "magistrates of the people" reiterated the demands uttered earlier by Robespierre, The Assembly, dominated by its left wing, acquiesced. The King was imprisoned and deprived of his remaining functions. The election of a National Convention was agreed. An executive council of the Assembly was chosen to take over the Government, headed by Jacques Danton, a leading Jacobin, who was appointed Minister of Justice. A week later the enemy crossed the frontier, and on September 2 Verdun, less than two hundred miles from Paris, fell to the invaders.

The dramatic events which took place in France during 1792–94 (far too complicated to unravel here) and which highlighted the "second French Revolution" have to be appreciated against the background of European war. A French Government, though uneasily divided at first between Danton's executive council, the revolutionary Paris Commune, and the new National Convention, was determined to repel invasion and repress rebellion at home. At the outset it seemed as if anarchy would prevail. During the first week of September a mob had thrust its way into the jails of Paris and murdered half the prisoners, most of whom were criminals but over two hundred of whom were priests. Who the leaders of this mob were is obscure, but Danton as Minister of Justice acquiesced in the massacre. Lefebvre says drily: "the collective mentality is sufficient explanation for the killing." Elsewhere in France, with the encouragement of the bloodthirsty demagogue Marat, men were murdered as suspected royalists or traitors. The

Terror subsided when it became known that almost miraculously the French army under the command of Dumouriez was winning victories on the French frontier.

How was this? The French army was more numerous than that of the enemy, was better equipped with artillery, and had acquired some training while awaiting the expected assault. The soldiers were inspired by a patriotic fervor. The invaders, on the other hand, were overconfident and bogged down by bad weather. The Battle of Valmy, east of the River Marne, in which Brunswick attacked the French in a strong defensive position, was the turning point. After receiving a whiff of grapeshot Brunswick ordered a retreat. Three weeks later he abandoned Verdun. On November 6 Dumouriez defeated the Austrians at the Battle of Jemappes and the whole of Belgium fell to him.

Thenceforward the French revolutionaries gave up the idea of war without conquests. They would, declared the Brissotins, liberate all the peoples of Europe and Latin America too. Later Victor Hugo recaptured the mood of the moment when he wrote:

> Volunteers, die to liberate all your brother peoples.
> Happily they said "Yes."

Others (such as Danton) were eager that their country should be extended to its natural frontiers—the Rhine, the Alps, and the Pyrenees. Already in November the inhabitants of Nice and Savoy—which belonged to the King of Sardinia—and of the Rhineland were asking that their territories be annexed by France. On December 15 the National Convention passed a decree to place conquered peoples under the guardianship of France. Belgium was to be annexed and Holland to be conquered. In February 1793 the archbishopric of Mainz, on the left bank of the Rhine, which had been occupied the previous October, was also annexed. Thus, the French revolutionaries changed in a flash from being the desperate defenders of their frontiers into military aggressors. Thereby they aroused against them the First European Coalition, organized by the British Prime Minister, William Pitt the Younger.

6. Great Britain and the French Revolution

The ideals which inspired the French Revolution had had their repercussions on Great Britain, as elsewhere; but, as in France, the doctrine of political equality had appealed more to the members of the middle classes than to the peasantry and working classes in the towns, who had been hit by the evils of the Industrial Revolution. The Society for Constitutional Information, which became sympathetic toward the French Revolution, had originally been founded by an Anglican clergyman, Horne Tooke, at the time of the Wilkes agitation, and it charged five guineas a year for membership. Less restricted and more far-reaching were the Corresponding Societies, started by a shoemaker named Hardy: these advocated manhood suffrage and annual Parliaments and carried out their propaganda among the masses who had economic grievances.

Tom Paine, author of a famous book in support of the Revolution entitled *The Rights of Man (1790-92),* contributed a large part of his royalties to these societies. Political agitation was particularly strong in Scotland. Tom Paine and Edmund Burke, both well-established political figures in their fifties when the French Revolution began, are generally regarded as the leading British apologists for and against the Revolution. But what they believed and wrote in 1790 has sometimes been exaggerated. Burke, for example, did not disapprove of revolutions as such: he had defended both the English Revolution of 1688 and the American Revolution. But he thought that social progress must be based on social experience: this was an empirical view, typical of much British political philosophy, and was consequently completely opposed to intellectual or abstract rationalism. Paine, for his part, was not unhistoric in his approach. He had lived for years in the United States and regarded that country as a model of the way in which Locke's theory of "natural rights" could be applied to politics. He therefore advocated republicanism, as in America, and the overthrow of monarchy, aristocracy, and the State Church. But *The Rights of Man* frightened the British governing classes far more than Burke's *Reflections on the French Revolution* had done. Unlike the other radical leaders, the author of *The Rights of Man* was condemned in absentia. He had in fact removed himself from London to Paris, where he was to be imprisoned during the Terror. Later he returned to the United States, where he was equally regarded as a dangerous and atheistic extremist.

When the war got under way the British radical leaders were rounded up and accused of high treason, but were mostly acquitted. It was not, however, anxiety over the effect of the Revolution on traditional British values, as expressed by Burke, that turned the British Government against France, but the invasion of Belgium, an area about which British governments have always been sensitive. At first, after the French National Convention had been provoked into declaring war on Great Britain in February 1793, Pitt followed his father's policy of concentrating British military effort against French maritime trade and overseas possessions while subsidizing other powers to fight on land against the French armies in Europe.

7. The French Republic Fights for Survival

In spite of the British entry into the war, at first during 1793 the French revolutionary armies carried everything before them. The Austrians and Prussians were distracted by the events in Poland. The annexation of Nice succeeded that of Savoy; Belgium, the Rhineland, and Basel were also annexed after French victories. Then war was declared on Spain. But the French overreached themselves. Dumouriez, who had been ordered to invade Holland, was driven back into Belgium and defeated by the Austrians at the Battle of Neerwinden on March 18, 1793. Intoxicated by his previous successes, he resolved to make a deal with the Austrians by handing back Belgium to them and then leading his soldiers to Paris to secure for himself a military dictatorship. But the National Convention, which was already shaken by peasant risings in the west of France (provoked not by royalism but by the religious policy of the revolutionary assemblies), had been forewarned about Dumouriez's intended treachery. Dumouriez was forced to desert to the enemy, as Lafayette had done earlier. It was now that the politicians in Paris decided to take ruthless measures to save the fatherland and preserve the Revolution.

The King was dead; he had been executed on January 21, 1793 after a mockery of a trial, still protesting his innocence; and a Republic was proclaimed. As has happened at the crisis in nearly all revolutions, power came into the hands of a resolute minority. The National Convention, which contained 750 members, could not in any case have made a suitable instrument of government. Though its social composition was much the same as that of the previous assemblies—over a third of its members had in fact sat in them—it was hopelessly divided in its political complexion: on the right sat Brissot and his friends, called by their opponents "Girondins" because some of them came from the department of the Gironde in southwestern France; on the left sat the Jacobins, known as "the Mountain," headed by Danton and Robespierre; and in the center sat the majority of the deputies known as "the Plain" or "the Marsh." Under the monarchy the Girondins had been reckoned men of the left; though they had no precise policy, they tended to be constitutionalists and had been reluctant to kill the King. The Mountain, which included all but one of the Paris deputies, on the other hand, consisted of convinced republicans who were prepared to act ferociously to save the fatherland. The Plain, the uncommitted majority in the middle, was wooed by both sides. But only one-third of the deputies regularly attended the Convention. The country as a whole was little moved by the struggle between the Girondins and the Mountain: the masses were more concerned over compulsory military service, which was about to be instituted, and with the danger of famine owing to the high price of food.

During March and April 1793 the Convention, under the impulse of the Mountain, agreed to a number of revolutionary measures. A revolutionary tribunal was established to deal expeditiously with treasonable offenses; an army of the revolution was formed to keep order at home; and "representatives on mission" were sent into the provinces to enforce the policies agreed on in Paris; finally—and most important of all—a Committee of

Public Safety was set up which was originally intended to supervise the actions of the Council of Ministers but gradually arrogated to itself the full power of government, although it was still responsible to the Convention. Afterward, as if to assure the Republic that it was not going to be permanently governed by a Parisian dictatorship, the Convention approved on June 24 a constitution based on manhood suffrage and providing for a referendum. But this constitution remained in abeyance; for the Convention voted that "the provincial government of France is revolutionary until peace has been achieved." Thus, the Committee of Public Safety ruled. It was headed by Danton; but the Committee decided that he was not ruthless enough for this time of crisis, and he was expelled on July 10. The Committee was then reduced from sixteen to nine members, the most influential of whom was Robespierre, who joined the Committee on July 24. Henceforward it acted as the real Government, the National Convention passing the decrees which it recommended.

The Committee was faced with three tasks: to achieve victory over the coalition that was attacking France; to put down risings which were spreading throughout the west of the country; and to assuage the grievances about the high price of food. So far as the war was concerned the French were given a breathing space because the Austrians (distracted by the second Partition of Poland, from which they were excluded) failed to press their advantage after the defeat of Dumouriez. Their general, the Duke of Coburg, lacked reinforcements and munitions. But by the end of July they had occupied Valenciennes on the eastern frontier of France; at the same time Mainz, which had become restless under French liberation, capitulated to the Prussians; and, most startling of all, an allied force was landed at the naval base of Toulon in southern France after a royalist rising had taken place there. While these events were occurring a *levée en masse* was decreed calling up unmarried men between the ages of eighteen and twenty-five to serve in the French armies. In Lazare Carnot (a member of the Committee of Public Safety) the French discovered an organizer of victory; in Jourdan, Pichegru, and Hoche were found capable generals; by the autumn the enemy were driven back on all the frontiers; in December a young artillery officer, Captain Napoleon di Buonaparte, helped to compel the evacuation of Toulon.

8. The Terror and its Aftermath

To ensure the internal security of France those who now controlled the Government determined to stamp out unrest by the exercise of terror. The revolutionary tribunal sitting in the so-called Hall of Liberty in the Tuileries dealt speedily with the suspects brought before it. The public prosecutor, Fouquier-Tinville, was given a free hand in ordering arrests so long as he did not touch deputies or generals. The Terror began slowly in April 1793 and continued until July 1794. The newly invented guillotine was used indiscriminately against all the enemies of the regime—royalists, provincial rebels, Girondins, even politicians of the extreme left. Marie Antoinette was followed to the guillotine by the Duke of Orleans, who had aspired to overthrow the Bourbons in the Revolution. Then came Barnave of the Feuillants and Brissot with other Girondin leaders. The Countess of Barry, the erstwhile mistress of Louis XV, was followed to the scaffold by eight Carmelite nuns. One of the few remaining *philosophes,* Condorcet, only escaped the guillotine by killing himself. Robespierre was to declare that the Terror had saved France; by the end of 1793, remarked Lefebvre, "Paris was becoming calmer."

But "the Great Terror" had still to come in the following year. In the spring of 1794 Hébert, a Paris journalist who had urged in violent language the more frequent use of the guillotine against profiteers and hoarders, went to the guillotine himself and was followed by Danton, who had advocated concluding peace abroad and dismantling the revolutionary machinery at home: he was condemned as "an indulgent." On June 10 Robespierre and his friends tightened up what Professor Rudé calls "the process of justice" by getting a law passed which deprived prisoners of defending counsel. The executions of suspects were not limited to those brought before the tribunal in Paris. Many "brigands" or rebels were put to death in the French provinces; for example, two thousand were condemned without trial at Angers, and two or three thousand were executed, mainly by deliberate drowning at Nantes. Altogether, some thirty-five to forty thousand persons are estimated to have died in the Terror and three hundred thousand suspects to have been put under arrest. The Terror, it has been asserted, supported the "planned economy" necessitated by the war and contributed to the feeling of national solidarity in face of the enemy.

The vast majority of the deputies in the National Convention, as in the earlier assemblies, were middle-class men who valued the institution of private property. Robespierre had originally resisted price control. It was only when inflation prevailed because of shortages inevitable in wartime, partly because the *assignat* had fallen in value, that the Convention agreed to prescribe a maximum price for wheat. This was in May 1793; and at the end of September, again under pressure from the Paris Commune, a maximum for all prices was voted. But even with rationing it was difficult for the Government to keep down prices, let alone wages, which were also supposed to be controlled under the September maximum law. The Convention had in fact to rely on appeals to patriotism and to the imposition of the Terror to prevent social unrest. To sustain the war some industries were in effect nationalized, and efforts were made to relieve the poor during the period of high prices. State socialism came in by necessity, not by conviction.

9. The Fall of Robespierre

While the home front in France was being dragooned by totalitarian methods, the democratized French armies were again victorious in the European war. No fewer than eight hundred fifty thousand men, partly regulars and partly volunteers, were thrown into the battle. The organizing genius of Carnot assured that they were adequately supplied with munitions and food. The tactics employed were those suited to a revolutionary army: instead of using the linear formation favored by Frederick the Great and attempting to roll up a flank, they attacked frontally in column and aimed to overwhelm their enemy by numbers. On the most vital front General Jourdan was given unity of command over the armies of the north, the Ardennes, and the Moselle. On June 25 he decisively defeated the allies at the battle of Fleurus. The Duke of York, son of King George III, who commanded the British contingent and troops in British pay, retreated to defend Holland, and the Austrians withdrew across the Rhine. Thus, once again the whole of Belgium was conquered by the French armies, which were soon to sweep into Holland. In 1794 the British won victories over the French at sea and in the West Indies, but in Europe the revolutionary armies were supreme.

Once the country was out of danger from abroad the totalitarian regime which prevailed in France lost its raison d'être. The narrow group of politicians who had been governing through two committees of the Convention, the Committee of Public Safety, and the Committee of General Security (which was virtually a Ministry of Police), began to quarrel among themselves. Maximilien Robespierre, the austere and incorruptible idealist who, with his friends Saint-Just and Couthon had carried great weight in the Committee of Public Safety, were opposed by practical men like Carnot and Lindet and extreme terrorists like Billaud and Collot. In May Robespierre, having seen his opponents Danton the "indulgent" and Hébert the socialist perish on the scaffold, appeared to be at the height of his influence. He had persuaded the Convention to adopt as the State religion the worship of a Supreme Being. For Robespierre disapproved of atheism and thought that the movement against Christianity had gone too far and too fast; like Voltaire and Rousseau, he believed that the French people needed a religion, "a reign of Virtue" if it was only a vague kind of deism. The Festival of the Supreme Being was held in Paris on June 8. It was presided over by Robespierre himself, who, wearing yellow breeches and a blue coat, set fire to a cardboard monument representing atheism. These antics did not endear him to his colleagues in the Convention or the Committee of Public Safety. When a group of women, following this or a cognate faith, who were alleged to have addressed Robespierre as the Son of God, were put under arrest for counterrevolutionary activities, he felt it his duty to save them from the guillotine. But after this he withdrew for a month from the Committee of Public Safety, which gave his enemies the opportunity to plot against him, accusing him of a dictatorship which he had never in fact wielded. On July 26 (8 Thermidor of the year II according to the recently instituted revolutionary calendar) Robespierre reappeared in the Convention and delivered a long rambling speech complaining of the persecution to which he had been subjected and uttering vague accusations against traitors who were "impure apostles of atheism."

Robespierre's enemies were frightened and at once took action. Next day he and his friends were shouted down in the Convention and then put under arrest. Although the majority in the Jacobin Club and the Paris Commune were loyal to Robespierre, the *"sans-culottes"*, who had once been enthusiastic supporters of the Jacobins but had been alienated by the wartime economic measures, failed to come to his aid. Nevertheless, after Robespierre and his friends had managed to evade imprisonment and taken shelter with the Commune in the Hotel de Ville, three thousand armed *sans-cullottes* gathered in his defense. Barras, the terrorist, was sent by the Convention to the Hotel de Ville with a contingent of National Guards. He arrived at two in the morning of July 28 (10 Thermidor). The *sans-culottes* had melted away. Robespierre vainly tried to commit suicide. That very evening he and twenty-one others were guillotined. Eighty-three more Robespierrists were executed on the following two days. "The great majority of the nation," remarked Lefebvre, "showed themselves satisfied" by the coup of Thermidor; "for they judged that the revolutionary government was mortally wounded; they were not mistaken."

10.   The Impact of the Revolution on Europe

When at the beginning of 1793 the French declared war on Great Britain, thus challenging the major naval power in Europe, and when in March Dumouriez after being defeated by the Austrians attempted to restore the monarchy and set up a military dictatorship, the enthusiasm of the Brissotins for world revolution cooled. But Robespierre was now convinced that Terror at home and revolutionary propaganda abroad would assist the survival of the Republic. He therefore had blamed Brissot and Dumouriez for betraying the international revolution: had not Brissot earlier told Dumouriez, "It is your glorious destiny to plant the tree of liberty everywhere"? When Belgium was annexed in February 1793, the Belgians became equal citizens of the French Republic, while the Dutch patriots wanted to form an independent Batavian Republic. But in 1793 and 1794 the Polish rebellion began to peter out. Kosciusco came to believe that the liberation of the Russian serfs was a necessary preliminary to Polish national liberation. But the French Revolution was no more than a distant battle cry in eastern

Europe. Not only in Poland but also in Hungary nationalist risings were repressed without much difficulty. In Holland, on the other hand, the approach of the French armies at the beginning of 1795 after the defeat of the Duke of York enabled the Batavian Republic to be set up and drove William V of Orange out of the United Netherlands into exile. Professor Palmer tells us that the Batavian Republic was the first to use the words, "Liberty, Equality, and Fraternity." Nevertheless, the price paid by the Dutch for their "liberation" was that they were compelled to make war on the British, to surrender Flushing and the mouth of the Scheldt to the French, and to lose all their colonies to the British. There was no real agreement among the Dutch middle and lower classes about what the new constitution of their country ought to be. Separatist traditions died hard, and when a National Convention was elected and met in March 1796 there were many disputes among the deputies, and a rising took place in Amsterdam which had to be suppressed by the French army. At the beginning of 1798 a coup d'état carried through with the support of the French troops resulted in a new constitution or "fundamental law" being successfully submitted to a referendum. For the next three years a moderate Government ruled. The so-called Batavian revolution was at an end.

In Great Britain the war with France united the House of Commons behind Pitt's Government. Charles James Fox, a wealthy aristocrat and fantastic orator who had been among the first to welcome the French Revolution (along with romantic poets like Wordsworth), privately deplored the "horrors" of the Terror and found nearly all his followers slipping away from him. In the country at large the radicals who sympathized with the Revolution and sought political and social reforms were, as in France and the Batavian Republic, mostly lower middle-class agitators who obtained some support from the masses owing to the high price of food that followed a bad harvest in 1794. Repressive legislation, including acts of Parliament controlling newspapers, trade unions, and secret political societies, were on the whole accepted with docility. The Foxites seceded from Parliament; it was widely regarded as unpatriotic to be pro-French when the kingdom was at war with its ancient enemy—not for ideological reasons but in the name of national security. Even the introduction of an income tax was received with comparative equanimity. Only in Ireland, where the mass of the agrarian population was Roman Catholic and had no reason to love the English Protestants, was there a rising in western Europe stimulated by the victories of the French revolutionaries. There nationalists planned an open rebellion in 1798, hoping to establish an independent Republic with French military aid; but it came too late.

Thus, as in Poland and Hungary the rebellions or attempted rebellions were essentially nationalist in character, not democratic or social. In Spain the majority of the population was revolted by the treatment of the Roman Church under Robespierre's regime. Nor did Jacobinism make much progress in the Scandinavian kingdoms. In Germany (outside Austria) the French

Revolution had remarkably small impact on intellectuals. Politically, it has been said that "German liberalism never accepted the doctrine of popular sovereignty," while Goethe and Humboldt thought that the Revolution was a menace to personal culture. Both Catholics and Lutherans disliked its atheist tendencies, and it was only welcomed by some Prussian officials and journalists because they regarded France as a natural ally against the Habsburgs. On the whole, the Revolution was not hailed for ideological reasons (except, to a limited extent, by Kant and his students), and there was much less appreciation of its social significance in Germany than among the lower middle classes in England and Scotland. In Italy, however, a middle-class and anticlerical movement was cleverly to be exploited by Napoleon, who was put in command of the army of Italy by the Directory, which replaced the Committee of Public Safety as the executive Government of France. Yet as even Professor Godechot admits, the pillaging, requisitioning, and levying of "contributions" wherever the French armies marched led to violent revolts above all in Belgium, Holland, and parts of Italy. The French conquerors might describe themselves as liberators, but, as Robespierre had observed, "liberty cannot be imposed by bayonets!"

11. The Achievement of the French Revolution

What did the Revolution achieve in France itself? It was effected in the first instance by a middle-class intelligentsia—of whom Robespierre was fairly typical—supported by a discontented peasantry and a Paris mob of *sans-culottes* consisting of men and women with articulate grievances. The original aim of the Third Estate was to draw up a liberal constitution which would establish political equality and abolish class privileges. But the revolutionaries were neither democrats nor socialists; only the Constitution framed in 1793 provided for complete manhood suffrage, and that was stillborn. Nevertheless, the Revolution did contribute to what later western democrats understood by political and social progress, equality of opportunity, and intellectual freedom. The nobility and the clergy were reduced to the position of ordinary citizens. Everyone was required to pay his fair share of taxation and became equal before the law. Liberty of conscience was attained. The State was laicized and Christian tradition uprooted. Henceforward France was to be divided between militant sceptics and militant Christians.

How did the "bourgeoisie," who are usually pictured as the real victors in the Revolution, fare? Not excessively well. Some of them had been the beneficiaries of the ancien régime either as venal officials of the monarchy or paid servants of the aristocracy. Many of them were hit by wartime inflation and actually left the country. As usually happens in such times, those who did best were not the dedicated but the unscrupulous: the *nou-*

veaux riches, the hard-headed men who knew how to profiteer. As for the mass of the French people—the peasants and the urban proletariat—unquestionably their position was considerably improved, in the case of the countrymen by the equalization of taxes, the abolition of seignurial dues and tithes, and the chance to buy more land. Working men in the towns gained less; though they were freed from indirect taxes like the *gabelle* and though real wages rose, the hated *octrois* were retained and the ordinary wage earner enjoyed little in the way of legal or social security.

Finally, the French people became proud of their nation as they had rarely been before: they marched to the strains of patriotic music; they could admire the republican virtues symbolized in the historical paintings of the adaptable David. In the nineteenth century the triumphs of the French Revolution were to inspire other European peoples to fight and die in the name of nationalism. Whether, as Lefebvre and other historians have maintained, the French people had to undergo the experience of the Terror—an experience unequaled until the Bolshevik Revolution—in order to try to fashion a victorious and united nation may be doubted. At least the Revolution was a unique historical event of far-reaching consequences for European history. It engraved the ideals of liberty, equality, and fraternity on the minds of men.

NINE

The
Napoleonic
Empire

1. The Aftermath of Thermidor

Once the Jacobin terrorists had been overthrown by the coup of Thermidor a gradual dismantling of the revolutionary system of government in France, originally justified by the needs of a country at war, took place. Before the end of August 1794 the two committees which had previously monopolized the executive power—the Committee of Public Safety and the Committee of General Security—had their functions reduced, and other committees were set up by the moderates in the Convention, which was thus able to exercise a wider degree of control. The Paris Commune was abolished, and later in the year the Jacobin Club was closed. The maximum laws were also, somewhat prematurely, brought to an end, for the lifting of economic controls was followed by inflation and famine in parts of France. By May 1795 the value of the *assignats* had fallen to 7½ percent of their original value. Thus, "the restoration of bourgeois supremacy," as the aftermath of Thermidor is described by left-wing historians, was hurtful to the masses. Twice in 1795 there were abortive mob insurrections in Paris motivated again by the scarcity of bread.

If the abandonment of a planned economy produced discontent, the loosening of authoritarian methods of government aroused a sense of political freedom. Suspects were freed from prison; more newspapers were allowed to appear; Robespierre's "reign of Virtue" was ended. The Red Terror was succeeded by a less ferocious White Terror. In Paris a group of middle-class youth, consisting in part of men whose parents had been arrested or guillotined during the Robespierrist regime, and who were known as *jeunesse dorée* ("gilded youth"), beat up *sans-culottes*. Outside Paris former terrorists were murdered and prisoners massacred. How far the White Terror was the work of royalists is not clear. But certainly a royalist revival began after Thermidor.

The Dauphin, the young son of Louis XVI, had been kept in prison after the execution of his parents, and owing largely to maltreatment and neglect died in June 1795, whereupon the late King's brother, the Comte de Provence, who was an *émigré* safe in Verona, assumed the title of Louis XVIII. But he failed to publish a declaration calculated to appeal to the French people. By now the ministry of William Pitt (which had been reconstructed in July 1794) had committed itself to the cause of the French royalists, although it had not originally been intended to enter the war in an ideological spirit. In June 1795 a British naval expedition landed a force of French *émigrés* at Quiberon Bay in western France aiming to link up with royalist rebels in the La Vendée area. This royalist rising was put down without difficulty. Later in the year a royalist revolt took place in Paris, after the introduction in September of yet another constitution: it was easily repressed.

The new constitution—known as the Constitution of the year III of the Revolution—was far from democratic as compared with that of 1793, which was never put into effect. Manhood suffrage was abolished and a system of indirect elections restored. Two chambers were created: the Council of Five Hundred, empowered to initiate legislation, and the Council of Ancients (men over forty), given the right to pass laws. Because of fears of royalist penetration into these councils the Convention decreed that two-thirds of the new deputies must be chosen from its own ranks. Executive authority was conferred upon five Directors appointed by the Ancients from a list drawn up by the Five Hundred. Under the Directors were seven ministers to run the machinery of government. One Director had to retire every year and also one-third of the deputies. The Constitution was well calculated to create confusion and disorder. But the new Government managed to survive for four years, partly because the harvests were good and prices fell, partly because the French armies won striking victories abroad.

During the campaigns of 1794 the French had gone over from defensive to offensive warfare. The whole of the Netherlands came under French control. In May 1795 the United Netherlands, renamed in January the Batavian Republic, concluded a humiliating peace with France, surrendering part of its territory and agreeing to pay for the upkeep of an occupation force. In October Belgium was annexed to the French Republic. The Prussians, finding no easy victories were to be won and more concerned over Poland than France, consented by the Treaty of Basel on April 6 to the French taking over the left bank of the Rhine. In July by another treaty concluded at Basel the Spaniards withdrew from the war and a year later entered into an alliance with France. By September 1795 only Great Britain, Austria, and Russia remained at war with France. But British troops had been thrust out of the Netherlands and the British navy had witnessed a fiasco at Quiberon Bay. Neither the Russians nor the Austrians were enthusiastic about the war, though the Austrians hoped to find compensation for their loss of Belgium and their failure to share in the second Partition of Poland. The British concentrated on maintaining their command of the sea and sending troops to the French West Indies, where they died like flies. Thus, it became possible for the French Directory to revive the so-called Girondin policy of wars of conquest in the name of republican freedom. The age of Bonaparte had arrived.

2. How Napoleon Came to Power

Napoleon, who was born in Ajaccio in 1769, described himself as "a poor Corsican squire." Educated at the École Militaire in Paris, he was at once commissioned a lieutenant and became an artillery officer, first distinguishing himself at the siege of Toulon in 1793. After that he was promoted Brigadier-General and his abilities impressed Augustin, the brother of Maximilien Robespierre. Owing to his connection with the Robespierres Napoleon was imprisoned at Antibes for a fortnight following the coup of Thermidor. Though he was engaged on the planning staff for the Army of Italy after his release, he again came under suspicion because of his Corsican blood, since the British captured the island in 1794. Devouringly ambitious, however, he was determined not to be sidetracked in his military career. He was on friendly terms with Paul Barras, one of the five Directors, whom he had met at Toulon; and his next opportunity came when Barras appointed him second-in-command to put down the rising that took place in Paris after the establishment of the Directory on October 9 (14 Vendémiaire), 1795. Subsequently he succeeded Barras as commander of the Army of the Interior; six months later, just before he was appointed to the command of the Army of Italy at the age of twenty-five, he married Josephine de Beauharnais, a widow six years his senior, who had formerly been the mistress of Barras.

Josephine is frequently described in disparaging terms by those of Napoleon's biographers, who believe that there is one law for a man and another for a woman. They cannot make out why their hero married her in the first place or kept up his marriage so long. The fact is that he fell passionately in love with a woman who was both experienced and seductive. If she was unfaithful to him once or twice, he was consistently unfaithful to her. His attitude toward women was extraordinary. They are "like muddy sticks," he once said, "one cannot pick them up without being soiled." Most of them he treated as mere conveniences. But it was said that "Josephine alone and almost furtively tried to encourage the display of feminine arts and graces" at his Court after her husband became Emperor. He owed more to her than he recognized.

Napoleon was a small man, five feet six inches tall, with a fine-drawn face and piercing eyes. One who saw him in 1799 wrote that "he is a little man, with straight black hair, a sickly shallow complexion, expressive features, and a terrifying look." He could be brutal or charming as the occasion arose. A quick and indefatigable soldier and administrator, with few outside interests, he was able to work for eighteen hours at a stretch and manage with four hours' sleep. He was at once a practical man and a romantic dreamer, who aimed to become another Alexander or Charlemagne.

Of what did Napoleon's military gifts consist, and how did he become so rapidly successful? In the first place, he had inherited a large and victorious army which had evolved revolutionary tactics, attacking their enemy in column after heavy preliminary bombardment and behind a line of skirmishers. The French artillery was the best in Europe. Napoleon's aim was always the maximum concentration of forces at the right place and the right time. Fire, he said, should be concentrated at a single point (or hinge) to upset the enemy's equilibrium. He stressed the need for speed and mobility, and in time he developed a complete mastery in the swift handling of huge forces of men. He believed in acting offensively: *"toujours l'attaque."* Napoleon's methods have sometimes been contrasted with those of Frederick the Great, whom he much admired. The most obvious contrast is that whereas Frederick the Great could only draw on a total population of 2 million for his army, Napoleon could in the end put a million men into the field. It is also said that Frederick preferred the indirect approach and was not battle-minded. But Napoleon, like all sensible generals, did not favor headlong attacks on the enemy's center if they could be avoided (but he was reduced to frontal assaults as at Borodino and Waterloo). "It is by turning the enemy, by attacking his flank," he once said, "that battles are won." And although Napoleon realized that the decisive defeat of the enemy's main army could win a war, just as Frederick did, like Frederick, he admitted (after the Battle of Wagram) that "battle should only be offered when there is no other turn of fortune to be hoped for, as from its nature the fate of a battle is always dubious." Most of Napoleon's numerous *obiter dicta* can be paralleled by those of other great soldiers. As a modern military historian has observed, Napoleon was a perfecter rather than a creator.

As to the reasons for his swift success, this was due to luck, partly to favoritism, and partly to sheer hard work. The Revolution offered equality of opportunity and a career open to talent. Most of the royalist officers had been aristocrats who emigrated; consequently, there was a dearth of trained officers. Secondly, Napoleon had been fortunate in impressing first the Robespierres and then Barras, who overthrew them. His marriage to Josephine helped him to enter the most intimate circles of the Directory. Lastly, Napoleon was a voracious reader of military treatises and a close student of topography. It was his staff appreciations and memorandums on possible Italian campaigns that aroused the interest of the Directors and induced them to appoint him in place of General Schérer when he asked to be relieved of his command at the end of 1795 after a not-unsuccessful campaign in Italy. This was Napoleon's first big step on the road to imperial power.

3. The End of the First Coalition

It had been the intention of the Directors (of whom the most active was Carnot) that Italy should be only a secondary front in the war against Austria. The main offensive was to be undertaken by two other French armies, one commanded by General Jourdan on the Lower Rhine, the other by General Moreau in Alsace. The ultimate aim was that the armies of Moreau and Napoleon should link up in the Tyrol and advance on Vienna. However, in actual fact Italy became the chief front. An armistice had been temporarily concluded with the Austrians in Germany on December 22, 1795; it was not until July 1796 that Jourdan and Moreau moved forward, and then Jourdan was defeated by the Archduke Charles in command of the Austrians. But Napoleon began winning a series of victories. First he knocked the Sardinians, who had allied with the Austrians, out of the war. On May 15, 1796, the King of Sardinia agreed to peace and surrendered Savoy and Nice to France. After a diversion southward during July, on orders from Paris, in consequence of which the governments of the Papal states, the duchy of Tuscany, and the kingdom of Naples were obliged to sign agreements with him, Napoleon resumed his thrust eastward and, many hard-contested battles having been fought, concluded an armistice on April 18, 1797, with Austria at Leoben, only seventy-five miles from Vienna.

Almost the whole of northern Italy fell into Napoleon's hands. He plundered the divided peninsula unmercifully, sending money and many art treasures to Paris. Then at the end of 1796 he formed out of Modena and the Papal states of Bologna and Ferrara, surrendered by the Pope, a Cispadane Republic friendly to France; in the middle of July 1797 this was expanded by the addition of Lombardy and later part of Venetia into a Cisalpine Republic, with a population of $3\frac{1}{2}$ million and with a constitution clearly modeled on the lines of the French Directory. At the same time Genoa was converted into the Ligurian Republic. A little earlier Napoleon picked a quarrel with Venice, as he believed that the territories of the ancient republic would provide a useful bargaining counter in his negotiations with Austria.

This indeed proved to be the case. For as in the spring of 1797 the two French armies had at last succeeded in crossing the Rhine and were also making for the Danube, the Holy Roman Emperor was ready to conclude peace. By the Treaty of Campo Formio (October 18) Austria surrendered Belgium, recognized the Cisalpine Republic, and supported the French claim to the left bank of the Rhine (except for Cologne). France and Austria divided Venetia between them, Austria's share comprising Venice itself, Istria, and Dalmatia. This treaty, providing for the partition of Venetia, was arranged by Napoleon largely in defiance of the wishes of the Directory and was marked by the realism and cynicism that colored most of Napoleon's negotiations in Italy. However, he might have argued that he had secured the "natural frontiers" of France and more; and that by creating sister republics he had upheld the principles of the Revolution. But in fact he came to regard these republics simply as satellites of France. This subject will be examined later.

Napoleon had not only made his own reputation during the Italian campaigns, but he had reestablished the renown of France as the greatest military power in Europe. With inferior forces he had exerted ceaseless pressure against his enemies. At the Battle of Lodi in May 1796 he had realized his own capacities and had earned the nickname from his soldiers of *Le Petit Caporal* because of his personal courage. Thenceforward he "believed that he was a superior being and conceived the ambition of performing great things"; after the armistice of Leoben he behaved like a conqueror and said to a confidant:

> Do you believe that I triumph in Italy for the Carnots, Barras *et cetera?* I do not want peace. A party is in favour of the Bourbons. I wish to undermine the Republican Party but only for my own profit and not that of the ancient dynasty.

What had happened in Paris during Napoleon's absence? There had been a shift to the right. When, owing to the collapse of the *assignat*, the swift rise in prices took place and there was an increase of poverty, a journalist named Gracchus Babeuf had attempted to overthrow the Directory and establish the first Communist society in modern Europe; but his conspiracy was quickly crushed, and Babeuf and his principal lieutenants were tried and guillotined. On the other hand, at the elections held in April 1797 many royalists were chosen as deputies, while General Pichegru, who had been a secret monarchist, was appointed President of the Council of Five Hundred. The majority of the Directors, led by Barras, alarmed at this royalist revival, determined to scotch it; aided by General Augereau, who had been sent by Napoleon to Paris for the purpose, the councils were purged of the royalist deputies on September 4 (18 Fructidor), and Pichegru was put under arrest. Thus, not only was the constitution of the year III shown to be unworkable, but hopes aroused among the enemies of France abroad that the Bourbons would be restored were blasted.

During 1797 and 1798, largely as the result of Napoleon's victories, the whole situation in Europe had changed. In November 1796 Catherine the Great had died and been succeeded by her eccentric son, Paul I, who, at the beginning of his reign, inclined to reverse his mother's policies; Frederick William II of Prussia died in November 1797, leaving a young and well-meaning son who acquiesced in the French acquisitions on the left bank of the Rhine. The British Government, on which Spain had also declared war in defense of its overseas empire in October 1796, not only suffered setbacks in Europe but, overstretched by the war, was experiencing social unrest and financial difficulties. In 1797 the Prime Minister, William Pitt, was compelled to introduce the income tax, which has survived until the present day; and the Bank of England was obliged to suspend the gold standard. Although in February 1797 the Spanish fleet was defeated at the battle of Saint Vincent in the Atlantic, all British naval forces had been withdrawn from the Mediterranean at the end of the previous year; and in the spring of 1797 sailors began to mutiny. In July 1797 Pitt was forced to try to open peace negotiations with France, though nothing came of them. At the Conference of Rastatt, held in March 1798 where Napoleon represented France, Great Britain's former allies, the Prussians and Austrians, quarreled. The occupation by the French of the Netherlands and their control of the left bank of the Rhine and of northern Italy were finally recognized; France was deemed the arbiter of Europe; the Germans and Russians having withdrawn from the war, the First Coalition collapsed; and for a year Great Britain was left to fight alone against the triumphant French.

4. Revolutionary Europe at the End of the Eighteenth Century

What, then, was the structure of western Europe after the Peace of Campo Formio? Only Great Britain resolved to go on fighting Napoleon, just as it was to continue fighting Hitler's empire alone in 1940. This had little to do with ideology, but Pitt's Government had in effect committed itself to an alliance with the French royalists once it had enlisted their support in the unsuccessful attack on Toulon. The original sympathy in England and Scotland for the French revolutionaries had somewhat evaporated. But economic causes existed for internal discontent. Wages lagged behind prices, and by 1795 the justices of the peace who were concerned with the parish of Speenhamland in Berkshire decided to supplement appallingly low wages with contributions from the poor rate. This decision was directly linked with the high price of bread; and the so-called "Speenhamland decision" was copied elsewhere throughout England. Furthermore, in 1797 the sailors of the English Channel fleet, stationed at Spithead, mutinied because of their poor food, low wages and inadequate medical services. Later the sailors stationed at the Nore also mutinied, although not exactly for the same reasons. But this unrest was not directly related to the French revolutionary propaganda, and when Napoleon extended French aggression into the Mediterranean, the kingdom was still fairly solidly behind the British Government. Patriotic feelings should not be underestimated.

In other countries patriotism took a different form. In Switzerland, for example, there were patriots who were inspired by the French precedent to overthrow the yoke of their old oligarchic masters. In 1798 Switzerland was not the political entity it has since become; it consisted of thirteen German cantons with different politics and religions; Geneva was not then part of Switzerland, nor was Neuchâtel, which came under the suzerainty of Prussia;

and there was also an area called the Valais southeast of Lake Geneva, and the Grisons bordering on the Tyrol. With the aid of French arms General Brune had occupied Berne in February 1798 and a Helvetic Republic was set up, comprising much of modern Switzerland except Geneva and Valais, which were annexed by France. The French pressed the Helvetic Republic to join them in the war against the Second Coalition, which began in October 1798. The Helvetic Republic was in fact kept in being by victories won first by General Masséna and then by General Bonaparte. Though there was considerable resistance to the French occupation, especially of a religious character, liberty and unity were to a marked extent introduced into Switzerland by French bayonets.

In Italy, as has been seen, the Cisalpine Republic (centered on Milan) was set up to cover much of northern Italy and was recognized by all the European powers except Great Britain in October 1797. And Pitt would in fact have been willing to recognize the Cisalpine and Batavian republics if his country had been allowed to retain its overseas conquests from the Dutch. To the Cisalpine Republic was added in Italy a Roman Republic, proclaimed on February 15, 1798, which had a constitution drawn up for it by a group of Frenchmen after General Berthier had marched on the Papal capital. Although a revolt took place in Rome against Masséna, who replaced Berthier, the Roman Republic survived for a year or more, and the aged and sick Pope Pius VI was exiled to France, where he died in August 1799. Finally, in the winter of 1798 another French general, Championnet, created in Naples, from which the Bourbon King and Queen had been expelled, another Italian republic which was called the Parthenopian, though the French Directory hesitated to recognize it. Like the Roman Republic, it soon collapsed in anarchy.

These revolutionary transformations in western and southern Europe may be regarded in two ways: first, from the French point of view, and secondly, from that of the inhabitants of the new republics. The main objective of the French rulers was to win the war against Great Britain and to safeguard themselves against a renewed attack from Austria by asserting complete control over Italy. Secondly, it seemed to the Directory that if it could stir up revolutions in the lands of its enemies by appealing to revolutionary principles of liberation, it would contribute to its own hegemony as "La Grande Nation" of Europe. Lastly, there were idealists among the French revolutionaries who were eager to see the establishment of "sister republics"; the Girondins had wanted this and so later had Robespierre. But the Directors were cautious and Napoleon was an empiricist. Talleyrand, later to be a realist Foreign Minister, thought the "sister republics" were "feeble roots of liberty."

As to the "patriots" in the new republics or annexed territories, it has been recognized that they were for the most part middle-class intellectuals (as were the republican leaders in France). In the Batavian Republic the

Dutch were deeply divided, and though they were undoubtedly proud of their independence, they longed for the departure of the French army of occupation. French ideas may have contributed to Dutch administrative unification, but the economy was damaged and the once-prosperous trading middle classes undermined. In Belgium the only Francophiles were the middle class; the bulk of the peasants and artisans hated the French. In the Rhineland, another occupied territory, although the French were not liked, the abolition of feudal burdens attracted many peasants; consequently, there were no revolts against the French army of occupation like those which took place in Italy and elsewhere.

With regard to Italy, here was a unique case, as Napoleon realized. From as early as the middle of the eighteenth century (some say as early as the days of Machiavelli) the idea of a united Italy had been adumbrated. Buonarroti, one of the Italian patriots, who was born at Pisa in 1761 and was a descendant of Michelangelo, held out hopes of an independent Italian nation, just as men like La Harpe and Ochs were doing in Switzerland. Napoleon's decision to divide the ancient Venetian Republic between the French Directory and the Austrian Habsburgs created disillusionment almost everywhere throughout Italy. Thus, there were insurrections against the French generals in Italy fiercer than anywhere else.

The truth would appear to be that one is wrong either to be too romantic about French aspirations for the spread of revolutionary ideals throughout Europe or to be too confident about the extent of democratic republican patriotism expressing itself freely outside France. At most times in the history of Europe one can discover "patriots" who are willing to fight for their own independence with the assistance of outside Great Powers. (And not in Europe only—witness French support for the Americans and Russian support for the Cubans.) The Balkans are a startling case in point. Before the war of 1939 most of the Balkan states became subject to German National Socialism; after the war these same states described themselves as socialist democracies which looked to Soviet Russia for leadership and protection. In accordance with how a historian views the question, he can describe such collaborators or noncollaborators with conquering powers as "fifth-columnists" or as "patriotic resistance movements." For the most part, the French were not loved, and the only republics that were reasonably stable and that endured for any length of time were those that were occupied by French armies. The British Government, though it had its faults, had never believed in the virtues of a Europe dominated by a single power, whatever its professions. As the great Dutch historian Pieter Geyl once observed, England made a stand both against Louis XIV and against Napoleon (as later against Hitler) for the salvation of European freedom. For what is Europe without liberty? William III of Orange, William Pitt the Younger, and Winston Churchill form a sequence of leaders who considered—rightly or wrongly—that Europe could only be permanently united by agreement, never by conquest.

5. The Consulate

The French Government was only too anxious to dispose of Great Britain, which had been the organizing force behind its enemies. But how to get at the obstinate islanders? On his return from Italy, though before he attended the Congress of Rastatt, Napoleon had been appointed by the Directory as commander of the Army of England. The original idea was an invasion across the Channel with fifty thousand troops and fifty warships. But Napoleon was soon convinced that such a project was not then feasible in view of British naval supremacy. Instead, he dreamed of destroying the second British Empire by landing in Egypt (part of the Ottoman Empire) and marching thence across Syria, Persia, and Afghanistan into India. In August 1797 he had written to the Directory: "The time is not far distant when we shall feel that, in order truly to destroy England, we must occupy Egypt." But some historians argue that the concept of the Egyptian expedition originated not with Napoleon himself but with Talleyrand, who was now Minister of Foreign Affairs under the Directory. He had urged in a lecture given in that year that France should conquer Egypt; earlier still this had been a notion of the Duke of Choiseul. Probably Napoleon and Talleyrand had concocted the scheme together. At any rate the Directory accepted it. At a relatively small cost the British should be kept out of the Mediterranean.

On May 19, 1798, Napoleon sailed from Toulon; on June 12 he occupied without meeting resistance the island of Malta, then in the effete hands of the Knights of Saint John. On July 2 he captured Alexandria; on July 21 he defeated the Mamelukes, the ferocious people descended from the slaves of former Arab rulers, at the Battle of the Pyramids. A year later the Ottoman Sultan having declared war, Napoleon, after a fruitless expedition to Syria, destroyed the Turks at the Battle of Alexandria. But in 1798 William Pitt sent a British fleet under the command of Vice Admiral Horatio Nelson back into the Mediterranean. Nelson shattered the French fleet at the battle of the Nile on August 1, 1798. Thus, Napoleon's army was cut off from France and ultimately doomed. More important from the point of view of European history, Nelson's victory contributed to the renaissance of France's enemies and the formation of the Second Coalition against it.

The Tsar of Russia, who was nothing if not volatile, now had ambitions to follow in the footsteps of his mother by extending Russian power into the eastern Mediterranean. He took the French occupation of Malta as a personal affront and, after he had accepted the title of Protector and Grand Master of the Order from the exiled Knights of Saint John, he prepared to fight the French. An Anglo-Russian alliance was signed at the end of 1798. Meanwhile, the Austrians were also growing restless, especially over what they considered was French imperialism in Italy.

The events in Italy galvanized the Russians and the Austrians into action. A Russian army under General Suvoroff was allowed to march through Austria into northern Italy. The French demanded the withdrawal of the Russians and, when this was refused, thrust two armies across the Rhine. Thus to William Pitt's satisfaction the Second Coalition came into operation. But its successes, though at first striking, faded away. After French armies had been defeated both in Swabia and in northern Italy, the Russians were overthrown by General Masséna at Zurich, while during the autumn the good old Duke of York marched an army into Holland and then marched it out again. Thus, by the time Napoleon returned from Egypt (he landed in France on October 9, 1799) the Second Coalition had already been checked.

Before the close of 1799 the French Directory had proved itself unstable, inefficient, unpopular, and corrupt. It had offended the Roman Catholics by driving Pius VI from Rome and creating a Roman Republic; it had alienated the rich by imposing a special income tax on them; it had frightened critics by introducing a law of hostages reminiscent of the law of suspects during the Terror. After Napoleon's return a coup d'état was organized against the Directory. The Abbé Sieyès, who had managed to survive the Terror, drew up a complicated and unworkable constitution for a consular government. The constitution (modified by Napoleon) was forced through the two councils meeting at Saint Cloud in November (18-20 Brumaire) with the aid of Napoleon's brother Lucien, who was then President of the Five Hundred, and a column of grenadiers. Sieyès was thrust to one side and Napoleon was appointed First Consul for ten years with overriding powers. Under the Consuls (there were three) an extremely able group of ministers was chosen. The chief organ of government became a Council of State. There was also a Senate, Tribunate, and Legislature. The consular setup fulfilled a saying of Napoleon that a constitution should be short and obscure. In February 1800 it was accepted by a plebiscite.

The period of the Consulate, which lasted until 1804 (Napoleon was made First Consul for life in May 1802 with the right to nominate his successor), was the most constructive era in Napoleonic France. The Revolution, it was announced, was now at an end; the law of hostages and the special income tax were abolished; the churches were reopened; the *émigrés* were allowed to come home if they wished; republican festivals were terminated. Reconciliation and order became the objects of the new Government. On the positive side, peace was concluded with the leaders of the revolt in La Vendée. A Bank of France was established and public finances were put upon a sound footing. Local government was reorganized: *départements* were placed under the direction of prefects by the central Government, while *arrondissements,* replacing the districts, were put in charge of subprefects. The prefects chose the mayors of the communes. Thus, local government was centralized under the Minister of the Interior, the astronomer

Laplace, who was later succeeded by Lucien Bonaparte. An elaborate Civil Code was worked out and finally completed in 1804; Napoleon took an active part in the preparation of the Code, and although he stressed the importance of family ties, he also insisted on the right to divorce. It became known as the Code Napoleon in 1807. The Code also reflected to some extent Napoleon's belief that the struggle of 1789 had been in favor of equality, while liberty was only a pretext. The First Consul was by no means a ruthless dictator, but he exerted his influence to restrict political opposition.

As a contribution to internal peace Napoleon pushed through a Concordat with the Papacy, thus restoring the Roman Catholic Church in France. Napoleon considered that the majority of the people were still Catholics at heart, though he himself was no Christian (when in Egypt he pretended to be a Muslim). The negotiations for the Concordat were long and complex. Pope Pius VII, a former Benedictine monk, was devoted and guileless. Not only had Napoleon to persuade him to consent to terms, but he had to overrule the objections of many French politicians and *philosophes*. However, it was eventually agreed that the Roman Catholic religion should be accepted as that of the majority of French citizens—though not as the State religion and that the First Consul was to nominate the bishops, who were to be instituted by the Papacy. In the end Napoleon neither subordinated the Church to the State nor the State to the Church.

Another decision taken by Napoleon as First Consul, which met with criticism, was his institution of the Legion of Honour. This was a civil and military order, divided into ranks, chosen by a Grand Council presided over by Napoleon. The objection was that it was an inegalitarian measure which in effect created a new aristocracy. Napoleon argued that "soldiers perform great deeds largely through a sense of honour. . . . It was the same under Louis XIV." But he also maintained that it was compatible with the idea of "a career open to all talents." At the same time Napoleon persuaded the Senate to make some changes in the Constitution: henceforward a newly created Privy Council could draft senata-consulta and sanction treaties. Thus, though Napoleon had in fact acquired dictatorial powers, he gave the impression of being a progressive and liberal-minded statesman. He seemed to be in the line of Caesar and Cromwell. It was in 1802 that Ludwig van Beethoven, a child of the *Aufklärung*, dedicated his *Eroica* symphony to Napoleon.

6. The End of the Second Coalition

Before Napoleon's supremacy in France was finally achieved, he had to bring the European war to an end. Italy, which during his absence in Egypt had been overrun by the Austrians and Russians, needed to be reconquered. On June 2, 1800, Napoleon entered Milan, and on June 14 he won the Battle of Marengo: this was a close-run thing. Napoleon was saved from defeat by the opportune arrival of General Desaix, who had served him well in Egypt and was killed in the battle. On December 3 Moreau defeated the Archduke Charles at Hohenlinden and Austria withdrew from the war. So later in 1801 did Russia and Turkey, as Spain had done earlier. The Cisalpine Republic was renamed the Italian Republic, of which Napoleon became President in January 1802; in August Piedmont and Elba were annexed to France; and in February 1803 Napoleon imposed a federation on Switzerland.

It only remained for peace to be concluded with Great Britain. William Pitt had been replaced as Prime Minister by Henry Addington in February 1801, partly because Pitt had resented a refusal by George III to emancipate the Irish Roman Catholics, partly because the kingdom was wearying of war. The Tsar Paul I had turned against Great Britain and formed an armed alliance to enforce neutral rights at sea. But Admiral Nelson, by bombarding Copenhagen and destroying the Danish fleet, reasserted British naval superiority in the Baltic, while the Tsar was conveniently assassinated. In June 1801 the remnants of the French forces in Egypt surrendered to the British army there. So both to the north and south of Europe any threat to the British command of the seas was removed. By the Treaty of Amiens (March 25, 1802) Addington agreed to restore all the British conquests oversea except Ceylon and Trinidad. Malta (which had been captured by the British) was to be returned to the Knights of Saint John. The French, for their part, undertook to evacuate southern and central Italy. Thus, superficially Great Britain gained little from the War of the Second Coalition. On the other hand, by the Treaty of Luneville, which the French concluded with Austria in February 1801, France had agreed to respect the independence of the Helvetic, Batavian, Cisalpine (or Italian), and Ligurian republics. The independence of Portugal was also to be respected. France retained its "natural frontiers." It thus appeared as though a new Europe had come into being.

When he was a prisoner at Saint Helena Napoleon was to declare:

> At Amiens I believed, in perfectly good faith, that my future and that of France was fixed. I was going to devote myself solely to the administration of France, and I believed that I should have performed miracles. I would have made a moral conquest of Europe. . . .

In fact, Addington's Government was to declare war again on France in May 1803 (modern historians have accepted that it was the British and not the French fault), and a new European conflict opened.

In February 1804 a plot against Napoleon's life, in which a royalist, landed by the British in France, was joined by two of Napoleon's generals precipitated a movement to create him hereditary Emperor of the French Republic, a paradoxical title. This was decreed on May 18 and confirmed by a plebiscite. On December 2, 1804, Pope Pius VII, now restored to his temporal dominions, arrived from Rome and anointed Napoleon Emperor in Notre Dame Cathedral. Napoleon himself placed the crown on his own head and then on that of the Empress. The Pope, however, made it clear that he would not officiate at the coronation of a man and woman who, in his view, had been living in sin. So, on the day before, Napoleon and Josephine were married according to the Catholic rite by a Cardinal in the palace of the Tuileries.

7. From Amiens to Tilsit

The war between Great Britain and France that began in May 1803 was the product of an antagonism between neighbors which had endured through many years of European political history. Open hostilities between the two countries had begun in 1689, but British public opinion, as expressed in the Parliament of King Charles II's reign, had been consistently critical of French policies and ambitions. This antagonism was accentuated after Napoleon became First Consul: he was regarded in England as "Boney" or "the Corsican ogre," an upstart and greedy tyrant. Napoleon, for his part, thought that Great Britain was ruled by a selfish and drunken aristocracy which maltreated soldiers and exploited the proletariat. He once declared that had he conquered Great Britain, he would have overthrown the aristocracy and established an egalitarian system.

Thus, the Treaty of Amiens proved a mere armistice, since the governments of each country were suspicious of the movements of the other. Although Addington, a mild and perhaps underestimated Prime Minister, immediately set about cutting down the size of the army and navy and reducing taxation, it was his Government which first provoked and then declared war on France. The reason why it was decided to declare war was that Napoleon was thought to be upsetting the balance of power in Europe and endangering British supremacy on the seas and outside Europe. Within Europe the French not only extended their control over Italy but continued to interfere in the affairs of the Swiss and the Dutch; economic privileges were secured for French merchants in Tunisia; the huge area of Louisiana was purchased by France from Spain; and an expedition was dispatched to reassert French authority in the West Indian island of San Domingo. This suggested that Napoleon intended to create a new colonial empire. Napoleon was annoyed by insulting attacks on him published in British newspapers, by the protection given in England to his enemies, including *émigré* royalists, and, above all, by the British failure to evacuate Malta. Unquestionably, the British Government broke the letter of the treaty and did not improve matters by refusing an offer of Russian mediation.

It was extraordinary that the Addington Government, which had disarmed and economized, should have embarked on war so cavalierly. Addington evidently thought that the war could be fought on the cheap: that command of the sea would bring pressure to bear on the French and that

Napoleon in His Study
JACQUES LOUIS DAVID
National Gallery, Washington, D.C.

militia and volunteers would be sufficient to cope with any isolated French attempts at invasion. It is scarcely surprising, once it was realized what Addington had taken on, that he was replaced by Pitt in May 1804: the new Cabinet included Lord Castlereagh who, like Pitt, had earlier resigned office over the question of Catholic emancipation in Ireland, and who was later to prove a great Foreign Minister. Napoleon accepted the challenge and assembled an army of one hundred thousand men at Boulogne, known as the Army of England, while two thousand transports were gathered to carry them across the Channel. He knew that in order to invade, he had to obtain temporary command of the sea. In the spring of 1804 he ordered Admiral Latouche-Tréville, in charge of the Toulon fleet, to prepare to join up with French warships in the Channel ports, and on July 20, after he had been proclaimed Emperor, Napoleon personally inspected the preparations at Boulogne. But in August Latouche-Tréville died; and Napoleon abandoned the invasion scheme for the time being.

Meanwhile, Pitt had been laboring to form a Third Coalition against France. In fact, the French were the first to acquire an ally; in December 1804 Napoleon persuaded Spain to declare war on Great Britain. Thus, he hoped to collect sufficient naval resources to gain his ends. "If only we can be master of the Channel for six hours," he declared, "we shall be masters of the world." Throughout the first half of 1805 Napoleon tried to weaken British naval protection of the Channel by a series of feints at sea. But none worked. Finally, on October 21 the Franco-Spanish fleet was largely destroyed by Nelson at Trafalgar off Cadiz. Nelson himself was killed and the French admiral committed suicide. Thenceforward Napoleon aimed to defeat the British by economic warfare and by crushing any allies they obtained.

The first ally got hold of by Pitt was Tsar Alexander I of Russia. Alexander was nothing if not eccentric. He has been described as a Christian liberal and also (more accurately) as a schizophrenic. Certainly he was anxious to become an outstanding European statesman. After his offices as a mediator had been rejected, he entered into an alliance with Great Britain on April 11, 1805. Then in August the Emperor Francis II, eager to regain Austrian influence in Italy, adhered to the alliance. Frederick William III of Prussia, however, being tempted by an offer from France of the Electorate of Hanover, which Napoleon seized as soon as the war began, preferred to remain on the sidelines. But Napoleon gained Bavaria and other German states as allies. In August 1805 the French Emperor "turned his guns round." On August 26 the *Grande Armée* began to leave Boulogne: altogether, nearly two hundred thousand men were thrown across the Rhine and gathered in seven corps on the Upper Danube. "My intention," announced Napoleon on October 3, "when we meet the foe is to envelop him on all sides." This he did. On October 20 the Austrians were outmaneuvered and surrounded. Napoleon took thirty thousand prisoners. On November 14 he entered Vienna unopposed.

The victorious *Grande Armée* had yet to contend with the Russians, who joined the Austrians at Austerlitz in Moravia fifty miles northeast of Vienna. But Napoleon also had another enemy in mind; for on December 1 he declared in an order of the day: "it is vitally necessary to conquer these paid lackeys of England." The Battle of Austerlitz, which is immortalized in Tolstoi's *War and Peace,* was also known as the Battle of the Three Emperors, since, besides Napoleon, Francis II and Alexander I were present. The Russian general, Prince Michael Kutusoff, an able veteran, was in command of the allies, but was subject to the instructions of the young Tsar. By brilliant tactics Napoleon pierced his enemy's center and enveloped his left. Though the French casualties were relatively light, Kutusoff lost a third of his strength. Seven years later he was to exact his revenge. But now the Russians withdrew into Hungary and Poland, while on December 27, 1805, Francis II signed the Treaty of Pressburg, giving up the Austrian gains from Venetia and recognizing the independence of Napoleon's German allies. In July of the following year the Holy Roman Empire of the German nation was declared at an end. Napoleon had shattered the Third Coalition.

So from 1805 Napoleon became "a European statesman" and the architect of a Grand Empire. But in order to secure his Empire he still had to defeat Prussia, Russia, and Great Britain. For the King of Prussia, angered by the extension of French power across the Rhine and convinced that he had been deceived over Hanover, surprisingly resolved to take on Napoleon virtually single-handed, though Russian and Saxon contingents joined his army. On August 7, 1806, Prussia declared war; on October 14 and 15 the Prussian armies were overwhelmed at Jena and Auerstadt; on October 25 Napoleon came to Berlin as a conqueror; and finally the kingdom of Prussia was dismembered, losing half its territory. But Great Britain and Russia were harder to beat. Napoleon's idea was to ruin Great Britain by what was erroneously described as a blockade, but was in fact an attempt to boycott the sale of British exports into Europe. The Berlin Decree, issued by Napoleon on November 21, 1806, aimed to close all ports and coastlines under French control to British trade. Although some success was obtained by this so-called Continental system in 1807 and 1808, British exports recovered by 1809 and 1810. Not only did they expand outside Europe, but a vast amount of contraband was connived at by Napoleon's own satellite rulers. The British, now governed by a "Ministry of All the Talents," Pitt having died in January 1806, retorted with orders in council forbidding neutral ships to carry specified goods into French-controlled territories on penalty of forfeiture of their cargoes and the sale of their ships. The supremacy of the British at sea enabled them to carry out a "right of search" pretty effectively, while Napoleon was driven into enforcing his Continental system by fighting all over Europe. Historians who stress the economic interpretation of history incline to attribute to the failure of this system the ultimate downfall of Napoleon.

At the end of 1806 Napoleon prepared to tackle the Russians but proceeded cautiously. The Tsar's generals, though mostly old, were by no means as incompetent as the Prussians had been; his infantrymen were tough, his cavalrymen, especially the Cossacks, were dashing, his artillery was excellent. In December Napoleon entered Warsaw, which had formed part of the kingdom of Prussia. There he had an agreeable time, reminiscent of Paris, taking as his mistress the charming Marie Walewska, who was to bear him a son. He wrote to Josephine telling her he was too far away for him to allow her to join him. But he had no intention of restoring the independence of Poland; he thought that lacking public spirit, the Poles had deserved to lose it; nevertheless, he persuaded many of them to swell his army. He first clashed with the Russians at Pultusk in the winter mud; then on February 7-8, 1807, he fought a bloody and inconclusive battle at Eylau in East Prussia during a snowstorm; finally, on June 14 he decisively beat the Russians at Friedland, east of Eylau. Alexander I sought an armistice, and on July 7-9 the two emperors met on a raft moored in the River Niemen near Tilsit to discuss peace terms.

At Tilsit Napoleon did not treat Alexander as a vanquished foe but as an equal. They resolved to divide Europe between them into western and eastern spheres (much as the Americans and Russians did in 1945). Napoleon abandoned the Turks, who had been fighting against the Russians. Alexander promised to join the Continental system. The unfortunate King of Prussia, who was also at Tilsit, got short shrift. Before Tilsit Napoleon had confided to Talleyrand, his Foreign Minister, his intention of next attacking Spain at the other end of Europe. Talleyrand, who thought that Napoleon was developing megalomania, prepared first to resign and then to conspire the downfall of his master.

8. The Organization of the Empire

"The work of Tilsit will rule the destinies of the world." That is what Napoleon believed. For the next six years, from 1807 to 1812, he concentrated on expanding, protecting, and reorganizing his federative Empire in Europe. The period of the Empire offers little to compare in any important way with the reforms of the Consulate. Lefebvre considered that since at least 1803 the national interests of France had ceased to count with Napoleon: "the only thing that mattered to him was to rule the Continent and the world." Jacques Bainville wrote of a kind of vertigo, a delirium of power. Marshal Masséna, looking back from 1814, thought he "was passionate in his ambition, hard as iron in everything else."

Of what in fact did the Napoleonic Empire consist at the height of its glory and what were its characteristics? By 1812 it covered about seven hundred fifty thousand square miles of territory and contained some 44 million inhabitants. This was "the Grand Empire" or French Empire proper, consisting of the original kingdom and later annexations. Except for Piedmont and Liguria (Genoa), the kernel of the Empire corresponded with the "natural frontiers" of France, to reach which had been the desire of French statesmen for generations. Thus, Belgium, the Rhineland, and Geneva were all annexed states ruled by prefects on a common pattern. These annexed states benefited in several ways; for example, they got better roads. Since the British ruled the seas, the safest method of intercommunication was by new roads and great canals built to fulfil the Imperial needs. The "routes Napoleon" survive until the present day. The firm rule of prefects over the departments into which the Empire was divided, the more equitable distribution of taxation, and the reduction of poverty within the central Empire were all material advantages. In particular, the middle classes were better off then they had been in the Europe of the ancien régime.

But outside this kernel there were French vassal kingdoms and allied states. The vassal kingdoms included Italy, Holland, Westphalia, Naples, and Spain. They were mostly ruled by Napoleon's relations. Italy was the most

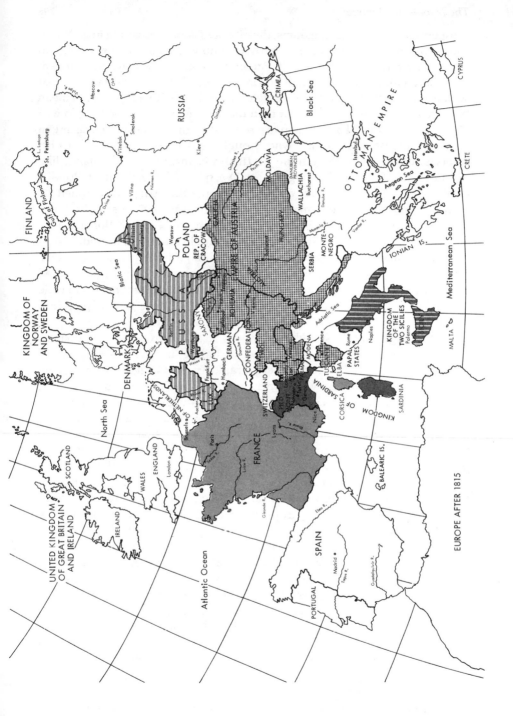

EUROPE AFTER 1815

prosperous of the vassal kingdoms, despite occasional peasant risings. Napoleon's son-in-law Eugène de Beauharnais, who was made viceroy of Italy in 1805, was a brilliant young man. Italian exports of silk and cereals expanded; a standard language (Tuscan Italian) was spoken; *lycées* were set up. A great sculptor, Canova, flourished (he sculpted Napoleon with a naked Herculean body, a statue for which the great man did not much care). The kingdom of Holland, over which Louis Bonaparte reigned from 1806 to 1810, was much less of a success. His brother, who thought that he was too tender to his subjects, obliged him to abdicate in 1810 and incorporated Holland, like Belgium, into France. The kingdom of Westphalia, carved out of Prussia, created in 1807, and ruled for a time by Jerome Bonaparte, was ruined by French financial and economic demands. Spain was never a satellite kingdom except in name. Naples, when ruled by the mild Joseph Bonaparte *(r. 1806–1808)*, was given a cultural and intellectual stimulus, and under Marshal Murat (married to Napoleon's sister Caroline) was relatively prosperous. But Napoleon was annoyed when Murat in the interests of his subjects tried to impose taxes on French imports. Napoleon may or may not have had wide visions for his satellite kingdoms, but he never had time to put them into effect.

After defeating Prussia Napoleon was also able to create vassal states within the Confederation of the Rhine, including, besides the kingdom of Westphalia, the grand duchies of Berg, Frankfort, and Würzburg. In 1807 he carved out the Grand Duchy of Warsaw, partly from Prussia, and later added bits of Austria. Finally, Napoleon's more or less willing allies included the remains of the kingdom of Prussia, Bavaria, Saxony, Württemberg, and Baden, all within the Confederation of the Rhine; the Swiss Confederation; Sweden; and Spain (until taken over as a vassal kingdom by Joseph Bonaparte in 1808). They were all obliged to accept the Continental system and to that extent came within the Imperial orbit. Only Great Britain and Russia, both of which, at least until the twentieth century, some historians have considered not to have been part of the traditional Europe at all, lay clearly outside the Napoleonic sway.

Within the Grand Empire reforms went steadily ahead. For example, in 1807 a commercial code was introduced, and this was followed in 1808 by a criminal code. None of these codes were as well considered or as effective as the civil code, which was applied throughout the Empire. Indeed, reactionary tendencies were to be detected reminiscent of the worst days of Bourbon rule. The penal code reestablished branding, the use of an iron collar, and the loss of hands as punishments. The judges were purged, and the Grand Judge, the Minister of Justice, or the Minister of Police could order prisoners to be interned by proceedings held in camera. Napoleon disliked lawyers and feared the printed word. Newspapers came either under the control of the police or, after 1810, were subjected to censorship. "The imperial administration," observed Lefebvre, "perfected the work of the Consulate and accentuated its arbitrary features." Only liberty of religious conscience remained untouched.

But Napoleon, despite the Concordat, did not leave the Roman Catholic Church in peace. In a megalomaniacal way Napoleon wanted to become a new Constantine and summon Church councils. He claimed in effect the right to institute bishops everywhere, and when this was refused he made Pius VII his prisoner. He disapproved of monkish orders as being wasteful of manpower, though he permitted the existence of nuns because he thought they were useful nurses. Napoleon also showed favor to the Freemasons, the ancient opponents of the Jesuits; his brother Joseph was Grand Master of the Lodges of Paris.

So far as education was concerned, Napoleon was prepared to leave primary education to the priests, but he took an active interest in secondary education, which he regarded as essential for the steady output of good officers and trained civil servants. For this purpose he introduced *lycées* in which military discipline was imposed. Although private schools were taxed to subsidize the *lycées,* they never made the headway for which he hoped. In 1808, in order to secure a larger measure of State control over education, a "University of France" (in effect a Ministry of Education) was set up with power to license teachers, fix their pay, and supervise higher education. Napoleon was, above all, a believer in vocational education and in the teaching of logic; but curiously, both modern languages and experimental science were neglected; as for women, Napoleon hardly thought they needed education at all.

Inevitably, the Continental system was damaging to the development of Imperial commerce, and many ports within the Empire were severely injured. On the whole, State intervention in industry was limited except for factories producing weapons of war, which became monopolies. Both strikes and trade unions were forbidden, but that, after all, was common form in eighteenth-century Europe. So far as foreign trade was concerned Napoleon was a bullionist. "My object," he once said "is to export French manufactures and import foreign *specie.*" Agriculture was more or less left alone. But what was important was that an egalitarian fiscal system relieved both the middle classes and the wage earners of the unfair burdens fastened upon them during the ancien régime. The poor were probably better off in the Empire than ever before, and opportunities were given to the peasantry to acquire small landed properties. The national finances were kept in extremely good order. Napoleon was not as exceptionally extravagant as his predecessors among French rulers, and because of the Revolution he had few or no aristocrats to trouble him. He allowed *émigrés* to return to France if they wished and inevitably—like Oliver Cromwell before him—he created his own nobility, ranging from princes to counts. But it was because he did not have to contend with the resurgence of the old aristocracies that had swept over Europe in the latter days of the eighteenth century that he could be claimed as "the most powerful of the enlightened despots."

Although as Emperor Napoleon reacted against republican esthetic austerity, his artistic tastes did not envelop Europe in the way that the Roman baroque had done or the classical style of Louis XIV. The fact was that, though he had been born on the small (and delightful) isle of Corsica, he thought of himself first and foremost as a Frenchman. To him the important place was Paris, the imperial capital, which he wanted to become (or might one say remain?) the artistic and intellectual heart of Europe. He had not much use for poets laureate or architectural dictators. He wanted Paris to contain reminders of his triumphs in splendid arches and broad roads lined with trees. The Arc de Triomphe was one of his monuments; but his Temple of Glory became the Church of the Madeleine. It was under his regime that the rue de Rivoli, the most fashionable street in Paris, was built. Gas lamps were introduced, new quays opened upon the Seine, the Pantheon and Bourse constructed. Though the standard of opera was raised, it was no great age for literature. Chateaubriand and Germaine de Staël received little or no encouragement from the Emperor. The Empire put society above the indi-

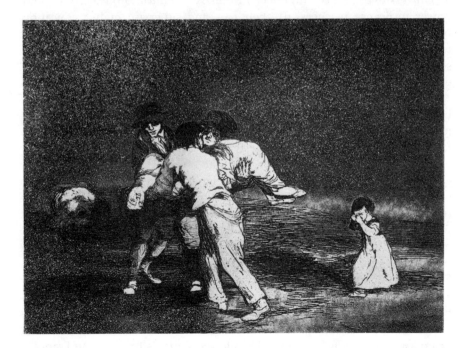

Unhappy Mother
Etching and Aquatint by Francisco Goya
The Metropolitan Museum of Art, Schiff Fund, 1922

vidual with or without a soul. The mood reflected first by Jean-Louis David, who was deeply influenced by the neoclassicism preached by Winckelmann and whom Napoleon regarded as "a master," and later by David's pupil, Antoine-Jean Gros, was one of Roman grandeur lauding honor and patriotism. David was not a bad painter, especially of portraits, but he was no colorist, and his achievement cannot be compared with that of the foremost painters of the century such as Gainsborough and Goya. The architecture of the First Empire was also conceived in terms of Greco-Roman motifs: its buildings were often rectilinear and merely utilitarian or imitative. The Arc de Triomphe and the Madeleine are simply imposing examples of the neoclassic style. Only Empire furniture, said to have been inspired by David, showed originality. It was a barren period in the noble history of French art.

9. Napoleon's Mistakes

In the hectic years of the Empire Napoleon tried to centralize everything upon himself and his family; the result was that he exhausted his own energy and came to commit more and more mistakes. His first mistake was to overestimate the significance of Portugal and Spain. To enforce the Continental system he thought it necessary to lay hold of Portugal. In September 1807 war was declared on Portugal, and by the secret Treaty of Fontainebleau between France and Spain the partition of Portugal was agreed. But then, taking advantage of a quarrel in the Spanish royal family, Napoleon decided to annex Spain as well. On December 1, 1807, Marshal Junot entered Lisbon and on March 23, 1808, Marshal Murat occupied Madrid. But neither takeover went smoothly. A revolt broke out in Madrid, and on July 21 a Spanish army compelled eighteen thousand French soldiers to lay down their arms at Bailen in Andalusia, an episode that caused a sensation throughout Europe. Ten days later Sir Arthur Wellesley landed at Montego Bay with a small British force, defeated Junot at Vimiero, and induced him to agree by the Convention of Cintra (August 22) to evacuate Portugal.

Napoleon was furious at these setbacks. In November he gathered an army of nearly two hundred thousand men and himself marched on Madrid, where he restored his brother Joseph to the throne. He also sought to chastise the British army, now under the command of Sir John Moore, which had advanced from Lisbon to Salamanca and thence northeast to cut the French communications. However, Napoleon himself was obliged to return to France, while Moore managed to evacuate his army at Corunna, though he was killed in the process. In May 1809 Wellesley (now Lord Wellington) returned to Portugal and lent support to Spanish resistance. During 1810–12 Wellington gradually got the better of the French armies in Portugal and Spain. In 1812 he decisively defeated the French under King Joseph at the Battle of Vittoria on the edge of the Pyrenees; by 1814 he was ready to cross the Pyrenees and invade southern France. Napoleon was never able himself to return to Spain, but he lost hundreds of thousands of Frenchmen in the peninsular campaigns.

The reasons why Napoleon had to return to Paris at the beginning of 1809 were first that he heard rumors of plotting against him there; secondly, he received information that the Austrians, stimulated by the events in Spain, were preparing to resume war against him. It appears that two of Napoleon's most capable servants, Talleyrand (who, though he had ceased to be Foreign Minister, held the office of Grand Chamberlain) and Joseph Fouché, the Minister of Police, concerned over Napoleon's megalomania, were contemplating substituting Marshal Murat (whose wife was Talleyrand's mistress) for Napoleon as Emperor. Napoleon was content to demote Talleyrand and warn Fouché. But the Austrian business was more serious. Napoleon now had to fight on two fronts. Though he defeated the Austrians, it proved a costly campaign. The Battle of Wagram (July 6, 1809) was won at a terrible price after sixteen hours of fighting. Napoleon himself showed signs of lethargy. But Austria was obliged by the Treaty of Schönbrunn (October 14) to lose 3½ million inhabitants and pay a large indemnity. By surrendering the Illyrian provinces, Austria was cut off from the sea, and by gaining Galicia Napoleon was able to increase the size of the Grand Duchy of Warsaw. During the same summer the French annexed the Papal states in Italy and interned the Pope.

Though the Napoleonic empire had thus once more been extended, the French Emperor was annoyed that his ally, Tsar Alexander, had refused to restrain the Austrians, after he and Napoleon had met in conference at Erfurt in October 1808, and failed to give any support to him during the Wagram campaign. During 1810 the relations between Alexander and Napoleon deteriorated. Napoleon, encouraged by the birth of illegitimate sons, decided to divorce Josephine and marry into the European dynastic circle so as to obtain a princely heir to his throne. Alexander refused to allow him to wed his sister, and instead Napoleon married Marie-Louise, daughter of the Emperor Francis I, in March 1810. Alexander was irritated by the enlargement of the Duchy of Warsaw. Furthermore, at the end of 1810 he repudiated the Continental system.

During 1811 Napoleon determined to make war on Russia and completed elaborate preparations. An army of over six hundred thousand men was assembled, only half of whom were French, the rest consisting of Austrians, Prussians and other Germans, Poles, Swiss, Italians, and even a few unwilling Spaniards. Napoleon insisted on being not only commander-in-chief but his own Chief of Staff. The Russians had some four hundred thousand troops, who were ultimately to be under the supreme command of Prince Kutusoff, a dedicated foe of Napoleon, who verged on seventy. The Russians slowly withdrew before the French hordes. Napoleon thought all could be settled by a single battle. But Borodino, fought on September 7, was a costly and inconclusive victory. Napoleon then decided, perhaps unwisely, to push seventy-five miles farther on to Moscow, the occupation of which he believed would compel peace. But Napoleon lived in a dream world. Moscow was set on fire by its own civil governor on September 15; although sufficient shelter remained for the Napoleonic army, neither warm clothing nor fresh horses were to be found. Napoleon lingered there too long before resolving on retreat. The weather was fine when he left Moscow, and it was not so much "General Winter" as overstretched communications and low morale that destroyed his armies. Of the six hundred thousand men who set out fewer than forty thousand managed rather luckily to cross the Berezina River in Lithuania at the end of November. On December 6 the French Emperor handed over the command to Marshal Murat, still known as the King of Naples. Napoleon reached Paris on December 18, 1812, conscious that his *Grande Armée* was no more.

The decision made by Austria to fight Napoleon again in 1809 had been caused largely by patriotic propaganda. Napoleon's enemies brought pressure to bear on the Austrian Emperor and the Archduke Charles, his commander-in-chief. Napoleon's *bête-noire,* Madame de Staël, leader of the French middle-class liberals, came to Vienna; so did Augustus Schlegel, who had been advocating cultural patriotism as a professor in Berlin, while the great statesman, Freiherr von Stein, who had served Frederick William III of Prussia and been dismissed on Napoleon's order, was an exile in Prague. All of them contributed to stirring up Austrian patriotism. In 1813 much the same thing happened in Prussia. Here the leadership was assumed by Fichte and other intellectuals and students in the newly founded University of Berlin. Patriotic societies were formed and a popular militia or *Landsturm* recruited. The King of Prussia was forced rather unwillingly to conclude an offensive treaty with the Russians at Kalisch (February 25, 1813), thus changing sides. By April Austria declared itself in favor of armed mediation, and on June 14 Russia and Prussia signed subsidy treaties with Great Britain promising to conclude no separate peace.

10. The Fall of Napoleon

Through stupendous efforts Napoleon gathered together a fresh army of two hundred thousand men in Germany ready for a campaign in 1813 (apart from his forces left in Italy and the Iberian peninsula), but his soldiers possessed neither the skill nor the equipment of the *Grande Armée* destroyed in Russia. After hard battles had been fought, an armistice was agreed and lasted until August 10. Seven weeks earlier, on June 24, Austria had agreed by the secret Convention of Reichenbach on the preliminary terms that were to be sought from Napoleon. If these were not conceded, Austria promised to enter the war. In pursuit of this, on June 26 the Austrian

Chancellor, Prince Metternich, had a long interview with Napoleon during the course of which the French Emperor proved himself intransigent and proclaimed: "I may lose my throne, but I shall bury the whole world in ruins." Peace negotiations broke down, and the Austrian Emperor, Napoleon's own father-in-law, declared war upon him. Sweden, now ruled by one of Napoleon's former marshals, Bernadotte, also joined the new coalition. Fiercely contested battles between huge armies took place in Germany during August and September, but at the Battle of Leipzig, which lasted four days (October 16–19), Napoleon was overwhelmed and withdrew across the Rhine.

There is some argument about whether the allies, meeting at Frankfort on Main in December 1813, did or did not offer Napoleon peace terms, based on the "natural frontiers of France." Napoleon himself certainly believed that they had done so, but in any case he failed to grasp the opportunity. As Stendhal percipiently pointed out, Napoleon could not believe that his former friend, Alexander I, and his father-in-law, Francis I, would subject him to the severest terms: "he possessed the defect of all *parvenus:* that of having too great an opinion of the class into which he had risen." In 1814, as the Prussians and Austrians prepared to invade France, Napoleon himself planned a patriotic war. He commended to the National Guard of Paris the charge of his son (born on March 20, 1811), known as the King of the Romans: "I place this child, the hope of France, in your care," he said. "As for me, I go forth to battle, my only thought the salvation of the country." But he rejected the idea of a complete *levée en masse.* "If fall I must," he exclaimed, "I will not bequeath France to the revolutionaries, from whom I have delivered her." Such was the ironic retort to those future historians who have portrayed Napoleon as a revolutionary. With remarkably small forces Napoleon fought during the first three months of 1814 one of the most brilliant of his campaigns, keeping the Prussians and Austrians apart inside France. Finally, Alexander I insisted upon a direct march on Paris. The allies entered the French capital on March 31. On April 2 the Senate invited Louis XVIII to return; on April 6 Napoleon abdicated; and on April 12 he signed the Treaty of Fontainebleau, which allowed him to retain the title of Emperor, to obtain the sovereignty of Elba, and his wife, Marie-Louise, to retire with her son to the duchy of Parma. Before he signed this treaty he vainly tried to commit suicide. By the first Treaty of Paris, accepted by the new French Government, France was reduced to the frontiers of November 1792, her "ancient frontiers," but was not asked to pay any reparations nor even to restore the art treasures pillaged by Napoleon. A congress was to meet in Vienna on October 1 to settle the political future of Europe.

But Napoleon was not yet ready to acquiesce in his fate. In Elba he learned that the allies were quarreling and that Louis XVIII was not popular. On March 1, 1815, he landed at Antibes and made for Paris, from which the King hastily withdrew. Napoleon was proclaimed an outlaw and another coalition was formed against him. A competition was held to win over French opinion: on June 1 Louis XVIII issued a charter; on June 4 Napoleon published a supplementary decree promising a constitutional monarchy and universal suffrage. In no time at all Napoleon collected an army of two hundred thousand men, better trained than the conscripts of 1813, and led over one hundred, twenty thousand of them into Belgium. Here he was confronted by a mixed army, including British, under the command of the Duke of Wellington, based at Brussels, and a larger Prussian army under the seventy-three-year-old Field Marshal Blücher with headquarters at Namur. Napoleon aimed to defeat his enemies separately; while he attacked Blücher at Ligny, he sent Marshal Ney to occupy Quatre-Bras, some eight miles to the northwest on the Brussels road. Napoleon drove back Blücher, but Ney failed to take Quatre-Bras. Napoleon then divided his army into two parts, sending nearly a third to pursue Blücher and concentrating the remainder against Wellington. But when, at two in the afternoon of June 17 Napoleon reached Quatre-Bras, he found that Wellington had withdrawn his army down the Brussels road and deployed it on what was to be known as the battlefield of Waterloo.

The Battle of Waterloo began at 1:30 in the afternoon of June 18. Napoleon left the tactical command to Marshal Ney and sent late and confused orders to his detached force under Marshal Grouchy. First of all Ney

Battle of Waterloo
By courtesy of the Trustees
of the British Museum

threw in infantry, unprotected by cavalry, and later he sent in cavalry without infantry or artillery support. Although both these assaults were repulsed, Wellington might have been beaten if Blücher's Prussians had not arrived unexpectedly on the field of battle at four in the afternoon, thus outflanking the French right wing. As evening approached and when it was too late, Napoleon sent forward his elite Imperial Guard, who had been back as reserves. The British redcoats concentrated their firepower on the advancing enemy and then charged with their bayonets. It was not long before the dreadful news spread through the French army: "La Garde recule!" ("The Guard is retreating!") Panic followed; that was the end. On June 22 Napoleon again abdicated; in July Louis XVIII came back to Paris and Napoleon surrendered at Rochefort to the commander of the British warship the *Bellerophon*. By the second Treaty of Paris, signed by Louis XVIII on November 20, France lost more territory and promised to pay an indemnity, to restore the stolen art treasures, and to accept an allied military occupation, which was in fact to be ended after three years. Napoleon was dispatched as an honorable prisoner to the isolated island of Saint Helena in the South Atlantic. There he died, though of precisely what disease is not known, on May 5, 1821, at the age of fifty-one. His last words were said to have been: "France, armée, tête d'armée, Joséphine." He was the victim of his own limitless ambitions and blind self-confidence.

11. Child of the Revolution?

How far was Napoleon the child of the French Revolution? How far did his Grand Empire transform the character of Europe? Admirers of the French Emperor set much store upon the Code Napoleon, which, they claim, confirmed the destruction of feudalism and upheld the principles of social equality fought for in 1789. The Code was applied, with some modifications, throughout most of Europe: it was introduced into the kingdom of Italy, for instance, as early as 1806. Even if Napoleon's aim was primarily to amass men and money to maintain his armies, he wanted, so Lefebvre argued, to sweep away any institutions that distorted or interfered with the ascendancy of France. Therefore, civic equality, religious liberty, the abolition of feudal privileges, and the sale of Church property composed his policy. The effete aristocracy of the ancien régime should, he thought, be extinguished everywhere, above all in Great Britain, and a new aristocracy, open to all the talents, be constructed subject to the sovereigns.

As to Napoleon's foreign policy, it did not differ materially from that of any other conqueror who attempted to subjugate Europe or was beckoned on by romantic dreams of power. Whatever legends may have been manufactured in Saint Helena, no historian today believes that Napoleon deliberately fostered the concept of nationalism which was to dominate Europe in the nineteenth and early twentieth centuries (as it now dominates Asia and Africa). The Emperor stimulated nationalism only by opposing it. By his menaces he aroused British, German, Austrian, Italian, Russian, Spanish, and Portuguese patriotism. But this passionate nationalist spirit, as it was engendered by the French Revolution, invariably brought dictatorship in its train. Stein's Germany was ultimately to become the totalitarian state of Hitler, Garibaldi's Italy that of Mussolini; the Russia which fought against Napoleon was equally to fight at the orders of the half-insane Stalin; the heirs of the Spanish and Portuguese revolutionaries were to find political stability only under Franco and Salazar. Today we Europeans are starting to cease thinking in terms of nationalism. We look forward, at least for our children and grandchildren, to a united Europe. We have seen too many crimes committed and too much blood shed in the name of nationalism.

If dictatorship with all its defects for those who believe in political freedom stemmed from the Revolution itself, it can be argued that the middle classes and, to a lesser extent, the peasantry, at any rate in France itself, were at least given equality of status in society. Marxist historians contend that this was indeed so, that the very universality of the French Revolution, as its tenets were spread by the wars of Napoleon, gave birth to the realization that a world social revolution was a possibility. It also, they insist, provided an impetus to industrial and financial capitalism. Great Britain's victory over France, they say, was a victory for capitalism. Other non-Marxist historians take the view that the contribution of the Napoleonic age to the evolution of modern capitalism was minimal: this would have come about in any case. Against the determinist attitude toward history may be contrasted the more old-fashioned liberal approach which prevailed until the Age of Guilt in the Europe of the 1920s and 1930s. Pieter Geyl was of the opinion that Napoleon rejected the highest ideals which animated the French Revolution—those of democracy and human dignity. He sacrificed individual freedom to a somewhat spurious social equality. Like all ambitious dictators, he at once exploited and despised the mass of the people.

TEN

Epilogue

"What a romance my life has been!" Napoleon once exclaimed. Perhaps it was; but the romantic enthusiasm which had greeted the Revolution in many parts of Europe was killed stone-dead by the Napoleonic Empire. The Revolution had been welcomed in England by the poets Wordsworth, Coleridge, and Southey, all of whom changed their views after 1797. In Germany it had been hailed with rapture by Kant, Hegel, Schiller, Fichte; in Switzerland by the educationist Pestalozzi; in Scotland by the poet Robert Burns, who died in 1796; of all the great men of the time only Goethe was unmoved. To Kant the Revolution meant progress and peace; to William Godwin in England it heralded the beginnings of a new Age of Reason; to Fichte and Hegel it presaged the dawn of German nationalism.

But the rise of Napoleon brought with it disillusionment. Beethoven struck out his dedication of the Eroica symphony when he learned of the coming of the Empire and wrote instead that it was to celebrate the memory of a great man. Thus, the romantic movement in Europe, which received its original impulse from the writings of Rousseau and the events of the Revolution, suffered a setback; its story belongs much more to the second and third decades of the nineteenth century, the age of Shelley and Byron and the British reform movement.

Yet it was of course the French Revolution, not the construction of the short-lived Napoleonic Empire, that changed the political and social outlook of Europe, just as the long, drawn-out Industrial Revolution was starting to transform the European countryside, creating, for example, the ghastly slag heaps of Lancashire and Yorkshire that still deface northern England in the twentieth century.

Though one must not exaggerate the historical importance of the kings and aristocracies that governed Europe in the seventeenth and eighteenth centuries, it was a more or less gentlemanly world. Until the Revolution, war and diplomacy were games played by accepted rules with much bowing and scraping. The royal families were all related to one another, and dynastic wars, boring enough to latter-day historians, did comparatively little damage

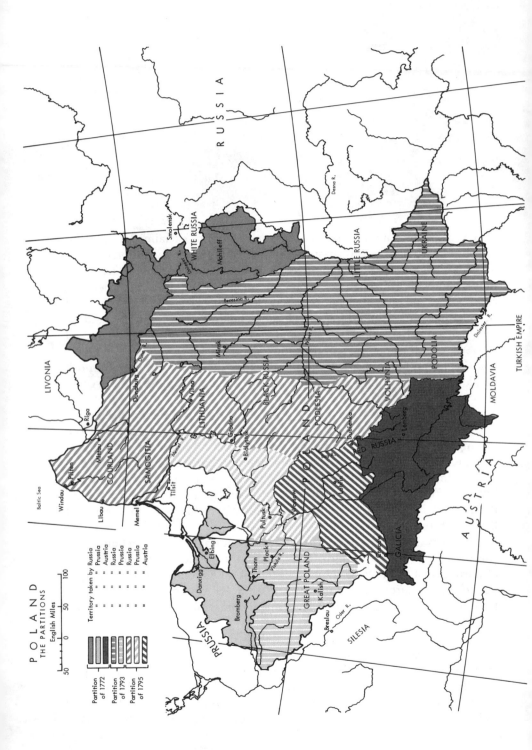

POLAND
THE PARTITIONS

English Miles

50   0   50   100

Territory taken by Russia
                   "   Prussia
                   "   Austria

Partition of 1772   Russia
                     Prussia

Partition of 1793   Russia
                     Prussia

Partition of 1795   Russia
                     Prussia
                     Austria

RUSSIA

Smolensk

WHITE RUSSIA

Mohileff

Minsk

LITTLE RUSSIA

UKRAINE

LIVONIA

Riga

Beresina R.

BLACK RUSSIA

PODLESIA

VOLHYNIA

PODOLIA

Dniester R.

TURKISH EMPIRE

Baltic Sea

Windau

Libau

Pillen

Mittau

COURLAND

SAMOGITIA

Dunaburg

Vilna

Grodno

Bialystok

Lemberg

Dubienko

RED RUSSIA

MOLDAVIA

Memel

Tilsit

P O L A N D

AUSTRIA

Danzig

Elbing

Pulwsk

GALICIA

PRUSSIA

Bromberg

Thorn

Plock

Vistula R.

GREAT POLAND

Kalish

SILESIA

Breslau

Oder R.

to the ordinary life of men and women. The peasants went on tilling their soil as the mercenary armies marched through. But at last the peasants of France rose in arms to help overthrow their old masters and began under the leadership of a professional middle class to destroy the remnants of feudal society. But the peasants failed to do the same in eastern Europe. The French Revolution was a catalyst and Europe was never to be the same again. Or, to vary the metaphor, the roads to modern capitalism and representative institutions were opened, though few realized they were to be dotted with "dark satanic mills" or with even more ruthless dictatorships based on terror, though disguised by plebiscites.

Thus, the story told in this book begins and ends with revolutions. Whereas the revolutions of the sixteenth century had been mainly over religion and of the mid-seventeenth century over unfair taxation that robbed the poor of their means to buy bread, the late-eighteenth-century revolutions were primarily nationalist and bourgeois in character, inspired by the French overthrow of their ancien régime and later fashioned out of resistance to the repression of the Bonapartes. The real revolution of the masses, however, had still to come.

The settlement of Europe that followed the fall of Napoleon scarcely reflected the romantic hopes which had inspired the Revolution or the

The Congress of Vienna, 1815
Watercolor by JEAN BAPTISTE ISABEY
The Granger Collection

nationalist ideals which had been conjured up by the revulsion against Napoleon's conquests. The Congress of Vienna was animated above all by the idea of creating a balance of power that would ensure European peace. As a congress in fact it never really met; for though hundreds of delegates gathered in the Austrian capital, the main decisions were taken by the Big Four (Great Britain, Austria, Prussia, and Russia) or by the Big Six (France and Spain being added) or occasionally the Big Eight (plus Sweden and Portugal). The internationally minded Prince de Ligne wrote: "Le congrès dance mais il ne marche pas." ("The Congress dances, but it does not move.") In fact, it concluded its business with impressive speed. All its work was done in nine months, despite the interruption caused by Napoleon's return from Elba, and the final act was signed on June 9, 1815.

According to the terms of the treaty Great Britain expanded its second Empire by the addition of Malta, Ceylon, and the Cape of Good Hope, the West Indian islands of Trinidad, Saint Lucia, and Tobago, Guiana in South America, and Mauritius off South Africa; it was also given a protectorate over the Ionian islands. When Napoleon heard about this in Saint Helena he was amazed. He said of Lord Castlereagh: "the peace he has made is the sort of peace he would have made, if he had been beaten." How, asked Napoleon, could a sensible nation allow itself to be governed by such a lunatic? Russia, the other most successful opponent of Napoleon, obtained Finland and Bessarabia and retained three-fifths of the old Poland or Congress Poland, as it was called; though nominally independent this soon became in fact part of the Tsar's Empire. Prussia regained most of its former Polish possessions, including Danzig, and acquired Swedish Pomerania, the kingdom of Westphalia, much of the Rhineland, and three-fifths of Saxony, which it was awarded in return for such parts of Prussian Poland as it surrendered to Russia. Austria retained all its Polish possessions and secured in Italy Lombardy and Venetia as well as Illyria and Dalmatia. From Bavaria Austria acquired the Tyrol and Salzburg. Altogether, 4 or 5 million inhabitants were added to the subjects of the Austro-Hungarian Empire.

Thus, the Big Four did not emerge too badly from the treaty. Among the smaller powers, Sweden obtained Norway from Denmark as compensation for the loss of Finland to Russia; Switzerland was formed into a confederation of twenty-one cantons and its neutrality guaranteed by five Great Powers; Holland, Belgium, and Luxembourg were amalgamated into one kingdom. In Italy, outside the area acquired by Austria the Pope was restored to his secular dominions, while he finally lost Avignon to France; the Bourbon King Ferdinand IV became King of Naples and Sicily; Victor Emmanuel I, the King of Sardinia, got back Piedmont and most of Savoy was awarded Genoa. The Grand Duke Ferdinand III, who was related to the Habsburgs, ruled in Tuscany; Duke Francis IV of Este, another friend of Austria, acquired Modena, Reggio, and Mandola. The vast number of small states which had constituted the Holy Roman Empire were now reduced to thirty-eight, Bavaria, Hanover, Saxony, and Württemburg all becoming kingdoms. These states were formed into a weak and loose Confederation of Germany under the presidency of Austria with a Diet at Frankfort. But Prussia was a powerful member of the new confederation, and Austria was never to dominate Germany as for a time it did Italy.

What were the principles, if any, that guided the Congress of Vienna in drawing up these terms? It used to be said that it was the idea of legitimacy, which had been advocated by Prince Metternich, the president of the Congress. Certainly the old dynasties were restored in France, Spain, Portugal, Sicily, Sardinia, Sweden, and, one might say, Holland. But the chief concern of all the leading diplomatists was to sustain a balance of power in Europe and prevent the renewal of European war. Most of them were less worried over a revival of French power, once Napoleon was safely in Saint Helena, than over the aggrandizement of Russia. It was hoped that just as the new kingdom of the Netherlands would become an independent buffer state against France, so the new kingdom of Poland (formed out of Napoleon's Grand Duchy of Warsaw) would act as an independent buffer state against Russia. Thus, the trickiest problem for the Congress was how much of the old Poland should go to Russia and how much of Saxony to Prussia. The problem was not solved until Castlereagh, Metternich, and Talleyrand (for France) signed on January 3, 1815, a secret treaty of alliance, promising that if any one of them were attacked on account of the proposals they had agreed upon for solving the Polish-Saxony dispute, they would lend each other mutual support. But Castlereagh's hope that the new Poland would be truly independent was not to be realized; for the Tsar of Russia was to become also King of Poland and was soon to abandon any pretense of allowing Poland independence.

Today most of these political changes may seem of minor importance, since if another inter-European war were to break out, Europe might destroy itself. What has to be sought is not rival nations but a united Europe. So far as the settlement of 1815 was concerned, might not Napoleon be said to have had the last word when he remarked in Saint Helena, apropos British predominance in the world, "there are two Hercules in their cradles, Russia and the United States of America"?

At Vienna Russia, Austria, and Prussia entered into a Holy Alliance, based "upon the sublime truths which the Holy Religion of Our Saviour teaches" to maintain "a true and indissoluble fraternity." Castlereagh thought this "a piece of sublime mysticism and nonsense" and refused to join it. It was inspired by Alexander I, whose vanity and neuroticism were among the difficulties confronting the realist statesmen in Vienna. However, Castlereagh also concluded a quadruple alliance which aimed to guarantee the settlement so far as France was concerned.

The Treaty of Vienna became the basis of international law for the next fifty years, and whatever its defects may have been, no war engulfing the whole of Europe took place for a century. Apart from averting immediate wars, it can hardly be said that the settlement benefited the mass of the European peoples. Indeed, the Belgians resented being subjected to the Dutch, the Poles to the Russians, and the Italians to the Austrians. Fresh revolutions were to break out in 1830 and 1848. When in the latter year Prince Metternich, who thought of himself as a rock of order, was obliged to flee from Vienna to England and later learned of the revival of Bonapartism in France, he had survived into a world he failed to understand. Thus, the revolutionary age was to continue into the Europe of the mid-nineteenth century.

Genealogies

Spain and the Spanish Succession

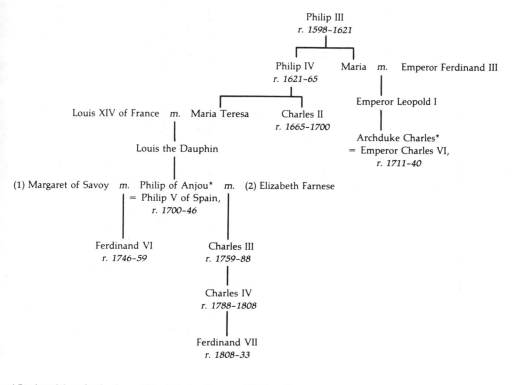

Philip III
r. 1598-1621

Philip IV   Maria   *m.*   Emperor Ferdinand III
r. 1621-65

Louis XIV of France   *m.*   Maria Teresa   Charles II
r. 1665-1700

Emperor Leopold I

Louis the Dauphin

Archduke Charles*
= Emperor Charles VI,
r. 1711-40

(1) Margaret of Savoy   *m.*   Philip of Anjou*   *m.*   (2) Elizabeth Farnese
= Philip V of Spain,
r. 1700-46

Ferdinand VI   Charles III
r. 1746-59   *r. 1759-88*

Charles IV
r. 1788-1808

Ferdinand VII
r. 1808-33

* Rival candidates for the throne of Spain during the war of the Spanish succession, 1701-13

The Hohenzollern House (1415–1840)

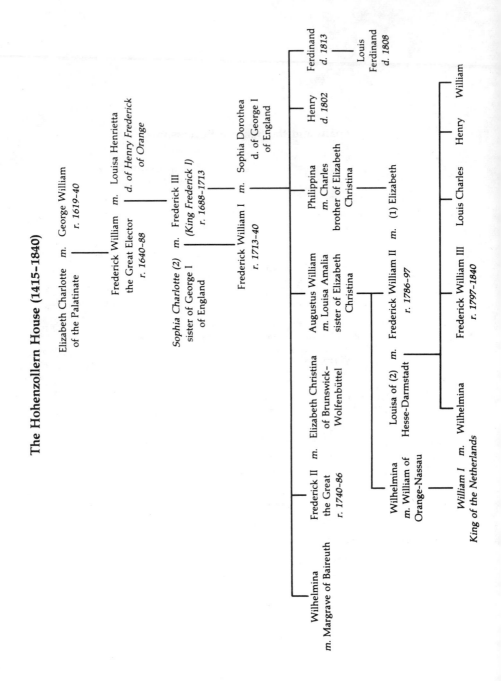

England

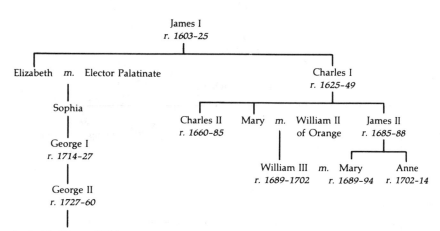

James I
r. 1603–25

Elizabeth   *m.*   Elector Palatinate

Charles I
r. 1625–49

Sophia

Charles II
r. 1660–85

Mary   *m.*   William II
of Orange

James II
r. 1685–88

George I
r. 1714–27

William III   *m.*   Mary
r. 1689–1702   *r. 1689–94*

Anne
r. 1702–14

George II
r. 1727–60

Frederick, Prince of Wales

George III
r. 1760–1820

France

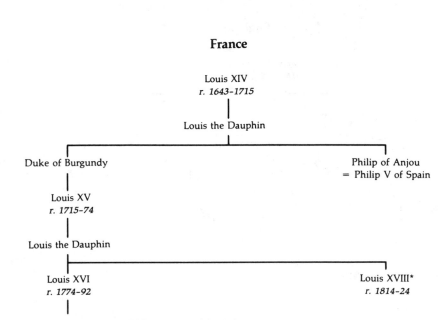

Louis XIV
r. 1643–1715

Louis the Dauphin

Duke of Burgundy

Philip of Anjou
= Philip V of Spain

Louis XV
r. 1715–74

Louis the Dauphin

Louis XVI
r. 1774–92

Louis XVIII*
r. 1814–24

* Louis XVII, son of Louis XVI never reigned; he died a prisoner in 1794.

Austrian Habsburgs

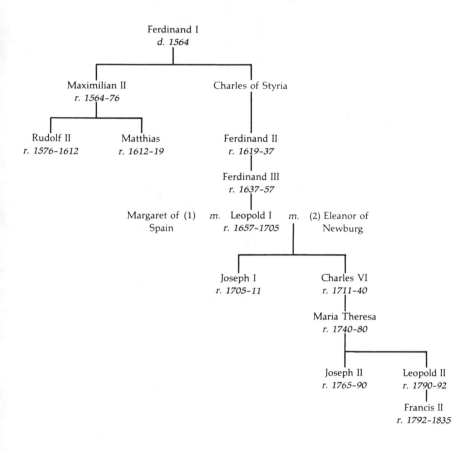

Ferdinand I
d. 1564

Maximilian II
r. 1564-76

Charles of Styria

Rudolf II
r. 1576-1612

Matthias
r. 1612-19

Ferdinand II
r. 1619-37

Ferdinand III
r. 1637-57

Margaret of (1)   *m.*   Leopold I   *m.*   (2) Eleanor of
Spain   *r. 1657-1705*   Newburg

Joseph I
r. 1705-11

Charles VI
r. 1711-40

Maria Theresa
r. 1740-80

Joseph II
r. 1765-90

Leopold II
r. 1790-92

Francis II
r. 1792-1835

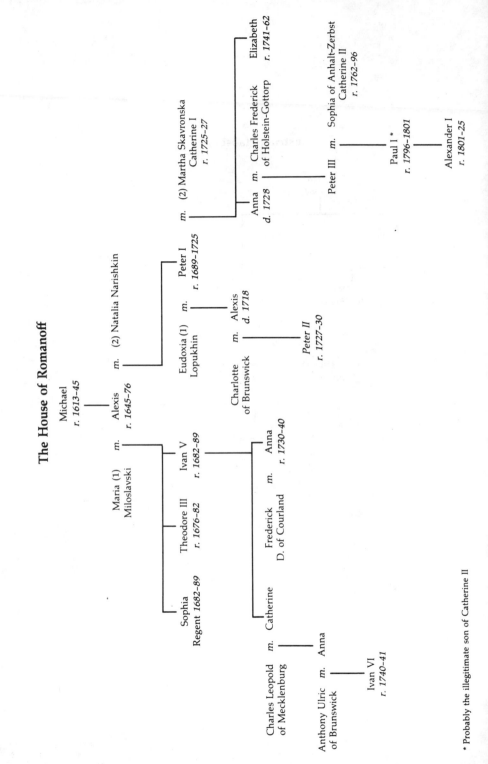

The House of Romanoff

Michael
r. 1613–45

Alexis
r. 1645–76

Maria (1) m. (2) Natalia Narishkin
Miloslavski

Sophia   Theodore III   Ivan V   Peter I
Regent 1682–89 r. 1676–82   r. 1682–89   r. 1689–1725

                                                    Eudoxia (1) m.
                                                    Lopukhin

                                                    Alexis
                                                    d. 1718

Catherine   Frederick m. Anna   Charlotte
            D. of Courland r. 1730–40 of Brunswick m.

                                        Peter II
                                        r. 1727–30

Charles Leopold m. Anna
of Mecklenburg

Anthony Ulric m.
of Brunswick

Ivan VI
r. 1740–41

m. (2) Martha Skavronska
       Catherine I
       r. 1725–27

                                    Elizabeth
                                    r. 1741–62

Anna m. Charles Frederick
d. 1728 of Holstein-Gottorp

                Peter III m. Sophia of Anhalt-Zerbst
                             Catherine II
                             r. 1762–96

                    Paul I *
                    r. 1796–1801

                    Alexander I
                    r. 1801–25

* Probably the illegitimate son of Catherine II

The House of Orange

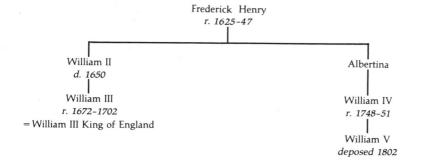

Frederick Henry
r. 1625-47

William II
d. 1650

William III
r. 1672-1702
= William III King of England

Albertina

William IV
r. 1748-51

William V
deposed 1802

King William I of the Netherlands
r. 1813-43

The Popes

INNOCENT X	(1644-1655)
ALEXANDER VII	(1655-1667)
CLEMENT IX	(1667-1669)
CLEMENT X	(1670-1676)
INNOCENT IX	(1676-1689)
ALEXANDER VIII	(1689-1691)
INNOCENT XII	(1691-1700)
CLEMENT XI	(1700-1721)
INNOCENT XIII	(1721-1724)
BENEDICT XIII	(1724-1730)
CLEMENT XII	(1730-1740)
BENEDICT XIV	(1740-1758)
CLEMENT XIII	(1758-1769)
CLEMENT XIV	(1769-1774)
PIUS VI	(1775-1799)
PIUS VII	(1800-1823)

Note on Authorities

A full bibliography of this long period in European history would require a volume in itself. What I have done is to confine myself mainly to books published in Great Britain, France, and the United States which I have found of value. These books, unless otherwise stated, were published in London, Paris, and New York respectively. Books published first in the United States are marked with an asterisk. For the most part I have not included books published more than forty years ago: lists of these will be found in the bibliographies given in Section I below.

I. Bibliographies

Bibliographies are published periodically in the American Historical Association's *Guide to Historical Literature* and the English Historical Association's *Annual Bulletin of Historical Literature*. *A Select List of Works on European and Europe Overseas, 1715-1815* (ed. J. S. Bromley and A. Goodwin, Oxford, 1956) and *A Select Bibliography of Modern European History, 1494-1788* (ed. Alun Davies, Helps for Students of History no. 68, 1966), published by the English Historical Association, may be recommended, although Davies's list contains rather a high proportion of oldish books. *A Bibliography of Modern History* (ed. John Roach, Cambridge, England, 1969), although it is unquestionably the latest full bibliography of European history in this period, is disappointing for two reasons: first, it is linked to the *New Cambridge Modern History* and is difficult to find one's way about; secondly, it contains no index of authors' names, which is irritating. Comprehensive lists of older books on European history will be found at the end of each volume of the old *Cambridge Modern History*. Valuable and up-to-date bibliographies are to be found in the *Nouvelle Clio* series published by the Presses Universitaires de France in Paris.

II. General

A good general introduction to modern European history is Ernest John Knapton, *Europe, 1450-1815* (1958).* R. R. Palmer, *A History of the Modern World* (1961)* is written by a distinguished American historian whose views about "the democratic revolution" are, however, controversial. Pierre Chaunu, *La civilisation de l'Europe classique* (1966) has been widely praised. It covers the years 1620 to 1760. It is not organized chronologically and, in my view, pays insufficient attention to political history. It is lavishly illustrated and contains many useful tables. Probably the *New Cambridge Modern History*, vols. v-ix is the most up-to-date survey of all aspects of European history between 1648 and 1815. The volumes are vol. v, *The Ascendancy of France, 1648-1688* (ed. F. L. Carsten); vol. vi, *The Rise of Great Britain and Russia, 1688-1725* (ed. J. S. Bromley); vol. vii, *The Old Regime, 1713-1763* (ed. J. O. Lindsay); vol. viii, *The American and French Revolutions, 1763-1793* (ed.

A. Goodwin); and vol. ix, *War and Peace in the Age of Upheaval* (ed. C. W. Crawley). All of these were first published during the last ten years. Owing to the number of different editors and contributors its quality varies and, like most collaborative volumes, it is not always easy to read. But it is a useful work of reference, though the individual volumes contain no bibliographies and one has to refer to Roach (see Section I above). The old *Cambridge Modern History,* vols. v–ix are still extremely useful for facts about political history.

The American series on the *Rise of Modern Europe* edited by W. L. Langer— comprising C. J. Friederich, *The Age of Baroque, 1610–1660;** F. L. Nussbaum, *The Triumph of Science and Reason, 1660–1685;** J. B. Wolf, *The Emergence of the Great Powers, 1688–1715;** P. Roberts, *The Quest for Security, 1715–1740;** W. L. Dorn, *Competition for Empire, 1740–1763;** L. Gershoy, *From Despotism to Revolution, 1763–1789;** C. Crane Brinton, *A Decade of Revolution, 1763–1789;** and G. Bruun, *Europe and the French Imperium, 1799–1814**—cover the ground comprehensively. Most of these volumes were published originally between thirty and forty years ago, but revised editions have been published since and are available in paperback. A more up-to-date American series edited by Felix Gilbert has recently been published by W. W. Norton of New York, and includes Richard S. Dunn, *The Age of Religious Wars, 1559–1689,** Leonard Krieger, *Kings and Philosophers, 1689–1789,** and Charles Breunig, *The Age of Revolution and Reaction, 1789–1850.** Another up-to-date series is in the process of being published in paperback under the title of the Fontana *History of Europe* by Collins of London. These include John Stoye, *Europe Unfolding, 1648–1688* (1969), Stephen Baxter, *Europe, 1689–1715,* David Ogg, *Europe of the Ancien Régime, 1715–1783* (1965), and George Rudé, *Revolutionary Europe, 1783–1815* (1964). The approach of the authors differs somewhat, but they are all good.

Two French series are *Peuples et Civilisations* and the *Nouvelle Clio.* Included in the latter are Frederick Mauro, *L'Expansion européenne, 1660–1870,* Robert Mandrou, *La France aux XVIIe et XVIIIe siècles,* Pierre Jannin, *L'Europe et de nord-ouest,* and Jacques Godechot, *L'Europe et l'Amerique a l'epoque napoléonnienne, 1800–1815.* These works represent the modern French school, which concerns itself with a deep exploration of society, chiefly from the demographical, social, and economic points of view. Modern German general histories of Europe include Fritz Wagner, *Europe in Zeitalter des Absolutismus, 1648–1789* (Munich, 1948) and G. Mann and A. Nitischke (eds.), *Von der Reformation zur Revolution* (Berlin, 1964). Two books dealing with diplomatic relations in Europe in a broad sweep are Ludwig Dehio, *The Precarious Balance: The Politics of Power in Europe, 1494–1945* (1963)* and Gaston Zeller, *Les Temps modernes de Louis XIV à 1789* (1955). E. N. Williams, *The Ancien Régime in Europe: Government and Society in the Major States, 1648–1789* (1970) may be strongly recommended; it contains an excellent, up-to-date bibliography. Herbert H. Rowen (ed.), *From Absolutism to Revolution, 1648–1848* (1968)* is a well-chosen collection of extracts from contemporary writers about ideas and institutions. Another useful American collection of extracts from contemporary European writings about the seventeenth and eighteenth centuries is Eugen Weber, *The Western Tradition* (1965).* Friederich Heer, *The Intellectual History of Europe*

(English trans. 1966) is a survey by a distinguished Austrian historian. Finally, those who are not obsessed by the modern sociological approach may refer back to works by two great British liberal historians of the past: LORD ACTON, *Lectures on Modern History* and H. A. L. FISHER, *History of Europe.* These were first published in 1906 and 1936 respectively.

III. General: Seventeenth Century

There are several sound books covering this period. One of the latest and best is JOHN STOYE, *Europe Unfolding, 1648-1688* (1970) in the Fontana series. D. H. PENNINGTON, *Seventeenth Century Europe* (1970) in Longman's *General History of Europe* has good bibliographies. RAGNHILD HATTON, *Europe in the Age of Louis XIV* (1969) is brief, brilliant, and fully illustrated. MAURICE ASHLEY, *The Golden Century: Europe, 1598-1715* (1969) in Weidenfeld's *History of Civilisation* series has over a hundred illustrations. Even more heavily illustrated, in color as well as black-and-white, is HUGH TREVOR-ROPER (ed.), *The Age of Expansion* (1967), a "coffee-table book" which contains a number of essays by leading authorities. Two older books by noted Oxford historians are SIR GEORGE CLARK, *The Seventeenth Century* (Oxford, 1947) and DAVID OGG, *Europe in the Seventeenth Century* (latest revision, 1965). SIR GEORGE CLARK has also written a brief conspectus, *Early Modern Europe, 1450-1720* (Oxford, 1966). TREVOR ASTON (ed.), *Crisis in Europe, 1560-1660* (1965) may be said to represent the work of the "Past and Present" school of historians, several of whom are Marxists. ANDREW LOSSKY, *The Seventeenth Century, 1600-1715* (1967)* consists of extracts from "sources in western civilization" with a stimulating introduction. ROLAND MOUSNIER, *Les XVIᵉ et XVIIᵉ siècles,* vol. iv in the *Histoire Générale des Civilisations* series, is the work of a distinguished French historian.

IV. General: Eighteenth Century

This is better covered in French than in English. In the *Peuples et Civilisations* series are P. MURET, *La Prépondérance anglaise, 1713-1763* (1937) and P. SAGNAC, *Le Fin de l'ancien régime et la révolution americaine, 1763-1789* (1947). R. MOUSNIER and L. LABROUSSE, *Le XVIIᵉ siècle: Révolution intellectuelle, technique, et politique* (1953) is the work of two considerable French historians. E. PRECLIN and V. L. TAPIÉ, *Le XVIIIᵉ siècle* (1952) is dull, but contains comprehensive bibliographies. Possibly the best surveys in English are M. S. ANDERSON, *Europe in the Eighteenth Century, 1713-1783* (1961) and (briefer) *Eighteenth-Century Europe, 1713-1789* (Oxford, 1966). Another such book by Anderson is promised in the Longman series. ALFRED COBBAN (ed.), *The Eighteenth Century* (1969) is an excellent coffee-table book, heavily illustrated, with essays by different writers. For the French Revolution and the Napoleonic era, the books by GEORGES LEFEBVRE, *The French Revolution* (English trans. 1962-1964) and *Napoleon* (English trans. 1969) are perhaps the best introductions: the Marxist bias of this great French historian is not conspicuous.

V. Economic and Social History

Ultimately, the *Cambridge Economic History of Europe,* still in the process of publication, should become the standard authority, but vol. iv, E. E. Rich and Charles Wilson (eds.), *The Economy of Expanding Europe in the Sixteenth and Seventeenth Centuries* (Cambridge, England, 1967) is rather disappointing. One-volume books include S. B. Clough and C. W. Cole, *Economic History of Europe* (Boston, 1952)* and H. Heaton, *Economic History of Europe* (1948).* For agrarian history, B. H. Slicher van Bath, *The Agrarian History of Western Europe, 1500-1950* (1963) is a valuable source. For population there are D. V. Glass and D. E. C. Eversley (eds.), *Population in History* (1965) and Carlo Cipolla, *The Economic History of World Population* (1967), but it must be remarked that estimates of population before the nineteenth century differ widely. There are no general books on social history (apart perhaps from Chaunu, see Section II above), but G. N. Clark, *Science and Social Welfare in the Age of Newton* (1937) and A. Goodwin (ed.), *The European Nobility in the Eighteenth Century* (1953) are useful.

VI. Philosophers and *Philosophes*

Bertrand Russell, *A History of Western Civilization* (1946) is extremely entertaining, but W. Windelband, *A History of Philosophy* (English trans. 1893) is considered to be sounder. There are a great many books on the so-called Age of Enlightenment. Curiously, while Stuart Hampshire, *The Age of Reason* (1956)* contains extracts from seventeenth-century authors, Harold Nicolson, *The Age of Reason, 1700-1789* (1960) is concerned with eighteenth-century authors. Henry E. Allison, *Lessing and the Enlightenment* (1956), Isaiah Berlin, *The Age of Enlightenment* (1956),* also consisting of extracts, Ernst Cassirer, *The Philosophy of the Enlightenment* (English trans., Princeton, 1960),* Basil Willey, *The Eighteenth Century Background,* and Earl R. Wasserman (ed.), *Aspects of the Eighteenth Century* (1965)* are all to be recommended. For the *philosophes,* besides Ernst Cassirer's book, R. J. White, *The Anti-Philosophers* (1970) is a recent lively approach to the subject. Paul Hazard wrote two books on the period which have been widely acclaimed: *The European Mind, 1680-1713* (English trans. 1952) and *European Thought in the Eighteenth Century* (English trans. 1954). The first is more readable. For the impact of the Age of Reason on the Church see G. B. Cragg, *The Church in the Age of Reason, 1648-1789* (1960).

VII. The Arts

Good general books are Frederick B. Artz, *From the Renaissance to Romanticism: Trends in Style in Art, Literature, and Music, 1300-1830* (Chicago, 1962),* Kenneth Clark, *Civilisation* (1969), the text of a series of television talks, lavishly illustrated, and V. L. Tapié, *The Age of Grandeur: Baroque and Classicism in Europe* (English trans. 1960). For baroque see also Michael Kitson, *The Age of Baroque* (1966), which also covers rococo, and V. L. Tapié, *Le Baroque* (1961). For music I have found Paul S. Lang, *Music in Western Civilization* (1942) the most stimulating book. Useful short books are Alfred Einstein, *A Short History of Music* (1953), D. J. Grout,

A Short History of Opera (1961), and Alfred Percival, *History of Music* (1961). Among recent books on painting Anita Brookner, *Watteau* (1967) and F. Haskell, *Patrons and Painters* (1963) are to be recommended. There is an excellent Pelican series on painting and architecture.

VIII. Science and Technology

Herbert Butterfield, *Origins of Modern Science, 1300-1800* (1949) and A. R. Hall, *The Scientific Revolution, 1500-1800* (1954) are admirable; the first is by a general historian, the second by a scientific historian. S. F. Mason, *A History of the Sciences* (1953) also touches on technology. C. Singer et al., *A History of Technology*, vols. 3 and 4 (1957-58) is comprehensive, but the relevant chapters of David S. Landes, *The Unbound Prometheus* (1969)* are more concise, readable and stimulating. For medicine see C. Singer, *A Short History of Medicine* (1922) and Lester S. King, *The Medical World of the Eighteenth Century* (1958).

Chapter Notes
and References

Chapter 1

R. B. Merriman, *Six Contemporaneous Revolutions* (1938) and Trevor Aston (ed.), *Crisis in Europe, 1560-1660* (1965) discuss the European revolutions of the mid-seventeenth century. Professor John Elliott of King's College, London, and Professor Ivor Roots of the University of Exeter have both in their inaugural lectures criticized the idea of "a general crisis" at that time. Professor Elliott's lecture, "Revolution and Continuity in Early Modern Europe," is printed in *Past and Present*, no. 42 (1969), and Professor Roots's lecture, "The Late Troubles in England," was published by the University of Exeter in 1969. Randolph Starn, in "Historians and 'Crisis,'" *Past and Present*, no. 52 (1971) regards "crisis" as an ambiguous term. R. R. Palmer, *The Age of Democratic Revolution, 1760-1800* (2 vols., 1959-64)* expounds his theory of a general revolution during the last forty years of the eighteenth century. See also Jacques Godechot, *La Grande Nation* (1956) and *Les Revolutions, 1770-1799* (1963). Their arguments have not been universally accepted: e.g., they are criticized by G. Rudé in his *Revolutionary Europe, 1783-1815* (1964) and by E. J. Hobsbawm in his *Age of Revolution, 1789-1848* (1964). For the ancien régime in general C. B. A. Behrens, *The Ancien Régime* (1967) is a stimulating introduction. I have borrowed the phrase "the Age of Daylight" from R. J. White, *Europe in the Eighteenth Century* (1965), which is also good on the ancien régime. The quotations about Louis XVI (p. 1) will be found in Saul K. Padover, *The Life and Death of Louis XVI* (1939), p. 324, and about Voltaire in Gustav Lanson, *Voltaire* (1906), p. 52, and Theodore Besterman, *Voltaire* (1969), p. 120.

Chapter 2

1. For the Thirty Years' War see C. V. Wedgwood, *The Thirty Years War* (1938), G. Pagès, *The Thirty Years War, 1618-1648* (English trans. 1970; original French ed. 1938), and S. H. Steinberg, *"The Thirty Years War" and the Conflict for European Hegemony, 1600-1660* (1966), a short but valuable book critical of both Wedgwood and Pagès. The standard book on the Treaty of Westphalia is Fritz Dickmann, *Der Westfälische Frieden* (Münster, 1965). R. Ergang, *The Myth of the All-Destructive Fury of the Thirty Years War** was published at Pocono Pines, Pennsylvania, in 1956.

2. For the mid-seventeenth-century revolutions see the books mentioned in the notes to Chapter 1, and also for the English Revolution, IVAN ROOTS, *The Great Rebellion, 1642–1660* (1966), now under revision, which has a good bibliography. There are many books and violent controversy over the causes of "the English Revolution." For the Frondes see E. H. KOSSMANN, *La Fronde* (1954); for Spain see JOHN ELLIOTT, *Imperial Spain, 1596–1716* (1963) and J. LYNCH, *Spain under the Habsburgs* (1969). For the United Netherlands P. GEYL, *The Netherlands in the Seventeenth Century* (English trans. 1961, 1964) is the standard work. For Russia V. O. KLYUCH-EVSKY, *A History of Russia* (English trans. 1966) may be called a standard authority.

3. For the United Netherlands, besides Geyl's books G. J. RENIER, *The Dutch Nation. A Historical Study* (1944) and B. H. VLEKKE, *The Evolution of the Dutch Nation* (1945)* are both reliable introductions. See also CHARLES WILSON, *Profit and Power* (1957), who deals with the English and Dutch wars in the seventeenth century. The quotations from WILLIAM CARR (pp. 16, 19) are in his book *An Accurate Description of the United Provinces* (ed. 1728), pp. 8 and 46. The quotation of PROFESSOR C. R. BOXER (p. 19) is in his book *The Dutch Seaborne Empire, 1600–1800* (1965), p. 60. For France see P. GOUBERT, *Louis XIV and Twenty Million Frenchmen* (English trans. 1972; French ed. 1966); C. W. COLE, *Colbert and a Century of French Mercantilism* (1939);* GEORGES DUBY and ROBERT MANDROU, *A History of French Civilization* (English trans. 1965); ROLAND MOUSNIER, *La France classique* (1950); GEORGES MONTGREDIEN et al., *La France au temps de Louis XIV* (1965); and JACQUES GOIMARD, *La France au temps de Louis XIV* (1965). The quotation from GOUBERT (p. 21) is on p. 27 of his *Louis XIV* (French ed.). For England see CHARLES WILSON, *England's Apprenticeship* (1965), which is the best introductory book on English economic and social history in the seventeenth and eighteenth centuries; the quotation (p. 22) is on p. 145. For the argument that there was an agricultural revolution in seventeenth-century England see E. KERRIDGE, *The Agricultural Revolution* (1967).

4. Besides Klyuchevsky see for Russia BERNARD PARES, *A History of Russia* (1965): Pares was a great British scholar. The quotation (p. 25) is taken from chap. 9. R. WITTRAM, *Peter I: Czar und Kaiser* (Göttigen, 1964) is accepted as being the best biography. For Peter the Great see also a useful collection of extracts about him by various historians, mainly Russian, in MARC RAEFF (ed.), *Peter the Great: Reformer or Revolutionary?* (Boston, 1963). See also P. I. LYASCHENKO, *History of the National Economy of Russia* (1949)* and R. E. F. SMITH, *The Enslavement of the Russian Peasantry* (Cambridge, 1968). For Prussia see F. L. CARSTEN, *The Origins of Prussia* (1954), the most up-to-date introduction to the subject, and S. B. FAY, *The Rise of Brandenburg-Prussia to 1786* (1937), revised by Klaus Epstein in 1964. For the Great Elector see FERDINAND SCHEVILL, *The Great Elector* (Chicago, 1947),* with a useful bibliography. The quotation about King Frederick William I (p. 26) is taken from J. A. R. MARRIOTT and C. G. ROBERTSON, *The Evolution of Prussia* (1946), p. 111.

5. For Scandinavia R. BAIN, *Scandinavia* (1905) is still the best general introductory political survey. For Sweden INGVAAR ANDERSON, *A History of Sweden* (1956) may be recommended and also CARL HALLENDORF and ADOLF SCHUCK, *A History of Sweden* (1928). For Denmark PAUL LAURING, *A History of the Kingdom of Denmark* (English trans. 1960) and J. H. S. BIRCH, *Denmark in History* (1938) are good introductions. For

Turkey I. S. Stavrianos, *The Balkans since 1453* (1958) is the best book in English; a more recent book is P. Coles, *The Ottoman Impact on Europe* (1968). The best introduction to the history of Poland is O. Halecki, *History of Poland* (1955); the *Cambridge History of Poland* has been severely criticized. For the Holy Roman Empire of the German nation there is nothing entirely satisfactory in English. Hugo Hantsch, *Die Geschichte Österreichs*, vol. ii, *1648–1918* (Vienna, 1962) is recommended in German. Books in English include H. Holborne, *A History of Modern Germany*, vol. ii, *1648–1840* (1964) and Adam Wandruszka, *The House of Habsburg* (1964).

6. For Spain besides John Elliott's book see also Henry Kamen, *The Iron Century* (1971), passim. The quotation from Professor Reglá (p. 30) is in the *New Cambridge Modern History*, vol. v, p. 369, and from Professor Elliott, (p. 32), op. cit., pp. 358–59.

7. For Carlos II see J. Nada, *Carlos the Bewitched* (1962). "J. Nada" was the pseudonym of a British journalist.

Chapter 3

1. For marriages see Ragnhild Hatton, *Europe in the Age of Louis XIV* (1969) and Peter Laslett, *The World We Have Lost* (1965). For Professor Andrew Lossky's views on the privileged see his editorial introduction to *The Seventeenth Century* (1967). For Professor Lawrence Stone's arguments about the social pyramid see "Social Mobility in England" in *Past and Present*, no. 33 (1966). On Beauvais see P. Goubert, "The French Peasants in the Seventeenth Century: A Regional Example" in *Crisis in Europe, 1560–1660*, p. 147, and his great book, *Beauvais et le Beauvaisis de 1600 à 1730* (2 vols., 1960). Gregory King's statistics are reproduced in G. M. Trevelyan, *English Social History* (1944), p. 277, and elsewhere. The quotation about Italy (p. 40) is to be found in Francis Haskell, *Patrons and Painters* (1963), p. 133; on Prussia see F. L. Carsten, *The Origins of Prussia* (1964) p. 186ff.; for Sweden see Eli F. Hecksher, *An Economic History of Sweden* (1954), p. 115; Professor Mousnier's remark (p. 40) is in his book *Les XVIᵉ et XVIIIᵉ siècles* (1967), p. 145. The quotation (p. 41) from Gonzales de Cellorigo is given by J. H. Elliott, "The Decline of Spain" in *Crisis in Europe*, pp. 184–85. The quotation from F. L. Carsten (p. 43) is in op. cit., p. 184. For Russia see especially Jerome Blum, *Lord and Peasant in Russia* (1963).*

2. For the economies of England, France, and the United Netherlands see especially the books already cited by Charles Wilson, C. W. Cole, and C. R. Boxer; see also for England Maurice Ashley, *Financial and Commercial Policy under the Cromwellian Protectorate* (revised 1962); for France Georges Mongrédien, *La vie quotidienne sous Louis XIV* (1948); J. Lough, *An Introduction to Seventeenth Century France* (1954); H. Pigeonneau, *Histoire du commerce de la France* (1897), vol. ii. The article by D. C. Coleman, "Economic Evolution and Policies," in the *New Cambridge Modern History*, vol. v, chap. 2 is a useful conspectus. For mercantilism see E. F. Heckscher, *Mercantilism* (English trans. 1935), which has been criticized in D. C. Coleman, *Revisions in Mercantilism* (1969), which contains the quotation (p. 48) from Professor

CHARLES WILSON. The quotations from ADAM SMITH (p. 49) are in *The Wealth of Nations* (ed. DUGALD STEWART, n.d.), pp. 502 and 517. The quotation from D. C. COLEMAN (p. 49) is in the *New Cambridge Modern History*, vol. v, p. 46.

3. See especially G. N. CLARK, *War and Society in the Seventeenth Century* (1958); the quotations (p. 50, this work) are on pp. 74 and 83.

4. The quotation from PROFESSOR R. WITTKOWER (p. 50) is from chap. 7 of the *New Cambridge Modern History*, vol. iv (1961), p. 149. For baroque and rococo see the works quoted on p. 272 above and the chapters by SIR JOHN SUMMERSON and PROFESSOR L. D. ETTLINGER in *The Eighteenth Century* (ed. A. Cobban, 1969). For Bernini's visit to Paris see V. L. TAPIÉ, *Le Baroque et le classicisme* (1957), chap. 7. The quotation from SIR KENNETH CLARK (p. 53) is in his *Civilisation* (1969), p. 222; the quotation from SIR ANTHONY BLUNT (p. 53) is in *French Art and Architecture* (1953), p. 240.

5. The quotation from Spinoza (p. 56) is from BERTRAND RUSSELL, *A History of Western Philosophy*, p. 273. For "mixed governments" see *Chapters in Western Civilization* (New York 1961).* J. W. N. SULLIVAN, *Isaac Newton, 1642–1727* (1938) is an excellent introduction from which the quotations about Newton (pp. 58, 59) are taken (pp. 150 and 144). The quotation about Robert Boyle (p. 60) is in HERBERT BUTTERFIELD, *Origins of Modern Science*, p. 141. The quotation about statistics (p. 60) is from SIR GEORGE CLARK, *New Cambridge Modern History*, vol. v, p. 180.

6. The quotation from PROFESSOR A. R. HALL (p. 60) is in *The Scientific Revolution, 1500–1800*, p. 159.

Chapter 4

1. The most up-to-date biography of Louis XIV is by the American historian J. B. WOLF (1968), from which the quotations on p. 65 are taken (pp. 69, 77, 80). MAURICE ASHLEY, *Louis XIV and the Greatness of France* (1964) is a short introduction to the subject. PROFESSOR RAGNHILD HATTON has written two short but stimulating books, *Europe in the Age of Louis XIV* (1969) and *Louis XIV and his World* (1972). PROFESSOR GOUBERT's *Louis XIV and Twenty Million Frenchmen* is a sketch of the reign from the modern "annalist" point of view. JACQUES GOIMARD, *La France au temps de Louis XIV* (1965) is a collaborative work by various modern French historians of this school. The quotation from PROFESSOR LOSSKY (p. 66) is in *William III and Louis XIV* (eds. RAGNHILD HATTON and J. S. BROMLEY, 1968), p. 7.

2. For Leopold II see A. WANDRUSKA, *Leopold II* (Vienna, 1963, 1964) and *The House of Habsburg* (English trans. 1964).

3. For the diplomacy of Louis XIV see C. G. PICAVET, *La Diplomatie française au temps de Louis XIV* (1930) and LOUIS ANDRÉ, *Louis XIV et l'Europe* (1950). ERNEST LAVISSE, *Histoire de France*, vols. vii ff. (1910) has not been entirely superseded for diplomatic and political history, although modern French historians approach the subject from a different angle.

4. For Colbert see C. W. COLE, op. cit. and also his book *French Mercantilism, 1683-1700* (1943).* The quotation on p. 71 is from P. GOUBERT, op. cit., p. 104. JEAN MEUVRET's chapter on "Les Temps Difficiles" is in J. GOIMARD, op. cit.

5. For the building of the Palace of Versailles see PIERRE NOLHAC, *La Création de Versailles* (1925) and *Versailles: Residence de Louis XIV* (1925). For Louis XIV's relations with the Papacy see J. ORCIBAL, *Louis XIV contre Innocent XI* (1949), and for the revocation of the Edict of Nantes see, inter alia, WARREN C. SCOVILLE, *The Persecution of the Huguenots and French Economic Development* (Los Angeles, 1960).*

6. For Louis XIV and the arts see SIR ANTHONY BLUNT's book cited above. See also VOLTAIRE's *Le Siècle de Louis XIV* (many editions). For French literature G. LYTTON STRACHEY, *Landmarks in French Literature* (1923) remains a polished introduction. MARTIN TURNELL has written excellent books on the subject, including *The Classical Moment* (1946).

7. For the threat to Vienna see JOHN STOYE, *The Siege of Vienna* (1964) and also his *Europe Unfolding, 1648-1689* (1969).

8. For the decline of Louis XIV see, besides the standard works, LIONEL ROTHKREG, *Opposition to Louis XIV* (1965).

9. For the origins of the War of the Spanish Succession A. LEGRELLE, *La diplomatie française et la succession d'Espagne* (1885-89) is an enormous book written from a patriotic point of view. For a brief, up-to-date summary see M. A. THOMSON, "Louis XIV and the Origins of the War of the Spanish Succession" in *Transactions of the Royal Historical Society*, series v, vol. iv, 111ff. The war itself is well discussed, inter alia, in SIR WINSTON CHURCHILL's *Marlborough: His Life and Times* (1933-38).

10. Lavisse himself wrote vol. 8, i, of the *Histoire de France* (1902) which he edited. The views of this great historian about Louis XIV are acceptable.

11. Besides the books by F. L. CARSTEN and S. B. FAY cited above see W. H. BRUFORD, *Germany in the Eighteenth Century* (1935) and F. L. CARSTEN, "The Great Elector and the Foundation of Hohenzollern Despotism" in *English Historical Review*, lxv (1950).

12. For Peter the Great, besides R. WITTRAM, op. cit., see V. O. KLYUCHEVSKY, *Peter the Great* (English trans. 1958). An excellent introduction is *Peter the Great and the Emergence of Russia* (1950) written by the late B. H. SUMNER.

13. The only useful book in English is that by I. S. STAVRIANOS.

14. For Charles XI of Sweden see MICHAEL ROBERTS, *Essays in Swedish History* (1967), chap. 8, and R. M. HATTON, *Charles XII of Sweden* (1968), the latest book on the latter King.

15. The reference to R. R. PALMER's views about the aristocracy is in *The Age of Democratic Revolution: The Challenge* (1959).

Chapter 5

1. The quotation about Louis XIV (p. 103) is cited by C. B. A. Behrens, op. cit., p. 1, and that about William III (p. 103) is the theme of the book by Gerald M. Straka, *Anglican Reaction to the Revolution of 1688* (1962), passim. For an excellent introduction to the question of "enlightened despotism" see the pamphlet with that title written by F. Hartung (1957) and published by the English Historical Association. For the European aristocracy see A. Goodwin, *The European Nobility in the Eighteenth Century* (1953), from which the quotations by Habbakkuk and Professor Beloff are taken (p. 105). In his books *Europe in the Eighteenth Century, 1713–1783* (1961) and *Eighteenth Century Europe, 1713–1789* (1966) M. S. Anderson deals trenchantly with the whole question of "enlightened despotism." See also Geoffrey Bruun, *The Enlightened Despots* (1967)* and Stuart Andrews (ed.), *Enlightened Despotism* (1967), which contains useful extracts from contemporaries and historians which should be compared with the views of Anderson and Bruun.

2. For Catherine the Great see G. P. Gooch, *Catherine the Great and Other Studies* (1954) and Paul Dukes, *Catherine the Great and the Russian Nobility* (Cambridge, England, 1967). The quotation from Catherine the Great (p. 108) is in Jerome Blum, op. cit., p. 352. The text of Catherine's instructions is printed in W. F. Reddaway, *Documents of Catherine the Great* (1931).

3. Besides Gerhard Ritter's book (English trans. by Peter Paret, 1968), for Frederick the Great see G. P. Gooch, *Frederick the Great* (1947) and Pierre Gaxotte, *Frederick the Great* (English trans. 1941), and for a short introduction D. B. Horn, *Frederick the Great and the Rise of Prussia* (1964). See also W. O. Henderson, *Studies in the Economic Policy of Frederick the Great* (1963).

4. For Maria Theresa see Edward Crankshaw, *Maria Theresa* (1969) and the books by Hugo Hantsch quoted above. The quotation by E. Wangermann (p. 112) is from the *New Cambridge Modern History*, vol. viii (1968), p. 297. For Joseph II see F. Fetjo, *Un Habsburg revolutionnaire, Joseph II* (1953) and Saul K. Padover, *The Revolutionary Emperor: Joseph II of Austria* (1961). For Leopold II see Adam Wandruschka, *Leopold II* (Vienna, 1963–64).

5. For early eighteenth-century England see J. H. Plumb, *Sir Robert Walpole* (1956, 1960) and *The Growth of Political Stability in England, 1675–1725* (1967). For Louis XV see Hubert Méthivier, *Le Siècle de Louis XV* (1966).

6. For Portugal see H. V. Livermore, *A History of Portugal* (Cambridge, England, 1947), for Spain Richard Herr, *The Eighteenth-Century Revolution in Spain* (Princeton, 1958),* and for Italy G. Candelero, *Storia dell' Italia moderna* (Milan, 1954). C. M. Ady and A. J. Whyte, *A Short History of Italy* (Cambridge, England, 1963), is a good short introduction. For Pombal see M. Cheke, *Dictator of Portugal* (1938).

7. The dynastic wars of the eighteenth century are summarized best in Mr. Anderson's books; see also David Ogg, *Europe of the Ancien Régime, 1715–1783* in the Fontana series (1965). For Philip V and Elizabeth Farnese see A. Baudrillart, *Philip V et la cour de France* (1890–1901) and E. Armstrong, *Elizabeth Farnese* (1892).

8. For Frederick II's military achievement see the chapter by R. R. PALMER in E. M. EARLE (eds.), *Makers of Modern Strategy* (1944)* and also the quotations on pp. 55–60. For Cardinal Fleury see ARTHUR M. WILSON, *French Foreign Policy during the Administration of Cardinal Fleury* (Cambridge, Mass., 1936).

9. The quotations about great monarchies (p. 125) are from C. B. A. BEHRENS, op. cit., that about the Marxist view of enlightened despots (p. 127) is from F. HARTNUNG, op. cit.

10. For the *philosophes* see ERNST CASSIRER, *The Philosophy of the Enlightenment* (English trans. 1951), R. J. WHITE, *The Anti-Philosophers* (1970), and ARTHUR M. WILSON, *Diderot: The Testing Years, 1713–1759* (1957). The biography of Voltaire by THEODORE BESTERMAN is rather disappointing, coming as it did from the greatest living authority on the subject. PETER GAY, *Voltaire's Politics* (1959) is stimulating. For John Locke see the biography by MAURICE CRANSTON (1957), an admirable introduction. PROFESSOR JOHN LOUGH has written various works on the *Encyclopédie*. For Montesquieu see P. HAZARD, *European Thought in the Eighteenth Century from Montesquieu to Lessing* (English trans. 1954). For Lessing and other German thinkers see SIR ISAIAH BERLIN, *The Age of Enlightenment* (1956)* and ROGER PASCAL, *The German Stürm und Drang* (1953). For Rousseau see D. MORNET, *Rousseau: L'Homme et l'oeuvre* (1950), F. C. GREEN, *Jean-Jacques Rousseau: A Critical Study of His Life and Writings* (1955), and A. COBBAN, *Rousseau and the Modern State* (1934).

11. For the eighteenth-century philosophers, besides WINDELBAND and BERTRAND RUSSELL see ISAIAH BERLIN on Herder in EARL R. WASSERMAN (ed.), *Aspects of the Eighteenth Century* (1965),* and for a useful introduction to Kant see H. B. ACTON, *Kant's Moral Philosophy* (1970).

12. The quotation from Voltaire (p. 136) is in PETER GAY, op. cit., p. 171; the quotation from R. J. WHITE (p. 137) is in his *Anti-Philosophers*, p. 122; the quotation from Seguier (p. 137) is in S. F. MASON, *A History of the Sciences* (1953), p. 260, but compare ROBERT MANDROU, *La France aux XVIIe et XVIIIe siècles* (1970), p. 203.

Chapter 6

1. For this period in general see PIERRE MURET, *La Prèpondèrance Anglaise* (1937) and BASIL WILLIAMS, *The Whig Supremacy, 1714–1760* (ed. C. H. STUART, 1962).

2. For the "Diplomatic Revolution" see chap. 19 by PROFESSOR D. B. HORN in the *New Cambridge Modern History*, vol. vii (1966); H. BUTTERFIELD, *The Reconstruction of an Historical Episode: The History of the Enquiry into the Origins of the Seven Years War* (Glasgow, 1951); and R. WADDINGTON, *Louis XV et le renversement des alliances* (1896). For England see BASIL WILLIAMS, op. cit. For William Pitt the Elder see the biography by BRIAN TUNSTALL (1938). The quotation about the Anglo-Prussian treaty (p. 143) is from D. B. HORN, *New Cambridge Modern History*, vol. vii (1966), p. 449; the quotation from Frederick the Great (p. 144) is from G. P. GOOCH, *Frederick the Great*, p. 41.

3. For European relations with America see J. H. PARRY, *The Spanish Seaborne Empire* (1966), C. R. BOXER, *The Dutch Seaborne Empire* (1965), and L. H. GIPSON, *The Coming of Revolution, 1763–1765* (1954). The quotation about Batavia (p. 145) is in C. R. BOXER, op. cit., pp. 224–25; for the British point of view a good introduction to the subject is CHARLES GRANT ROBERTSON, *Chatham and the British Empire* (1946).

4. For the relations between Europe and America see, inter alia, MAX BELOFF, *The Debate on the American Revolution* (1949), R. R. PALMER, op. cit., vol. i; L. H. GIPSON, op. cit. The quotation from STEVEN WATSON (p. 150) is in his *The Reign of George III, 1760–1815* (1960), p. 38. The quotation from John Adams (p. 152) is in E. S. MORGAN and H. M. MORGAN, *The Stamp Act Crisis* (1953), p. 140, and that from Thomas Hutchinson (p. 152) is in MAX BELOFF, op. cit., p. 32.

5. For the impact of the American Revolutionary War on Europe see R. R. PALMER, *The Age of the Democratic Revolution*, vol. i (1959), pp. 282ff.

6. For the Industrial Revolution see E. J. HOBSBAWM, *The Age of Revolution* (1962), chap. 2, T. S. ASHTON, *The Industrial Revolution* (1954), and PHYLLIS DEANE, *The First Industrial Revolution* (Cambridge, England, 1965). For scientific progress see S. F. MASON, *A History of the Sciences* (1953), DAVID S. LANDES, *The Unbound Prometheus* (1969), and T. K. DERRY and TREVOR I. WILLIAMS, *A Short History of Technology* (1960). For medicine see C. SINGER, *A Short History of Medicine* (1928). DAVID LANDES's book is that referred to on p. 273. The quotation from Hugh Trevor-Roper (p. 162) is in his book *The Rise of Christian Europe* (1965), p. 194.

Chapter 7

1. In writing this chapter I must once more acknowledge my debt to PROFESSOR R. R. PALMER's masterpiece, *The Age of Democratic Revolution*, although I do not agree with all his conclusions. The quotation from Frederick the Great is taken from OTTO BÜSCH, *Militärsystem und Sozialleben in alten Preussen* (1962), p. 79. Arthur Young's quotation about the English peasant (p. 169) is taken from E. N. WILLIAMS, *Life in Georgian England* (1962), p. 90. For England at the time see STEVEN WATSON, *The Reign of George III*, especially pp. 134ff.

2. See especially JACQUES GODECHOT, *Les Révolutions, 1770–1799* (1963).

3. For the age of rococo see MICHAEL KITSON, *The Age of Baroque*, pp. 124ff., and JOHN SUMMERSON, "Royalty, Religion, and the Urban Background" in *The Eighteenth Century*, pp. 78ff. For Anton Watteau see the book with that title by ANITA BROOKMAN (1967). On the Louvre and Napoleon see CECIL GOULD, *Trophy of Conquest* (1963).

4. For music P. H. LANG, *Music in Western Civilization* (1942) is excellent. For the greatest composers recent books are PERCY YOUNG, *The Bachs* (1970), H. S. FISCHER and L. BESCH, *The Life of Mozart* (1969), and GEORGE A. MORETH, *Beethoven: Biography of a Genius* (1970).

5. For the long-term causes of the French Revolution see, inter alia, J. Égret, *La Prerévolution française, 1787-1788* (1962) as well as the books cited by Professor Palmer and Professor Godechot. Professor J. MacManners, "The Historiography of the French Revolution," chap. 22, vol. viii of the *New Cambridge Modern History,* is an excellent introduction to the subject. E. J. Hobsbawm, *The Age of Revolution,* part I, chap. 3, A. Aulard, *Histoire politique de la Révolution française* (1901) and Albert Mathiez, *The French Revolution* (English trans. 1922) are classical works; so is Georges Lefebvre, *The Coming of the French Revolution* (English trans. 1947). For the influence of Rousseau see Joan MacDonald, *Rousseau and the French Revolution* (1954) and various books by Alfred Cobban. Cobban wrote in *The Myth of the French Revolution* (1954), p. 6, "Now we know it began in 1787," but Égret said that the years 1787 and 1788 should be "detached" from the Revolution. Labrousse's book is *La Crise de l'economie française à la fin de l'ancien régime au debut de la Révolution* (1944), an important book linking economic and political history. G. Lefebvre wrote his book on *La Grande Peur* in 1932. The quotation from Lefebvre is in his *Études sur la Révolution française* (1954), p. 246.

Chapter 8

1. Besides the books cited for Chapter 7 see A. Goodwin, *The French Revolution* (1966), the latest book by a British scholar. G. Lefebvre, *La Révolution française* (1951) in the *Peuples et Civilisations* series was translated into English in 1962, and a revised French edition edited by A. Soboul was published also in 1962. Among older books Soboul himself published a *Précis de l'histoire de la Révolution française* (1962); Louis Madelin, *The French Revolution* (English trans. 1920) is a lively introduction to the subject by a French academician to offset the Marxist or semi-Marxist interpretations of historians like Hobsbawm, Lefebvre, Matthiez, and Soboul.

2. For these revolutions see the works by R. R. Palmer and Jacques Godechot cited before.

3. For the destruction of Poland see, besides Halecki, Herbert Kaplan, *The First Partition of Poland* (1962), R. H. Lord, *The Second Partition of Poland* (1915), and an article by R. H. Lord in the *Slavonic Review* (1925), 487ff., about the Third Partition. For a comparison between the French and Polish revolutions see C. E. J. Konic, *Comparison des constitutions de la Pologne et de la France de 1791* (1918) and L. R. Lewitter, "The Partitions of Poland" in the *New Cambridge Modern History,* vol. viii, pp. 343ff. For Kosciusco a good biography is that by M. Harman, *Kosciusco: Leader and Exile* (1946). The quotation of Catherine II (p. 199) is in R. H. Lord, op. cit., p. 274.

4. For Brissot and the "Girondins" see M. J. Sydenham, *The Girondins* (1961).

5. For the *sans-culottes* see A. Soboul, *Les Sans-Culottes parisiens en l'an II* (1958) and G. Rudé, *The Crowd in the French Revolution* (1959). Professor Rudé's book in the Fontana series is a useful summary of these events.

6. For aspects of the French Revolution's impact on Europe see *Occupants occupés, 1792-1815* (1969) published by the Université Libre de Bruxelles. I am indebted to PROFESSOR S. JOHNSON of University College, London, for lending me this book.

7. For the struggle between the Girondins and the Mountain see A. MATHIEZ, *Girondins et Montegnards* (1930) and M. J. SYDENHAM, op. cit.

8. For the Terror see D. GREER, *The Incidence of the Terror during the French Revolution* (1935).* There are good biographies of Robespierre by J. M. THOMSON (1939), G. WALTER (1950-52), and a short one by G. J. RENIER (1936).

9. The quotation from LEFEBVRE is in his *French Revolution* (English trans.), p. 419.

10. A good recent biography of Charles James Fox is by LOREN REID (1970).

11. H. A. L. FISHER in his *History of Europe* (1936) compares the French and Bolshevik terrors.

Chapter 9

1. For Thermidor and its consequences see GEORGES LEFEBVRE, *La Révolution française,* vol. iv, chap. 3.

2. The best short life of Napoleon is that by FELIX MARKHAM (1966); a fair book on Josephine is by HUBERT COLE (1962). The quotation about her and Napoleon's attitude toward women (p. 221) are from M. H. BEYLE (STENDHAL), *A Life of Napoleon* (English trans. 1934), pp. 115 and 112. (Stendhal was a contemporary of Napoleon.) The description of Napoleon (p. 221) is quoted from LOUIS MADELIN, *The Consulate and the Empire, 1799-1815* (English trans. 1934), p. 26. For Napoleon as a soldier see the excellent book by DAVID CHANDLER, *The Campaigns of Napoleon* (1967).

3. For the Napoleonic influence on other countries than France and the Napoleonic Empire in general see *La France à l'epoque napoleonienne* (1970) and OWEN CONNELLY, *Napoleon's Satellite Kingdoms* (1965).* Again I am grateful to Professor Johnson for lending me these books. The quotations from Napoleon in Italy (p. 224) are in FELIX MARKHAM, op. cit., pp. 28 and 38.

4. For the view about England's stand against Europe see PIETER GEYL, *Napoleon: For and Against* (rev. ed. 1969). This book by a great Dutch historian illustrates the many different approaches to the subject of Napoleon.

5. For the idea of an expedition to Egypt see A. DUFF COOPER, *Talleyrand* (1932), pp. 101-3. For local government under Napoleon see ALFRED COBBAN, "Local Government during the French Revolution" in *English Historical Review,* lviii (1943) and also JACQUES GODECHOT, *Les Institutions de la France sous la révolution et l'empire* (1951). For the Consulate, besides MARKHAM see LOUIS MADELIN's book on the subject.

6. For Pitt and George III see STEVEN WATSON, op. cit., p. 406, and for the quotation from Napoleon about his intentions after the Treaty of Amiens (p. 231) see MARKHAM, p. 95.

7. For "the Continental system" see GEORGES LEFEBVRE, *Napoleon: From Tilsit to Waterloo, 1807-1815* (English trans. 1969) and E. F. HECKSCHER, *The Continental System* (Oxford, 1922).

8. The quotation from Napoleon about Tilsit (p. 236) is from JACQUES BAINVILLE's biography, at one time the standard one-volume book on Napoleon in French (English trans. 1932), p. 248. The quotation from Massena (p. 236) is in FELIX MARKHAM, op. cit., p. 241. For Napoleon's domestic policy see GEORGES LEFEBVRE's book on Napoleon. For David see CLIVE BELL, *Landmarks in Nineteenth Century Painting* (1927), pp. 22ff.

9. The Russian campaign is excellently described by DAVID CHANDLER, op. cit.; for the stirring of Austrian patriotism see, inter alia, G. LEFEBVRE, op. cit., p. 52.

10. The quotation about Napoleon's interview with Metternich (p. 244) is taken from HAROLD NICOLSON, *The Congress of Vienna* (1946), p. 43; that from STENDHAL (p. 244) from his *Life of Napoleon*, p. 136, as also the next quotation (p. 244), p. 140. Napoleon's next quotation (p. 244) is in DAVID CHANDLER, op. cit., p. 959. Napoleon's last words (p. 244) are quoted by MARKHAM, op. cit., p. 240.

11. For a Marxist view of Napoleon see E. J. HOBSBAWM, *The Age of Revolution,* p. 91, and for GEYL's view *Napoleon: For and Against,* p. 448.

Chapter 10

The quotation from Napoleon (p. 251) is in MARKHAM, op. cit., p. 42. For the disappointment over the rise of Napoleon to supreme power see the chapter by H. G. SCHENCK in the *New Cambridge Modern History,* vol. ix (1965), pp. 91ff. For the Congress of Vienna see HAROLD NICOLSON, op. cit., and SIR CHARLES WEBSTER, *The Congress of Vienna, 1814-1815* (1919). The quotations by Napoleon about the Treaty of Vienna (p. 254) are in HAROLD NICOLSON, pp. 236, 253, 276-77.

Index

Adams, John, quoted, 152
Africa, West, 23, 46, 149, 153
Agriculture, 22, 38, 45
Aix-la-Chapelle, treaty of (1748), 125, 142
Alberoni, Cardinal Giulio, 118
Alexander I (Tsar of Russia), 234
Alsace, 10, 76
America, North
  Colonial wars, 144, 147–50
  War of Independence and Europe,
    150–55
Amiens, treaty of, 232
Amsterdam, 15, 16–17
Anne (Queen of England), 81
Anne (Tsarina of Russia), 105
Antwerp, 16
Architecture, 51–53, 174–75
Aristocracy, see Nobility
Asiento, 142
Assembly of Notables, 172, 184
Athens, 95
Augereau, General Pierre-François-
    Charles, 224
Augsburg, treaty of, 78
Augustus III (King of Poland), 119
Austerlitz, battle of, 234
Austria
  diplomatic relations, 141–43
  reforms in, 113–14, 124, 126
  social structure, 167
  war against France, 204
Austria-Hungary, 197, 234, 254
Austrian succession, war of, 118, 145

Babeuf, Gracchus, 224
Bach, Johann Sebastian, 177–78
Banks, 47
Barfleur (or La Hogue), battle of, 79
Baroque art, 11, 50–53, 173
Barras, Paul, 221–22

Basel, treaty of, 220
Bavaria, 123
Bayle, Pierre, 128
Beethoven, Ludwig van, 177–80, 230, 251
Berkeley, George, 134
Bernini, Giovanni Lorenzo, 52
Blenheim, battle of, 82
Blücher, Marshal Gebhart Liebrecht, 246
Bohemia, 123, 124, 126, 144
Boileau, Nicholas, 75
Borodino, battle of, 242
Bossuet, bishop, 76, 103
Bourgeoisie, 15, 41–42, 106, 194, 210
Brandenburg, see Prussia
Brazil, 115–16
Brienne, Loménie de, 172
Brissot, Jacques Pierre, 204, 205, 212
Brunswich, Duke of, 204, 206
Burke, Edmund, 151, 168, 181, 207

Campo Formio, treaty of, 223, 225
Canada, 147, 153
Carlos II (King of Spain), 32–37, 79–80, 88
Carlos III (King of Spain), 117, 119
Carr, William, quoted, 16, 19
Castlereagh, Lord, 233
Catalonia, 4, 14–15, 31–32
Catherine II (Tsarina of Russia), 25, 106,
    107–10, 127, 157, 167, 196–202, 224
Charles I (King of England), 3, 12, 23
Charles II (King of England), 13, 37, 67, 69
Charles VI (Holy Roman Emperor), 83, 84,
    119, 120, 122
Charles XI (King of Sweden), 43, 95–96
Charles XII (King of Sweden), 27, 54,
    96–98, 99, 103, 122
Charles Emmanuel III (King of Sardinia),
    142
Chemistry, 158
Choiseul, Duke of, 152, 170

291